ESSAYS ON SPIRITUAL BONDAGE AND DELIVERANCE

Willard M. Swartley, Editor

Occasional Papers No. 11

Institute of Mennonite Studies
3003 Benham Avenue
Elkhart, Indiana 46517

1988

POLICY STATEMENT FOR THE *OCCASIONAL PAPERS*

Occasional Papers is a publication of the Institute of Mennonite Studies and authorized by the Council of Mennonite Seminaries. The four sponsoring seminaries are Eastern Mennonite Seminary (Harrisonburg, VA), Goshen Biblical Seminary and Mennonite Biblical Seminary (Elkhart, IN), and the Mennonite Brethren Biblical Seminary (Fresno, CA). The Institute of Mennonite Studies is the research agency of the Associated Mennonite Biblical Seminaries.

Occasional Papers is released several times yearly without any prescribed calendar schedule. The purpose of the *Papers* is to make various types of essays available to foster dialogue in biblical, theological and practical ministry areas and to invite critical counsel from within the Mennonite theological community. while most essays will be in finished form, some may also be in a more germinal stage--released especially for purposes of testing and receiving critical feedback. In accepting papers for publication, priority will be given to authors from the CMS institutions, the College Bible faculties in the Council of Mennonite Colleges, the Associate membership of the Institute of Mennonite Studies, and students and degree alumni fo the four seminaries.

Because of the limited circulation of the *Occasional Papers*, authors are free to use their material in other scholarly settings, either for oral presentation at scholarly meetings or for publication in journals with broader circulation and more official publication policies.

Orders for *Occasional Papers* should be sent to the Institute of Mennonite Studies, 3003 Benham Avenue, Elkhart, IN 46517.

Editor: Willard M. Swartley, Director
         Institute of Mennonite Studies
Associate Editor:
         Elizabeth G. Yoder, Assistant Director
         Institute of Mennonite Studies

©1988, Institute of Mennonite Studies
ISBN 0-936273-12-7
Printed in U.S.A.

CONTENTS

PREFACE

The essays and responses in this volume were prepared originally for a three day consultation, July 30-August 1, 1987, on "Bondage and Deliverance" held on the campus of the Associated Mennonite Biblical Seminaries. The consultation was co-sponsored by five Mennonite agency or conference entities, described in Richard Kauffman's Introduction (note 3). In Marlin Miller's absence from campus due to sabbatical in 1986-87, Richard Kauffman chaired the Planning Committee during this interim and carried the extensive executive work that goes into a consultation of this type. Marlin Miller served excellently as moderator of the consultation, enabling the various points of view to be fruitfully discussed. As his "Afterword" indicates, several ongoing efforts to understand better this topic and ministry continue.

The understandings of conference participants varied in regard to evil spirits, oppression-possession, and how the church should minister to demonized persons. Some called for greater openness and commitment to deliverance ministry or exorcism; others called for pastoral care models which generally avoid use of exorcism. As several participants noted, we also need to give more attention to angels, and their role in the believer's protection and security.

The Findings Report of the Listening Committee identifies areas of agreement, areas of disagreement and areas in which more study and ongoing work are needed. I have included a briefly annotated *Bibliography* of selected sources to assist in this task of ongoing study. As indicated in Kauffman's **Introduction**, worship sessions, led by Rachel Fisher and James Waltner, were an important part of the consultation. These consisted of grateful praise to God, Jesus Christ and the Holy Spirit for God's work of redemption and steadfast love amid suffering; the prayers enabled us to unitedly raise our voices to God. Another helpful part of the consultation not included in this collection was the extensive teaching outlines presented by John Hinson which he uses at the "Body of Christ" deliverance farm for spiritual rehabilitation of demonized persons.

I wish to thank all the contributors to the volume, Sue DeLeon for her typing of the manuscript and Elizabeth Yoder for her assistance in editing the essays. May our reading and study of these contributions on spiritual bondage and deliverance enable us to be more faithful servants of the liberating gospel of Jesus Christ: "If the Son sets you free, you shall be free indeed" (John 8:36).

Willard Swartley, Editor
March 27, 1988

INTRODUCTION

Richard A. Kauffman

It is clear from the Gospels that one of Jesus' ministries as Messiah was that of exorcism--i.e., the casting out of demons. His role as Messiah was not exclusively, nor even primarily, that of an exorcist. Nor was this the one function which made Jesus unique. Nevertheless, his deliverance ministry was a demonstration of the power of God and a sign that the kingdom of God was coming in the person and ministry of Jesus.

Today, however, many Christians are seriously divided over the issue of whether the church should continue this particular ministry of Jesus. Given a western mindset, many of us are inclined to say that where similar phenomena are manifest, it can be best explained and treated in terms of mental disorders and therapies.

Yet, when western missionaries go overseas, they encounter world-views and demonic realities remarkably similar to those described in the New Testament. And even here in North America some persons have felt called to a ministry of deliverance. Though their ranks may be small, even a few mental health professionals claim to have encountered clients whose symptoms are like that of demonic possession and for whom conventional therapies are not effective.

What are we to make of these phenomena both in Jesus' ministry and in our own time? What did Jesus mean when he said that his disciples would do even greater works than he did (John 14:12)?[1] Did he mean to imply that this would include his ministry of demonic deliverance--not to mention healing the sick, raising the dead, and walking on water? Was Jesus commissioning of his disciples to cast out unclean spirits and to heal every disease and infirmity merely a charge for that time or for all time?[2]

These and other questions, some of which come from the actual practice of deliverance, prompted us to say that what is needed is a face-to-face, heart-to-heart confrontation of these issues--a consultation such as was held on the campus of the Associated Mennonite Biblical Seminaries, July 30-August 1, 1987.[3] The committee which planned this consultation was much interested in the perspective of numerous view-points theologically, confessionally, and otherwise. They were also concerned to draw together the angles of vision which a variety of academic disciplines provides--not only the theological disciplines such as biblical studies, church history, theology and pastoral care--but also the human sciences: psychology, social science, and anthropology.

This volume, then, contains the papers which were prepared for this consultation. Readers will be disappointed if they expect a party line. They may be surprised to discover that there is yet more truth to be discovered about this most complex and controversial topic.

   The primary purpose of this consultation was to surface issues related to bondage and deliverance from a variety of perspectives with a view toward developing some kind of consensus across disciplinary lines. More specifically, the objectives were:
   1. To address the following questions: What is meant by demon possession? How do worldviews impinge upon our understandings of demonic possession and exorcism? How is it diagnosed? treated? What is the role of the exorcist? of pastoral care? of the mental health profession? What models of pastoral care and ministry are called for?
   2. To look at these issues in an interdisciplinary fashion and, though this consultation was largely a Mennonite one, to draw in the perspectives and experiences of persons from other traditions in order to enrich our own understandings.
   3. To try to pull together a statement which would reflect the points of convergence and divergence arrived at as a result of this consultation.
   We did not expect to answer all the questions involved with this topic. Likely, we raised more questions than we have answers for. But at least we wanted to make a beginning step toward raising consciousness about these phenomena and helping the church--congregations, pastors, and Christians in the helping professions--to know better how to respond to them.
   A word about the process of the event is in order. This was a working consultation. The papers were all distributed beforehand and the participants at the consultation consented to read the papers and come prepared to enter into dialogue and discussion about their contents.
   Additionally, two committees functioned during this event, a listening committee and a findings committee. The listening committee had its ear to the ground concerning process matters and served as a sounding board to the moderator (Marlin E. Miller) as the consultation developed. The findings committee concentrated on the substance of the consultation and facilitated preparation of the findings statement which summarized our learnings during these two and one-half days--points of convergence and divergence and areas which demand further work (see pages 212-14).
   Many of you have either heard or read the story of the nineteenth century pastoral-theologian, J. C. Blumhardt--a story committed to posterity and used by Karl Barth in the third movement of his doctrine of reconciliation. According to this story, Blumhardt worked with a young woman who was afflicted over a two-year period. From the beginning, Blumhardt's prayer was, "Lord Jesus, help me. We have seen long enough what the devil can do. We now desire to see the power of Jesus." When there finally was a breakthrough and the young woman experienced deliverance, it came with a remarkable statement which Blumhardt attributed to the departing angel of Satan. In an expression characterized as a shriek, the demon cried out, "Jesus is Victor!" In this story and affirmation Barth finds a cap-

sule summary of the New Testament message that in the work of Jesus there is victory over the powers of darkness.[4]

The consultation was not convened to see what works the devil can do or to look for a demon behind every bush; nor did we gather to wallow in the mire and muck of malevolent forces. Rather, our aim was to claim and proclaim the lordship of Christ over all the forces of evil and powers of darkness. Consequently, our coming together was also a time for corporate worship--in praise and thanksgiving for what God has done in Christ Jesus. "But thanks be to God, who in Christ always leads us in triumph, and through us spreads the fragrance of the knowledge of him everywhere" (2 Cor 2:14).

Notes

1. In *The Work of God Goes On* (Philadelphia: Fortress Press, 1987) Gerhard Lohfink makes some interesting connections between God's work in creation and the ongoing work of God in Israel's history, Jesus Christ, and the formation and activity of the church. In dealing with John's Gospel, e.g., he observes that "the miracles not only attend the whole of Jesus' public life; they continue, after Jesus' death, in the church. In this case the evangelist no longer calls them 'signs' (*semeia*) but 'works' into which the believers enter.... Jesus has, indeed, brought the saving work of the Father in its fundamental sense to its completion (4:34; 17:4; 19:30). But everyone who believes enters into the 'work' (6:29)" (p. 39). However, God's ongoing work is not restricted to the mighty signs and wonders manifest in healing or deliverance from demonic possession. God's miraculous work is that of the formation of a new "contrast society," the church, which is not "built on a basis of mistrust and lordship, but rather on trust and nonviolence" (61).

2. Another serious attempt to grapple with these and other issues is represented in *Ministry and the Miraculous: A Case Study at Fuller Theological Seminary*, edited by Lewis B. Smedes, 1987. In this faculty "consensus" statement there is a call for discernment where deliverance ministries are practiced. Five points on discernment are made:

"1. Discernment, unlike divine revelation, is the ability to detect the real differences between things that are otherwise not open to the view of everyone else. Since discernment does not confer infallibility it is therefore open to judgment and confirmation by disinterested critics who have their own views of the same phenomena. All discernment of the demonic in people, therefore, should be subject to the evaluation of wise, informed, and responsible members of the Christian community.

2. No one should ever be subject to exorcism without informed consent.

3. Only persons recognized by their communities to be spiritually mature, responsible, and wise Christians should ever be permitted to exorcise demons from anyone.

4. Wherever it is possible to do so, the Christian community

should seek the counsel and the active involvement of professional people trained to evaluate bizarre and destructive behavior; it should approve of no exorcism unless the person to be exorcised has been evaluated and treated by people trained and skilled in diagnosis and therapy. 5. Exorcisms should not be done in secret nor kept secret. For the protection of the persons involved, as well as for the later study, appropriate records should be kept of both the diagnosis and the actual exorcism. All such records should, of course, be subject to informed consent and should be kept in confidence (74).

3. This event was co-sponsored by Goshen Biblical Seminary and Mennonite Biblical Seminary (the two seminaries which comprise the Associated Mennonite Biblical Seminaries), Indiana-Michigan Mennonite Conference, Mennonite Board of Missions, and Oaklawn Psychiatric Center. Additional funding was provided through the Shalom Fund of Mennonite Mutual Aid Association. Members of the planning committee were Howard H. Charles, Paul M. Gingrich, David Helmuth, Gerald Kauffman, Richard A. Kauffman, Marlin E. Miller, Henry Poettcker and Willard M. Swartley. The consultation, by invitation only, was attended by 60 persons.

4. Karl Barth, *Church Dogmatics: The Doctrine of Reconciliation,* IV/3 (Edinburgh: T & T Clark, 1961), 165ff.

BONDAGE AND DELIVERANCE
BIBLICAL AND THEOLOGICAL PERSPECTIVES

by Thomas Finger and Willard Swartley

Introduction

The purpose of this paper is to present an overview of the biblical data relating to the demonic, and especially to demonic activity which results in personal bondage and thus calls for deliverance. We will not be focusing narrowly on bondage or deliverance, however, but will be relating these phenomena to the broader reality of evil and to deliverance from evil wrought through Jesus Christ. As we examine the biblical data we will also be raising (1) broader theological questions as to the reality and meaning of these phemonena in our "modern" world, and (2) implications of this study for exorcism[1] and the overall healing process of persons.

The First Century World View

The Greco-Roman Perspectives

In the centuries before and after Jesus' ministry, belief in demons and their power over human life flourished. In the 9th-4th centuries BCE the word *daimon* could refer to either a good or evil spirit. Plato conceived it primarily as good, but as time went on the word came to be associated more and more with evil spirits. Philosophers often associated the pagan religious rites with demons. Common belief held that demons occupied the intermediary regions between heaven and earth and thus assisted or thwarted communication between humans and gods. They were often identified with the souls of the dead and would avenge wrongs done against the deceased person in his or her lifetime. But they were conceived also as personal helpful guardian spirits or deputies of the gods. They could possess human beings, causing madness or affliction of the body. Hence many magical formulae and rites developed to assist in their exorcism (Ferguson: 58-59).[2]

Jewish Perspectives

Although Jewish literature, like the Greek, does not have a consistent doctrine of demons, it does speculate about their origins.[3] According to many intertestamental apocalyptic writings, Yahweh governs the universe through numerous spiritual beings, some governing natural forces.[4] Long ago, Yahweh placed such spirits in authority over all nations--except for Israel, which he ruled directly.[5] These beings were to teach humans the arts, crafts, and just government. Some of these spirits, however, formed a conspiracy to rule humankind to serve their own ends. One-third of the angel spirits rebelled and were expelled from the heavenly court. They were led by several "Satans," or by a "Satanail" who had previously sought to be equal with Yahweh.[6] Under their rule, justice was perverted and even crafts intended for peaceful purposes, such as metallurgy, were used for war.[7] These beings were also called "sons of God" who produced giants through unions with "the daughters of men." Drawing humans into their wars, the giants began killing each other off; yet when they were slain, evil spirits emerged from their bodies. These continued to incite people to warfare and to the worship of idols.[8] Since the nations--including Israel-- willingly followed these spirits, Yahweh then allowed them to afflict humankind. The Satans had access to "the Lord of Spirits;" they tempted humans to do evil and then denounced them before the heavenly court.[9] Although in pagan nations magic was often employed to ward off the power of these beings, Israel disapproved it. Proper antidotes were meditating on God's word, walking in God's commandments and praying.

It is commonly assumed that little is said about demons in the OT proper; speculations of this type arose during the intertestamental period and are reflected extensively in that literature. Early Jewish thought gave only marginal space to *spirits*; even the evil spirit that tormented Saul *was sent from/by the Lord* (1 Sam 16:14; cf. 1 Kgs 22:23; Jdg 9:23). Evil is attributed directly to God in Isaiah 45:7: "God makes peace and creates evil" (KJV). During Israel's wilderness period, we encounter the Destroyer Angel (Exod 12:24; 1 Cor 10:10 explaining Num 25), who executed judgment within God's overall providence. Further, in Israel's early history *the Lord's* anger incited David to take a military census (2 Sam 24:1). In the parallel post-exilic account *Satan* incited David to take the census (1 Chron 21:1). This parallel thus shows the influence of later Persian dualistic emphases upon Israel's conceptions of good and evil.

Satan thus appeared first in biblical literature as one of the ministering spirits, or "sons of God," within the heavenly court. His role was that of prosecuting attorney, or manager of God's wrath department. He was thus used to test humans, prove goodness, or even execute punishment (1 Chron 21:1; Job 1-2; Zech 3). Walter Wink's study of Satan argues that Satan was first of all a servant of God and only through human sinful choices became and becomes the "Evil One," and thus opposed to God's purposes (Wink, 1986:30-33).

A closer study of the biblical record, however, shows other conceptions of evil as well. In his exhaustive study, Edward Langton discusses seven forms of demon appearance in the earlier OT literature. These are (1) the "fiery serpents" which God sent to bite the people (Num 21:6)[10] and fiery flying serpents (Deut 8:15, Isa 14:29; 30:6);[11] (2) demons in the shape of hairy he-goats (*Se'irim*; as in Lev 17:7; 2 Chron 11:15; 2 Kgs 23:8; Isa 13:21; 34:14);[12] (3) other demonic animals, including wild beasts (*Ziyyim* in Isa 34:14), doleful creatures ('*Ochim*, also in Isa 34:14); ostriches (*Benoth ya'anah*); wolves ('*Iyyim*); and jackals (*Tannim* also in 34:14);[13] (4) Azazel, the goat sent out into the wilderness to take evil back to its headquarters as part of the atonement ritual (Lev 16:8);[14] (5) *Lilith* (in Isa

34:14c), a female demon, translated quite differently by English versions: screech owl (AV); night monster (RV); night hag (RSV); (6) the darkness-pestilence (Opel) and the noonday-destruction (Shud) demons of Psalm 91:6; both Opel and Shud are translated daimonia in the Septuagint[15] and (7) the Shedim, translated as demons in the RSV (Deut 32:17; Ps 106:37).

While this study of demonic-type animals is significant--and the Septuagint regards these as demons, yet the OT gives slim evidence of a world-view in which demons played a significant role. We might raise the question whether the conceptualization of demons as entities independent from God represents a psychological projection of the people's fears arising from the uncertainties and turbulence of the intertestamental times.[16] Certainly the influence of Zoroastrian Persian dualism upon Israel's thought, as well as the political crises of the intertestamental period, contributed to Israel's new expressions of the clash between good and evil in terms of good and evil spirits, in which the latter are headed up by Satan. To see whether there is any continuity between this view and earlier OT understandings, we shall now examine the OT on a broader theological basis.

Old Testament Theological Perspectives

In this section we will examine OT thought regarding the heavenly court, the relation between pagan kings, gods and Satan or the devil, the relationship between idols and demons, the OT view of sin and its relation to the demonic, the relationship between Israel's political infidelity and cultic adultery, and Israel's holy warfare practices.

The Heavenly Court

In Psalms 82:1-2; 89:5-18; etc., we see God surrounded by heavenly hosts. In Psalm 82 God takes his place in the divine council and holds judgment among the gods, accusing the pagan gods--and the kings they controlled--of oppressive rule. In Psalm 89, where Yahweh is again surrounded by heavenly beings, an image of warfare occurs in the phrase Yahweh Sebaoth (v. 8), which means "Lord of hosts" or "Lord of the Heavenly Armies." Battle imagery also occurs in the phrase, "Thou didst crush Rahab," which stands in parallel to "thou didst scatter thy enemies with thy mighty arm" (v. 10). Rahab refers to the sea monster of the ancient chaos (see Ps 87:4; Isa 51:9; cf. Leviathan in Job 41:1; Ps 74:14;106:26; Isa 27:1); Yahweh's triumph over Rahab highlights God's power to create order out of chaos (Gen 1 and Ps 33:6). These allusions to ancient primeval chaos affirm God's ultimate creative power over the forces of chaos. God is creator and sustainer of the universe. Psalm 89 moves on to affirm that the Lord is a God of righteousness and justice, of steadfast love and faithfulness (v. 14). God's nature thus affirms the qualities of life that maintain order and harmonious relationships among humans.

This prevailing OT theological conviction of the Lord God's transcendence over creation as creator and moral governor of the universe stands in contrast to both the Mesopotamian and Egyptian creation mythologies, in which the tired gods created humans to do their work, fought among themselves, and lived luxuriously off the people's tribute. In turn, the people's security depended on rightly discerning the capricious will of the gods, who oppressed their subjects, as Psalm 82:2 also noted. (Finger, II, ch. 7).

Relation Between Pagan Kings, Gods and Satan or Devil

Two important texts are Isaiah 14 and Ezekiel 28, oracles of doom spoken against the kings of Babylon and Tyre respectively. The imagery in these texts, including the "fall of Lucifer" (Day-Star, RSV, Isa 14:12, and the prince "in Eden, the garden of God," Ezek 28:13) is used in both later Jewish and Christian history for descriptions of Satan and the devil. The early Christian fathers used these texts also to refer to the pagan kings, but indicated that they are even truer descriptions of the devil (Ferguson: 108). Both Origen and Justin connected the worship of pagan gods with the worship of demons. Origen said, "the worship which is supposed among the Greeks to be rendered to gods at the altar, and images, and temples is in reality offered to demons." Justin explained this by saying that the pagan people "not knowing that these were demons, called them gods, and gave to each the name which each of the demons chose for himself." Tertullian had similar views; Minucius Felix says that "demons are involved in magic, idolatry, divination, oracles, healing cults, and sacrifice" (Quoted in Ferguson: 112-13).

In these texts and in the later church commentary we see the interconnection not only between the pagan kings with their gods and the devil/Satan, but also between the gods and the demons. We shall examine the basis of this connection in the OT itself.

Relation Between the Gods (Idols) and the Demons

Three OT texts put *idols* and *demons* in parallel thought structure and/or regard them as inchangeable:

"They sacrificed to *demons* and not to God,
to *gods* whom they knew" (Deut 32:17).

"For all the gods of the people are idols" (Ps 96:5); the Septuagint uses the word *daimonia* for the word idols.

"They sacrificed their sons and daughters to the demons" (*tois daimoniais*, Psalm 106:37; LXX, *gluptois*).[17] This statement occurs in the context of verse 36 which says they served the idols.

Several quotations from the Apocryphal Baruch are also instructive: "...you provoked him who made you, by sacrificing to demons and not to God" (4:7) and "For fire will come upon her from the Everlasting for many days, and for a long time she will be inhabited by demons" (4:35).

What is striking here is the interconnection between paganism and demonic realities. Not only are the kings the prototype of

Satan and the devil, but the idol worship of the nations over which
these kings rule is ascribed to demon inspiration. Isaiah (44:9-
22;46-47) and the Psalmist (115:3-8;135:15-18) boldly declare, however,
that the idols cannot speak and give direction for life. Regarding
these gods as non-entities, Isaiah 44:9-20 is a "put-down satire"
[read it aloud!] on the reality of such gods--yet all of this within
a historical context in which their functional power was all too
real.[18]

In this context the many "Complaint Psalms" take on profound
significance, for they often comment negatively against pagan belief
or practice, or gods directly. In many of these Psalms the psalmist
cries out for deliverance from the enemy which has now become a
form of personal oppression (Pss 3,5,12,18,68,118:5-18, etc). Friday
Mbon, in his study of the Lament Psalms, notes that the enemies are
not usually identified; they now transcend the original historical
situation and often refer to the godless, or the wicked. He cites S.
Mowinckel who suggests that these are "'supernatural beings, demons,
or evil spirits,' which he prefers to classify under the general term
'sorcery' (awen), and which, he further suggests, may have been
responsible for the psalmists' physical condition in some of the
'psalms of illness'" (1982: 9).

Sin and Its Relation to the Demonic
The OT has three words for sin: *chattath*, meaning "to miss the
mark"; *ayin*, emphasizing the subjective intention, guilt and corruption normally involved in sin; and *peshar*, which regards sin as
rebellion. By themselves, however, such words merely outline some of
sin's formal features. To apprehend sin's concrete reality, we must
ask: within what actual circumstances did sin manifest itself?
Against what kind of norms was it a transgression, a willful act, a
rebellion? In Israel's actual history, sin manifested itself
primarily in a turning away from Yahweh's covenant. Thus Israel's
sin consisted chiefly in idolatry.[19]

This view of Israel's primary sin is confirmed by the prophetic
judgment found in the primary history of Israel, from Deuteronomy
through 2 Kings, which underscores again and again that Israel's
faithfulness or faithlessness to Yahweh was measured by the extent
to which the kings destroyed or promoted the idolatrous pagan practices. Note the contrasting descriptions of Israel's most wicked
king Manasseh and Israel's ideal righteous king, Josiah:
> Manasseh, evil: And he built altars for all the host of
> heaven in the two courts of the house of the Lord. And he
> burned his son as an offering, and practiced soothsaying and
> augury, and dealt with mediums and with wizards. He did
> much evil in the sight of the Lord, provoking him to anger.
> And the graven image of Asherah that he had made he set in
> the house...But they did not listen, and Manasseh seduced
> them to do more evil than the nations had done whom the
> Lord destroyed before the people of Israel (2 Kgs 21:5-7a,9).

<u>Josiah, good</u>: Moreover Josiah put away the mediums and the wizards and the teraphim and the idols and all the abominations that were seen in the land of Judah and in Jerusalem, that he might establish the words of the law which were written in the book that Hilkiah the priest found in the house of the Lord. Before him there was no king like him, who turned to the Lord with all his heart.... (2 Kgs 23:24-25).

In later OT literature (Isa 47:10-15;57:3ff.; etc.) Israel was judged faithless because it engaged in sorcery practiced by pagan peoples. Paganism, sorcery, and idolatry were all part of one package, which according to the above sections was all under the power of the demons and ultimately Satan. Hence Israel's turning to idols was a paradigm shift affecting all of life:[20]

> By turning to other national gods, therefore, Israel turned away not only from the religious commands of Yahweh's covenant but from its social ones as well. Idolatry meant not only preference for another religious cult but for the whole way of ethical and cultural behavior which accompanied foreign cults. It meant asking the gods of Egypt, Canaan, and Assyria, etc., for economic prosperity and military protection in exchange for adopting the moral and social way of life which they represented. (Finger, 1985: 328).

Israel's Political Infidelity and Cultic Adultery

Faithfulness to Yahweh required a totally new way of life, with both religious and political distinctiveness. Israel's worship of idols (a cultic issue) and Israel's dependence upon politics of power (a political military issue) were inherently interconnected. A popular way of putting the point is: religion and politics were never separated in Israel's faith.

Of the many texts demonstrating this point, I will focus primarily upon a well-known text, Isaiah 2:1-22.

<u>Isaiah 2:1-22</u>. This chapter, a central one for understanding Isaiah's overall theological emphasis, presents a sharp contrast between Yahweh's politics of trust and shalom and Israel's idolatries, amassing of wealth, and power of politics. The alternative components look like this:

Yahweh's Politics	Israel's Politics
A Go to Yahweh's mountain to learn *the way* of Yahweh	A Went after diviners and soothsayers (v.6)
B To walk in Yahweh's paths	B Sought riches and war power (v.7)
C *Law* goes out from Zion	C Land filled with idols (v.8)
B' Yahweh's judgment	B' False abasement (v.9) [vv.10-19: haughty pride which Yahweh will punish]
A' Swords beat into plowshares learn war no more	A' Idols will be cast to the moles and bats (v.20)

In concentric structure, the central component C discloses the heart and accent of the composition. The Torah law, given by the prophet, is God's revelation to Israel (Deut 18:15-22); the idols with various forms of sorcery are the symbolic power center of the pagan world (Deut 18:9-14). The idolatrous ways of the nations produced pride and power, the power of military terror; their haughtiness and blasphemous claims, however, will reap disaster (Isa 47:8-10).

Yahweh's politics of "learning the way of the Lord and walking in Yahweh's paths" will lead to economic conversion: war technology will be converted into food-production technology. Trust in Yahweh's way stands in direct opposition to anxious scheming via diviners and soothsayers. The way of sorcery is against Yahweh's way; this is true at the very heart of things, both personally and systemically. The alternatives are two opposing ways of organizing both personal and corporate life. Against Yahweh's will Israel sought a king like unto the nations. This led to the amassing of military power and wealth; predictably, the history is replete with Yahweh's judgment upon the people's idolatry. God's fault with Israel was their unending desire to seek diviners, to worship Baal and the Asherah (which led to male and female sexually carved tree-groves and all the sexual paraphernalia, including cultic prostitution, that went with pagan worship). For these sins--messing with the ways of the nations--Israel and Judah both went into exile.[21]

Israel's Warfare Practices

The crucial texts are Deuteronomy 18:9-22 and ch. 20. The rationale for Israel's practice of holy war--and the only one given so far as we know--is the destruction of pagan idolatry that seeks guidance and power from gods other than the God of Israel. The list of abominations includes sorcerers, wizards, necromancers, augurs, soothsayers--in short anyone who practices divination, i.e., seeking power through evil or the pagan religions. Over against this is the command of God to listen to the voice of the prophet, one who shall be raised up like unto Moses (18:15-22). The command to exterminate pagan peoples (*herem*) is rooted in zeal to seek and listen only for Yahweh God's guidance and empowerment. Indeed, Yahweh will even speak through an ass to safeguard this trust from the divine side: "no divination against Israel" (Num 23:23)!

Deuteronomy 20 outlines the policies for Israel's holy warfare. Millard Lind's *Yahweh Is A Warrior* has shown the supernatural nature of this warfare. God is the Warrior; the people are to stand still and watch the salvation of the Lord (Ex 14:14). Indeed, at times God's people literally participate in war and fighting, but this is seen as a deviation from the divinely willed standard. Hence the fight is really between God and the gods; the people are to choose which God they will serve and then trust God's power to deliver from oppression.

It is possible, however, to distinguish between wars of liberation and wars of separation or nonconformity. In wars of liberation from oppression or defense from aggression the Lord fought for the people and they were only to be still. This model occurs in Exodus 14-15, 2 Kings 6:8-23 (God's miracle against Syrian invasion), and 2 Chronicles 20 (God's defense against Moabite, Ammonite and Meunite aggression). In the wars of separation or nonconformity from the pagan religions, wars against Canaanites in the land of promise, however, God's people were commanded to practice *herem*. In this model God also acted to decisively defeat the enemy through miraculous means, yet the people of Israel were commanded to destroy everything and take no booty; the survival of anything provided occasion for contamination from the pagan idolatry.

Conclusion

In sum, then, OT warfare reflects God's fight against paganism inspired by rebellious spirits linked with the gods of the nations. One thing is clear from this analysis: the topic of the demonic in the OT cannot be "creamed off the top" without taking hold of the total pattern of theological thought. Religious, political and social dimensions are all intertwined; sin and the demonic are part of the entire fabric. Our study shows clearly that the demonic can overtake an entire people's values, including social and political structures, and thus lead them into idolatry.

Perhaps, then, the demonic is to be understood *only* in social, political and religious structural categories, since this is the primary grid in which it expressed itself in the OT analysis above-- granted that we noted some expressions in the personal dimensions as well. We now look to the NT for further insight and shaping of our perception.

New Testament Perspectives

God's warfare against evil is a theme of basic continuity--and discontinuity--between the Testaments. Because this has been too easily overlooked by pacifists, it has also been difficult to adequately assess the Gospels' portrait of Jesus' combat both against demons and an ordering of society which fosters oppression. Jesus' call for a revolutionary new order continues the basic theological accent of the OT holy war concerns. Of the many recent contributions which show the holy warfare interconnection between the testaments,[22] William Brownlee points out well both discontinuity and continuity. Unlike the Maccabean warriors (167-130 BCE) whose blood pleaded "for vengeance like the blood of Abel," the warrior Jesus' "blood pleads only for forgiveness and redemption." Brownlee sees continuity, however, in that Yahweh's warfare is carried forward by Jesus as the human warrior-martyr who is also the divine warrior defeating demonic forces:

His exorcisms are the inauguration of a holy war which
reaches its climax in His death and resurrection wherein He
decisively defeated the Devil and his hordes. In this capacity He is acting as the divine warrior (Brownlee: 286).

In Christ the war against evil has been won, although the final
battle has not yet been fought (witness Revelation). Brownlee's summary of the continuity and discontinuity between the Testaments on
this crucial matter is well put:

> In the area of biblical theology, we often see modifications
> and enrichments as we move from the earliest to the latest
> Scriptures; but in the present case we have the most
> dramatic development and transformation of all, as we move
> from the institution of Holy War, with its *herem* of total
> destruction of the enemy, to the divine-human Warrior, Who
> gives His life for the salvation of the whole world, includ-
> ing His own enemies. Yet, between the *herem* and the Cross
> there is not simply contrast, a radical break with the sub-
> stitution of one for the other, but a theological continuity
> whereby in the history of Holy War the one led to the other
> (Brownlee: 291).[23]

Jesus and the Gospels[24]

From the above analysis it is clear that Jesus began his ministry within the context of distinctive OT holy warfare emphases as
well as the widespread beliefs about demon powers in the intertestamental period. We have also seen how God's battle against evil
expressed itself in many dimensions: creating order out of primor-
dial chaos, planting Israel as the covenant people to establish an
alternative to pagan idolatry, fighting for Israel against the pagan
nations, and calling Israel to a quiet trust in Yahweh's defense.
Moreover, a particular hope arose in Israel that in the eschatological messianic battle God would overthrow all the forces of evil,
headed up by Beliar or Mastema (alternate names for Satan, the cap-
tain of the demons).

Against this background of thought Jesus began his ministry,
announcing that the kingdom of God has come near. This in effect
was a proclamation that God's effective sovereignty over creation
and conquest over all evil powers was about to dawn in human history.[25]

The exorcisms, so prominent in Mark's Gospel, have been recognized by various scholars as the depiction of "a cosmic struggle in
history to inaugurate the eschatological reign of God" (Robinson:
38). Foster McCurley shows a trajectory of emphasis from God's triumph over the primeval-creation chaos, to God's victory over chaos
through Yahweh, the Warrior and King in Israel's history, to Jesus
as "The Son of God Versus Chaos" (McCurley: 12-71). To illustrate
continuity and transformation, McCurley parallels Yahweh's rebuke of
Satan in Zechariah 3 to Jesus' rebuke of the sea in Mark 4:35-41.
(This rebuke harks back to God's own rebuke of primeval chaos). In

rebuking and exorcising the demons Jesus carries forward God's purpose to establish sovereignty and victory over evil (46-52). James
Kallas holds that the Synoptic Gospels' emphasis upon exorcism is
one of the major theological themes in Jesus' ministry:[26]

The arrival of the Kingdom is simultaneous with, dependent
upon, and manifested in the routing of the demons. The
Kingdom arrives in a limited localized area as the demon's
rule is broken. The Kingdom will arrive on a world-wide
basis when the world-wide rule of Satan is broken. The
Kingdom's arrival is to be seen...in the cleansing of the
world which has fallen captive to and obeys the will of the
God-opposed forces of the evil one (1961: 78).

Immediately after his baptism certifying divine sonship, Jesus
was driven into the wilderness (which may be here seen as the locale
of demonic powers) in order to be tempted by Satan. Further, the
word for temptation (*peirazo*) may here carry the idea of Satan's
eschatological attack upon the One who comes to do eschatological
warfare against the evil powers. Jesus' encounter with and
resistance to Satan's temptations thus began in the wilderness and
continued until Gethsemane. His entire ministry was a clash between
the powers of God and the powers of Satan.

Immediately after the call of four disciples, Jesus' first public
action in Mark was an exorcism in the synagogue. An unclean spirit
cried out "'What have you to do with us, Jesus of Nazareth? Have
you come to destroy us? I know who you are, the Holy One of God.'"
Then Jesus rebuked the spirit, "'Be silent, and come out of him!'"
Then "the unclean spirit, convulsing and crying with a loud voice,
came out of him." Here, as in all Jesus' exorcisms, we see contrast
with many exorcisms reported in other contemporary literature, in
which the stories are elaborately embellished to accent the power of
the demons and the ensuing struggle. Jesus' *word* of power alone is
the weapon of victory. Brownlee suggests that the unclean spirit's
addressing of Jesus as "the Holy One of God" fits with the warfare
theophanies in which the Lord God goes forth to battle with all the
"holy ones" with him (286).[27]

While it has been said that about one-third of Mark's Gospel,
including such things as Jesus' rebuke of the sea chaos, reflects
exorcistic emphasis, it is important also to note that Jesus' defense
of his ministry to the religious leaders and his own family rests
upon his authority and power to cast out demons (Mark 3:20-28). The
Matthew/Luke parallel puts it sharply: "If it is by the Spirit of
God ('finger of God' in Luke 11:20) that I cast out demons, then the
kingdom of God has come upon you" (Matt 12:28). This saying, part of
the Beelzebul controversy, indicates clearly that Jesus' exorcisms
were a key sign that the kingdom of God had come and that the
Spirit of God was (and is) at work in Jesus Christ. The Scriptures
on this theme in Mark's Gospel are quite extensive: 1:13,22-
27,39;3:11-12,14,23-30;4:15,35-41;5:1-20;6:7,13;7:24-39;9:14-29.   In addition to the prominent function of Jesus' exorcism in the synagogue,

Jesus' exorcism of the Gadarene demoniac (5:1-20) and the healing of the epileptic boy (9:14-29) play especially significant roles in Mark's Gospel as well: the former extends the power of the kingdom to the Gentiles--the first in Mark--and the latter contrasts Jesus' kingdom power (just manifested in the Transfiguration) with the disciples' lack of faith in appropriating that power. Jesus had already assigned to his disciples the authority to cast out demons (3:14;6:7,13). Mark's Gospel, as well as Matthew, Luke and Acts, thus shows that Jesus shared this authority with his followers.

Jesus' rebuke of Peter, "Get thee behind me Satan!" (8:33) stands in the same stream of emphasis, for here Peter is Satan-inspired; both Peter and Satan must be rebuked. The tempting from the religious leaders is also part of the same satanic trap (8:11;10:2;12:15); Jesus wins these "tests" by clear perception and declaration of God's will.

The entry to Jerusalem, especially the temple confrontation, may be seen as God's holy warrior, Jesus, coming to reclaim the nation from its evil injustices and to reassert the sovereignty of God. Fulfilling the peace theme of Zechariah 9:9-10, Jesus rides upon a donkey which demonstrates that his victory is not by military means but by the longstanding model of quiet trust in God's sovereignty and power. Hence, the powers of evil expressed themselves not only in individuals who were oppressed by demonic powers, but also in the religious and political structures. The religious leaders and the political leaders became part of the satanic effort to detour Jesus from the course of his kingdom ministry (Finger, 1985: 291-98). Early on they sought to kill Jesus (Mark 3:6) and finally came up with a trap to frame a case for the cross (Mark 12:13-17). Standing against Jesus, the religious and political leaders became the mouth-pieces of the Tempter. The jeering taunt, "If you are the Son of God, come down from the cross" (Matt 27:40), may be seen as a repeat of the wilderness temptations, "If you are the Son of God,..." When Jesus cries out "My God, my God, why have you forsaken me," it appears as though the evil forces have won, but in response to Jesus' dying breath the Gentile soldier exclaimed, "Truly this man was the Son of God." This confession together with God's dramatic raising of Jesus on the third day testifies that the powers, who thought they had defeated Jesus, were themselves defeated by the power of Jesus' ministry of prophetic word and love. The crucifixion itself is thus a confrontation with the powers of evil and the resurrection proclaims God's sovereign victory through Jesus Christ over all evil foes.

While Matthew's and Luke's narratives do not contain as high a percentage of exorcisms as Mark does, those exorcisms reported, together with related accents, make the theme just as prominent. Conflict between Jesus and Satan is accented at numerous places: Matt 4:10;9:32;12:22; Luke 6:17ff.; 7:21;8:2;13:10-17,32;22:53 and especially 10:17-20 where the missionary work of the disciples is described in terms of cosmic exorcism, i.e., Satan falling from

heaven. Luke's account of the early church also continues the theme
as a specific aspect of the church's missionary experience (Acts
10:38;26:18). While John's Gospel contains no exorcisms as such (nor
parables for that matter!), the narrative as a whole presents Jesus'
ministry as a clash with the powers of evil: darkness (1:5;8:12),
unbelief and blindness (3:19-21;5:46-47;8:24;9:40-41;12:35-50), and the
"ruler of this world" whom Jesus' glorification "casts out"
(12:31;14:30; 16:11;18:30). Strikingly, in John's Gospel the Jewish
leaders accuse Jesus of having a demon (7:20;8:48;10:20-21), an irony
which serves only to highlight their own blindness.

Jesus' ministry then, in its entirety, is an encounter against
demonic power: demon possession of individual persons; temptations
from Satan, even through his disciples; the hostility and blindness
of religious leaders; and the political powers which crucified Jesus.
While the demonic had sabotaged God's shalom upon earth,[28] Jesus'
confronted and thus overcame the forces and ravages of Satan's work
in the world.

In this holistic ministry of Jesus against the forces of evil, it
is important to note two features of the earlier OT holy war tradition. First, God fights on behalf of the people; in the Gospels it is
Jesus who as God's Son has the authority to carry on this warfare
and who delegates that authority to his disciples, both to cast out
demons (Mark 3:15) and to "take up the cross" (8:34ff). Second, as in
the OT, the prophetic word is the primary instrument of warfare.
The word is the power of God that restores peace to the demonized
and calmness to the sea, heals the sick, raises the dead, proclaims
the kingdom and announces its coming through Jesus' death and
resurrection.

The Early Church's Preaching and Confession

The great Pentecost event climaxes with Peter's affirmation:
"Know you therefore that God has made this Jesus both Lord and
Christ" (Acts 2:36). Oscar Cullmann and others have argued that the
title "Jesus is Lord" (Kyrios), the earliest Christian confession,
proclaims the lordship of Christ over all enemy powers. In this
confession we again encounter a double dimension to the reality of
evil: the political leaders who claimed lordship and the demonic
powers which often inspired those leaders (1 Cor 2:6-8). This early
Christian confession is central to the church's self-understanding
and mission. It climaxes the great Christological hymn in Philip-
pians 2:5-11:

"Therefore God has highly exalted him and bestowed on him
the name which is above every name so that at the name of
Jesus every knee should bow, in heaven and on earth and
under the earth, and every tongue confess that Jesus Christ
is Lord, to the glory of God the Father."

This is a powerful sustaining confession in the face of both
political persecution and demon powers. In 1 Peter we note again
that the death and resurrection of Jesus is viewed as a proclamation

of Christ's victory to the spirits in prison (possibly the rebellious powers) and also as an exaltation of Jesus to the right hand of God so that he is Lord over all principalities and powers (3:18-22). Peter also reports ongoing Christian struggle against the devil and calls believers to resist him (5:8).

Acts reports exorcisms similar to those performed by Jesus (5:16;16:8;19:12) and conflicts between the gospel and pagan-demonic forces (8:9-24;13:6-12;16:16-18;19:13-19). In 17:18 the philosophers believed Paul to be a preacher of strange demons (*tsenon daimonion*).[29]

Hebrews also describes the work of Jesus Christ as conquest of the devil:

> Since therefore the children share in flesh and blood, he himself likewise partook of the same nature, that through death he might destroy him who has the power of death, that is, the devil, and deliver all those who through fear of death were subject to lifelong bondage (2:14,15).

Pauline Theological Perspectives

Paul's writings continue the theme of Christ's triumph over all forms of evil. Indeed, Paul's writings repeatedly proclaim "the gospel of Jesus Christ, which is the power of God unto salvation" (Rom 1:16-17). This salvation delivers persons from "the dominion of darkness...[in]to the kingdom of his beloved Son, in whom we have redemption, the forgiveness of sins" (Col 1:13-14). On this basis and by this gospel power, all discussion about deliverance from bondage rests. *Evangelism is the primary form of power encounter and deliverance from the bondage of sin.*

Paul speaks of evil powers in four ways (Finger, 1985: 322-33). The **first** of these is Satan or the devil. A most striking text occurs towards the end of Romans where Paul calls believers to be wise about what is good and guileless about what is evil: "...then the God of peace will soon crush Satan under your feet" (16:20). Notably, this pronouncement combines the unique NT term "God of peace" with the crushing of Satan's power. In one short declaration, it unites two major trajectories in biblical theology: God as Warrior and God as Peacemaker. They meet in the life of the Christian and the believing community when the power of Satan is crushed by the power of God through Jesus Christ. In this way God triumphs over evil and establishes peace. Klassen connects this text to the missionary proclamation of peace in Luke 10:

> There is a similar juxtaposition of joy, victory, fall of Satan, and "treading under foot snakes and scorpions and all the forces of the enemy..." in the commissioning of the disciples in Luke [10:18ff.]. They return having retained their identity as children of peace and this causes Jesus to become exuberant (Lk 10:21)....

Paul like his fellow Jewish apocalyptic writers sees peace coming through the conquest of evil, the conquest of Satan, a

conquest which is intimately related to the faithfulness of
the believers. But at the same time it is God, the God of
peace who destroys evil... (Klassen, 1987: ms 16-17).
Paul's letters speak of Satan or the devil numerous other times
as well. The incestuous man is to be turned over to Satan for the
"destruction of his flesh but in order that his spirit might be saved
in the day of the Lord Jesus" (1 Cor 5:5). When Paul speaks of ban-
ning a member from the community, he uses the word anathema (1 Cor
16:22; Gal 1:8-9). Rather than restoring a person to Christian community through deliverance from evil, this is a solemn deliverance of
one to the evil powers. A very severe form of church discipine, this
may be seen as the NT analogy to the OT practice of herem (see note
23). Many texts speak of the believers' resistance against Satan
(Eph 4:26f.; 1 Cor 7:5; 2 Cor 2:11;11:14;12:7; 1 Thess 2:18). The ways
of Satan are deceitful; he masks himself as an "angel of light" (2
Cor 11:14) and with deceitful designs seeks to get an advantage over
the believer (2 Cor 2:11). In 1 Thess 2:18 Paul says Satan hindered
the missionary team from visting the Thessalonians (if this refers to
persecution, it is thus another instance of Satan working through
political powers). Also the believer is to give no place to the
devil, thus not letting the sun go down on his or her anger (Eph
4:26f.).

The second face of evil appears in the forces that lie behind
pagan religions and philosophies, as well as behind the law as means
for self-justification. Paul speaks of being redeemed from under
the law and also from "the elemental spirits (stoicheia) of the
universe" (Gal 4:5,8-9; see also Col 2:8,18-23). These structures and
rituals were powers that dominated life and thus destroyed freedom.
For the Jews it was the law--not the law itself, but the works of
the law as a means of salvation; for the Greeks the stoicheia consisted of astrological fate and fortune, powers governing the cycles
of nature, imparted secret knowledge and other occult forms of
ordering life.

From these texts we gain a basic understanding of idolatry
itself. Structures that provide order for existence are turned into
ultimate values, ends in themselves, and thus elevated to powers over
one's life, and then worshipped as gods.[30] Romans 1 shows the same
pattern: through sinful impulses humans fail to see God's revelation
in nature and therefore turn to idolatry, worshipping the creation
and creature instead of the Creator. Hence, God gave them over--
repeated three times (vv 24,26,28)--to the course and consequences of
their wickedness. Only the power of the liberating gospel can free
humans from this chain of sin. Indeed, Jesus "gave himself for our
sins to deliver us from the present evil age."

The third way, related to the above, in which evil expresses
itself is through a variety of terms denoting types of rulership:
principalities, powers, dominions, thrones, etc. While these powers
have a positive function within the world outside of Christ--
restraining evil as agents of God's wrath (Rom 13:4, recall the OT

link between the wrath of God and the demonic), they readily become
instruments of the demonic. Indeed, these powers crucified the Lord
of Glory (1 Cor 2:6-9). The most explicit description of Christ's
triumph over the powers says he "disarmed the principalities and
powers, and made a public example of them" (Col 2:15). In his recent
study, Philip Bender regards the middle form of the verb *apekdusamenos* as significant. He holds that the middle form indicates
that Christ, rather than directly attacking the powers, stripped himself off from their power, thus eluding their grasp and creating a
new community of power independent of the powers. He sums up his
work on this text as follows:

...in the context of *apekdusamenos* as "stripping off from
himself," [Col 2:15] suggests that Christ's warfare against
the Powers consisted 1) of his obedience to God unto death,
resulting 2) in the unmasking of those Powers as adversaries
of God and humanity, leading 3) to their disarming through
the stripping away of their power of illusion, which now 4)
exhibits them as weak and humiliated captives. In Christ,
the Powers have been "deglorified," through the exposure of
their presumptuous and hostile claims. Relative to the
power of God as evidenced by Christ in his rejection of
their claims through obedience to God unto death, the power
of the Powers now appears as "weak and beggarly" (Gal 4:9).
For Paul, Christ's stripping away of the Powers was his
instrument of divine warfare and victory (Bender: 44).

In another important text (Eph 1:20-23) Christ is the head, the
church is his body, and all the powers are put under his feet. The
writer of Ephesians sees the new Christian community, composed of
previously hostile parties, as God's witness to the principalities
and powers, a demonstration of God's power over all other so-called
powers (Eph 3:9-10). The frequent use of Psalm 110:1 throughout the
NT, speaking of Christ's rule at God's right hand, further testifies
to Christ's victory over the powers (Hay: 59ff.).

The consummation also has consequence for the powers, but here
emerge two emphases not easily harmonized. In some texts the picture is that of "destroying every rule and authority" (1 Cor 15:24-28;
cf. 2 Thess 2:3-11), but other texts speak of reconciliation of the
powers to God's purpose (Col 1:19-20; Eph 1:9-10).

Paul uses the word *demons* on only one occasion (1 Cor 10:20-21,
occurring four times). Echoing the earlier connection between
idolatry and demon power, Paul draws a parallel between the
Israelites' worship of idols (vv 6-13) and the Corinthian believers
potential idolatry through participating in cultic meals, dedicated
to pagan gods (vv 14-22). Paul asserts, "you cannot partake of the
table of the Lord and the table of demons" (v 21). While in 8:5ff.
Paul indicated that pagan gods have actually no real existence,[31] in
chapter 10 he does not flirt with the power of demons. He recognizes their power and calls Christian believers away from their
influence.

The **fourth** way in which Paul speaks of evil is in the categories of sin, flesh and death. The evil impulse of "the flesh" (Rom 7:5-18) is in opposition to God's Spirit (Rom 8:3-9; Gal 5:16-18,24;6:8). Through the impulse of the flesh, the law itself becomes an occasion for humans to sin and come under the power of death (Rom 7:5-25). Indeed, Romans 7 reflects a deep psychological despair--fanned by a sin, flesh, law syndrome--which can be overcome only by deliverance through Jesus Christ. Paul frequently calls for a "putting off" of the old and a "putting on" of the new. That which is to be put off are the sins of the flesh; that which is to be put on is the fruit of the Spirit (Gal 5:16-23; Col 3:1-17; Eph 5:25-32). Paul nowhere calls any of these sins demons; yet his overall theology is such as to recognize that demonic power works through sin and preys upon human weakness.

While this analysis of Pauline literature has not shown any explicit use of exorcism, it is clear that Paul regards the Christian gospel as a frontal assault against the evil powers. The well-known Eph 6:10-18 text, a call to Christian warfare, emphasises this point. The spiritual armor listed here is derived mostly from Isaiah where it earlier described God's battle against chaos and evil. The list is as follows:

girdlebelt around waist	Isa 11:5
breastplate of righteousness	
helmet of salvation	Isa 59:17
feet shod with preparation of the	
gospel of peace	Isa 52:7
shield of faith	Isa 7:9b
sword of spirit	Isa 11:4
Word of God	Isa 49:2

Finally, prayer is the important means by which we appropriate God's armor for our victorious living.

Paul states the nature of the Christian's weapons clearly:
For though we live in the world we are not carrying on a worldly war, for the weapons of our warfare are not worldly but have divine power to destroy strongholds. We destroy arguments and every proud obstacle to the knowledge of God, and take every thought captive to obey Christ, being ready to punish every disobedience, when your obedience is complete (2 Cor 10:3-6).

Johannine Perspectives [32]

Like Paul, John speaks of sin as a suprapersonal power, a bondage of the devil (John 8:31-47). Jesus warns his opponents that "everyone who commits sin is a slave to sin," and that they are caught in this slavery because they carry out the desires of the devil. John's first epistle warns that whoever makes a practice of sinning is "of" the devil. Jesus, however, came to destroy the devil's works, and thus takes away our sins (1 John 3:5-9). John contrasts being "of" the devil, who is a liar, with being "of" God, or "in" Christ, who is the Truth (John 8:44,47; 1 John 2:14;3:8-10; 5:18-20). Indeed, Jesus came to bring the truth, and the truth sets us free from bondage to sin and lies (John 8:22ff).

John uses the term "world" (*kosmos*) in a two-fold way. Positively, the "world" was created through Christ and is the object of divine love. Negatively, however, the same word indicates a corporate way of life bitterly opposed to God (John 15:18-20;17:14-17; 1 John 3:3). "The world" in this sense is under the power of the Evil One (1 John 5:19; John 17:15). John depicts Jesus crucifixion and resurrection as a struggle against the "Prince of this world" (John 12:31;14:30;16:11), and as overcoming "the world" (John 12:31; cf. 1 John 5:4-5). For John, as in the Synoptics, Jesus' religious and political opponents are agents of the Prince of this world.[33]

John also throws some light on the psychological effects of sin. While Paul shows how consciousness of sin can lead to despair, John adds that it can produce a tormenting fear of future condemnation. Only the love which is perfected through abiding in Christ can "cast out" this fear (1 John 4:17-18; cf. 2:18;3:19-22).

One might see the Gospel of John as a grand exorcistic proclamation of Jesus' victory over the forces of evil, focused specifically in the collusion of the Jewish and Roman powers against Jesus and over the issue of his kingship. From this perspective, John 12:31 climaxes Jesus' public ministry: "Now shall the ruler of this world be cast out." This exorcistic language declares Jesus' victory over the Prince of this world, to be consummated in his imminent death and resurrection.

The book of Revelation, which breathes a different atmosphere than the Gospel and Epistles of John, is also marked by strong conflictual imagery. Here, however, the central conflict is between the devil/dragon allied with the empire, on the one hand, and the victorious martyr/Lamb and the faithful witnesses (believers), on the other hand. McCurley sees the line of battle clearly drawn. On the one side is the dragon and his beastly allies; and on the other, the Lamb upon Mt. Zion with his followers, whose foreheads are marked by the names of the Lamb and of the Father. The "opponent of the dragon is a Warrior on a white horse; he is the Word of God on whose robe is the name 'King of Kings and Lord of Lords.'" Thus, "On the basis of the adversary involved, the issue at stake is clearly the dominion of the cosmos; either chaos or order will reign after the battle" (71). The final visions of the new heavens and earth clearly affirm the triumph of God's order over chaos.

Though the struggle continues throughout the book, its outcome is clearly signaled by the bursts of praise and worship at the end of each major cycle (Swartley, 1987: 1-11). As in the Gospel of John, one might see the book as powerful liturgy--it is a Lord's Day vision--proclaiming the Lamb's triumph over the forces of evil. Jesus Christ is King of Kings and Lord of Lords (19:16)!

Conclusions and Assessment

Here we address some of the key issues that arise when we think our way from this NT study to our situation today.

1. Do the Gospels clearly distinguish between healings and exorcism? Some texts emphasize the healing ministry of Jesus, and include those demonized as a constituent part (Matt 4:24;15:28;17:17f; Luke 6:18;8:2;9:42; Acts 15:16). In Luke 4:39 a fever is rebuked as a demon and in Mark 4:39 the chaotic sea is rebuked as a demon. Acts 10:38 describes Jesus' entire ministry as "healing those who were oppressed by the devil." On the other hand, numerous texts clearly distinguish between sick persons and demonized persons (Mark 1:32,39; Matt 4:24;8:16;10:1,8; Luke 6:18;13:32; Acts 5:16;8:7). This issue is resolved, however, when we view Jesus' ministry as a conquest over all evil powers and manifestations. In the first century world-view all sickness and demonization were ultimately interconnected with "paradise lost." Hence the Messiah who will bring God's reign upon earth is one who comes to "preach good news to the poor, proclaim release to the captives, give sight to the blind, liberate those who are oppressed, and proclaim the acceptable year of the Lord" (Luke 4:18-19).

Since the Gospels thus distinguish between possession and illness, this raises two cautions for today: first, that we not rule out demon oppression in person's lives and, second, that we do not attribute all physical sickness, emotional illness, and various human handicaps to demons.

2. Since demons were so much a part of the first century world-view, shouldn't we as moderns leave them there?

We have seen that the exorcisms were not isolated phenomena in Jesus' ministry; they were integral to the main theme of the gospel's proclamation, the triumph of God's kingdom over Satan's power. Moreover, Graham Twelftree points out that there was already skepticism about demon possession in the first century (1986: 27). Further, the Gospels do distinguish between bondage and illness. Hence, to some extent it was a choice then also for Christian believers to accept this world-view and to narrate the gospel story within its framework. To conclude, therefore, that the evil spirits were simply first century superstitions is to regard Jesus and the earliest Christians as thoroughly captive to that world-view, and not in just a minor point, but in something quite central to the earliest presentations of the Gospels.

3. Does the fact that the Pauline letters mention no exorcism mean that it should not be part of the church's ministry today? Hamm cites this argument in his list of reasons why exorcism should not be seen as a continuing ministry for today (49-50)[34] and Miller makes the same point (171). Luke's account of Paul's missionary work, however, indicates that exorcism was practiced on occasion. Similarly, since the Synoptic Gospels were written in the last third of the first century, for pastoral and catechetical functions, their extensive attention to Jesus' exorcisms would present a very per-

plexing situation to readers who were not to make it a part of their ongoing ministry. Further, the above argument rests on silence and appears to be at odds with the church's practice in the second and third centuries. As Ferguson notes: "I am persuaded that an important factor in the Christian's success in the Roman world was the promise which it made of deliverance from demons" (1984: 129).

4. The demonic expresses itself in both individual and socio-political structural dimensions. This cautions us against an exclusive focus on personal deliverance ministry in our commitment to Christian warfare against evil. The confrontation between Jesus and the demonic powers took place at many levels; the case is similar in the Pauline and Johannine literature. A consistent pattern of response is also clear: the Christ-model is not a military conquest of any human enemy, but the disarming of the invisible demonic powers through the power of the prophetic Word. This Word issues from a life of humble servanthood which models the way of the cross and love for the person through whom the enemy is at work. It is clear that Christians are called to battle against evil. We must thus ask what forms that should take in our Christian ministry today.

5. Although the Gospel narratives depict deliverance for numerous demonized persons, we gain no clue as to the cause of such phenomena in those particular narratives. The person is not blamed for the situation, though the Pharisees are held culpable for their unbelief. In light of the theological interrelationship between demons, idolatry and paganism, it would be appropriate to surmise that some "opening" to those powers lies behind the phenomenon of possession, whether by the person directly, through ancestral influence,[35] or other means.

6. Is it possible for believers to fall captive to demon oppression or possession? The Calvinist tradition, which has emphasized the security of the believer in Jesus Christ, has tended to answer this question negatively. Indeed, when believers are living victoriously, praising God and witnessing to the gospel's power, any degree of demonization is nigh impossible. However, in nominal Christianity the situation is too often otherwise; through laxity in spiritual nurture and flirting with sin, openings are provided for demon powers. The OT covenant people were tempted toward idolatrous influences and all too frequently capitulated. Likewise, believers are warned against fellowship with demons (1 Cor 10). As Heinrich Schlier says, "Even Christians are not immune from the influence of these dumb idols if they venture near them, for though the idols are nothing, the demons control them" (27).[36]

Theological And Practical Applications

The Relation of the Demonic to Psychological and Sociological Understandings
Our study has shown that the demonic seldom appears in isolation, wholly unconnected with larger psychological, sociological and
political realities. In fact, Scripture presents its activity as so
intertwined with these that modern people often interpret biblical
references to demons as primitive, mythological ways of depicting
phenomena that now can be fully explained by medical and social
science. The Scriptures, however, represent demons as deceptive
(Matt 4:1ff., John 8:44; 2 Cor 2:11;4:3-6;11:14-15; 2 Thess 2:9; Heb
2:14). Demonic powers seldom appear in the open. Usually they
strive to appear as, and work under the guise of, something else.

This has profound implications for the church's healing work.
It means that outward resemblances between alleged cases of bondage
and forms of mental illness do not necessarily mean that the former
interpretations are fanciful. While they may be in some cases, it is
also possible that psychological illness and demon bondage are
intertwined. Demons may enter and take advantage of malfunctioning
psychological and social development, arising often from deep hurts
and disappointments in life (and here the devil does not play fair or
show mercy). The demonic intensifies and further distorts fears,
hostilities, projections, imbalances, etc. that are already there.

Those engaged in scientific forms of healing, then, should look
carefully beneath the surface of apparent mental illness to see if
other factors might be operating. At the same time, those involved
in exorcism should seriously consider the extent to which genuine
psychological disease may be involved. Attempts to explain *all* such
cases as wholly psychological are as misguided as attempts to
explain *all* of them entirely in spiritual terms. The positive
implication is that scientific and spiritual healers often need to
work hand-in-hand. Each needs the diagnostic abilities of the other.
Patients undergoing scientific treatment will need the spiritual
strength and community that science cannot give. Those from whom
demons have been exorcised will often need psychic and social healing all the more as well as spiritual nurture and pastoral care, lest
worse devils return (Luke 11:24-26).

The Role of Personal Responsibility
Spiritual interpretations of problems are often rejected because
those who suffer seem to blame everything on Satan, and thereby
avoid responsibility for things they really can control. But if the
demonic normally works in conjunction with psychic and social
processes, the latter dimensions will be to some degree under
peoples' control. There will be at least a limited area within which
an afflicted person can choose, and positive choices will be essential to healing. On the other hand, since evil has a binding power,
this means that once one has given in to it, even in little ways, one

tends to be afflicted by forces far stronger than one bargained for. If the demonic--Sin, Flesh, the World, Satan's hosts, etc.--are corporate, suprapersonal Powers, giving in to them is like stepping into a rushing river. One may only wade a few steps from the bank before being swept away by a current whose force one cannot break. Nevertheless, one can fight the current to some degree or struggle part way back to the bank, and doing so may be essential to coming within reach of help from anyone else.

In healing, it will be necessary to take both truths into account. Troubled persons must be encouraged to take responsibility wherever they can. Yet the magnitude of their bondage must also be recognized, and additional spiritual and personal resources enlisted against it.

Indications of Bondage

Our study suggests that the demonic may be active in personal psycho-social ways as well as in socio-cultural structures of economics and politics. Based upon above emphases, we suggest some possible diagnostic signs for demon presence in the personal psycho-social realm:[37]

1. A sense of being *ultimately* overwhelmed, swamped, trapped, victimized and unable to extricate oneself from the morass (Rom 7:7-25). Although the swamping seems to originate from outside, one feels so flooded or permeated, so thoroughly identified with the source of bondage, that no escape seems possible. Of course, such a feeling may occasionally assail anyone as a realistic awareness of evil power. But when this feeling recurs repeatedly, so that hope for deliverance through Jesus (Rom 7:25-8:2) seems impossible, the demonic is very likely at work.

2. A fear of *ultimate* condemnation (1 John 4:17-18), conveyed especially through fear of death (Heb 2:14-16). This is the persisting feeling of being inherently unworthy, unclean, unlikeable, deserving of punishment. This is far more than discouragement or even remorse over one's faults. For faults are perversions of abilities that are potentially good. But the feeling that not merely our actions, but the core of our being, is inherently polluted, cannot come from the Creator, but only from his opposite. By this we do not mean the problem of low self-esteem, but rather the crushing feeling of *no* self-worth.

3. Social marginalization. Many from whom Jesus exorcised demons were outcast from society or on its fringes. Of course, it cannot be determined to what extent their bondage led to marginalization, or to what extent marginalization originally left them prey to bondage. But whether as cause or consequence, isolation and alienation are often deeply intertwined with bondage. This underscores the importance of community in the healing process.

4. Response to the holy. Based analogically upon the outcries of the demons in the presence of Jesus, strong negative reaction to Christian symbols such as the Bible and the cross--symbols of the

holy--together with the inability to pray or hear the name Jesus are likely signals of demon oppression. This reaction may express itself in violence or cursing.

5. Unusual power and pre-knowledge. Both these features were evident in the Gadarene demoniac and are frequently evident in cases throughout history and currently as well.

Exorcism and Jesus' Love Command

A practical issue that arises in exorcism is how we apply Jesus' love command, even for the enemy, in violent situations. It is clear that we must distinguish between the individual and the demon powers oppressing the individual. Love, and indeed intense love, must be shown to the individual while at the same time we must have a Jesus-type "cleansing of the temple" response to the evil powers. Speaking various forms of Jesus' love command (Matt 22:37-39;5:44) is a powerful antidote to demon powers that present themselves. But when a person seeks self-destruction, physical restraint is necessary. A proposed guideline for our consideration is: physical restraint may/should be used when it is an expression of love to the one applied; the recipient of the same would acknowledge it as an expression of love when he/she is functioning normally.

Scripture's Primary Emphasis: God's Protection and Victory

While this study has focused on the demonic, as assigned, this topic must be viewed in the larger perspective of biblical revelation. While much of the biblical story can be seen as power encounter (see Kamps), the accent falls on God's sovereignty, protection and victory. The image of Zion, so central to Isaiah and many Psalms, connotes God's sovereignty and victory, on the one hand, and calls humans to faith, trust in God's care, and repudiation of pride and power (see Ollenburger).

Similarly, the prominence of angels throughout the biblical narrative calls us to confidence that God watches over and protects us.[38] God's angels, the Holy Spirit, and our union with Christ Jesus in his exalted position over all evil powers ensures us ample security and safety.

The primary emphasis of Scripture, therefore, is upon God's sovereignty and divine triumph over evil, not on evil itself. This should lead us as Christian believers to a strong life of worship, praise, and adoration of God and our Lord Jesus Christ. Our first emphasis should be on prevention of demonic oppresssion through full commitment of our lives to the worshipful praise of God. Revelation provides a model for us in that each of the cycles of oppressive persecution, inspired by the demonic, ends with the crescendo of worship bursting out in praise to the power of God and the victory of the Lamb. Hence this closing:[39]

"Worthy art thou, our Lord and God,
to receive glory and honor and power,
for thou didst create all things,
and by thy will they existed and were created."

"Worthy is the Lamb who was slain,
to receive power and wealth
and wisdom and might and honor
and glory and blessing!"

And I heard every creature in heaven
and on earth and under the earth and in the sea,
and all therein, saying,
"To him who sits upon the throne and to the Lamb
be blessing and honor and glory
and might for ever and ever!"

Then I heard what seemed to be the
voice of a great multitude..., crying,
"Hallelujah!
For the Lord our God the Almighty reigns."
(Rev. 4:11;5:12-13;19:1,6b)

Notes

1. We are aware that the term *deliverance* is preferred by most communities engaging in this ministry. However, the word exorcism is widely used in literature on the Bible as well as in anthropological studies more generally.

2. The recent publication by Hans Dieter Betz (*The Greek Magical Papyri*), e.g., shows the many magical formula that the Greeks used to ward off demon powers. In his phenomenological study of demonological beliefs of the Hellenistic world, Jonathan Smith compares beliefs in the Greco-Roman world with those in both the Orient and in more primitive animistic religions. In all systems of belief, the intermediary world between heaven and earth is very important; people do not relate directly to God but indirectly through intermediary spirits and powers.

3. For what follows, see Thomas Finger, *Christian Theology: An Eschatological Approach*, Vol. II, ch. 7, and Everett Ferguson, 94-95.

4. Jubilees 2:2; 1 Enoch 60:11-24, 82.

5. Jubilees 15:31.

6. The account of the "Satans," who persuaded some 200 "Watchers" to descend to earth for this purpose, is found in 1 Enoch 6, 40-71; "Satanail" appears in 2 Enoch 29:4-5, 31:30-6; cf. Life of Adam and Eve, 12-17.

7. Jubilees 4:15; 1 Enoch 8, 69.

8. 1 Enoch 15, Jubilees 11:2-7; cf. Gen. 6:2-4.

9. 2 Enoch 40:7.

10. It is striking that the Hebrew consonants for the word serpent in Gen. 3 may also mean "to divine." This would indicate that
the serpent is here already playing the role of counterfeit; hence
Eve's deception may have involved the difficult issue of discerning
whether the voice was really the voice of God or the voice of a
counterfeit.

11. Langton thinks that the seraphim (Isa. 6:1ff) were originally
also connected to the same notion although in Isaiah they are
angelic spirits. He bolsters this association by 1 Enoch 20:7 where
both the serpents and cherubim are under the rule of Gabriel in paradise (30:8).

12. The Greek Septuagint LXX regularly translates this word
daimonia.

13. The LXX translates almost all these daimonia.

14. Langton believes that Azazel may have first been a Semitic
god of the flocks and was later "degraded to the level of demon
under the influence of Yahwism" (46).

15. With this Langton mentions also the 'Alukah demon of Prov
30:15, translated leech (RSV), but which, Langton argues, might be
better translated vampire. This is a bloodsucking type demon, a
parallel to Babylonian texts that speak of "demons that spill the
blood of men, devour their flesh, and suck their veins" (50).

16. Another scholarly study points out that many passive means
of resistance to demons were employed. These consisted of various
forms of ascetic living: clothing, hygiene, fasting, sexual con-
tinence, sleeping regulations, covering of eyes, or silence (Böcher:
42-50).

17. A most interesting text occurs in Isaiah 65:3 where the LXX
adds a phrase not in the Hebrew text (nor the RSV or KJV). The
English translation would be: "burning incense upon the bricks to
the demons which are not (do not exist)." Although this comment is
not a part of the biblical canon as such, it reflects continued
reflection upon the status of demons, empirically and ultimately.
The statement both recognizes the reality of demons dominating
people's lives and religion and yet denies their ultimate reality.

18. Wisdom of Solomon 12-15 is an extended spoof on the gods of
nations. One part of this satire relates to some modern insight on
how people get hooked into demonic forces:

For a father, consumed with grief
    at an untimely bereavement,
made an image of his child,
who had been suddenly taken from him;
and he now honored as a god what
    was once a dead human being,
and handed on to his dependents
    secret rites and initiations.
Then the ungodly custom,
    grown strong with time, was kept as a law,

and at the command of monarchs
    graven images were worshiped. (Wisd Sol 14:15-16)
19. To punish Israel for such sin, Yahweh often handed Israel
over to the enemy. When Israel would repent and cry for help, Yahweh would raise up a deliverer (Judg 2:11-18). Or God would punish
through a plague (Num 16:41-50;25:1-13) or famine (2 Sam 21:1-8) or
exile itself (Jer 18:1-17).
20. Gerald Gerbrandt's dissertation on kingship substantiates
this point; Israel's kings were evaluated according to their record
of allowing or destroying pagan worship within Israel (264-73).
21. A study of Ezekiel 6-7, as well as chapter 16, would document the same points made above in the Isaiah 2 study. In his study
of "the knowledge of God," a formula occurring 81 times in Ezekiel,
Millard Lind points out that "the knowledge of God" is interconnected
with Israel's public political policies. The issue is whether they
will pursue quiet trust in Yahweh's sovereign Lordship or whether
they will amass military power and go the way of political pride
(hybris). Israel's cultic adultery and political infidelity are
deeply interconnected; they did not trust Yahweh but pursued the
pagan way of amassing military armaments.
    This crucial point is summed up in Hosea 14:3:
    Assyria shall not save us!
    We will not ride upon horses;
    And we will say no more, "Our God,"
    To the work of our hands.
22. Philip D. Bender's recent master's thesis, "The Holy War
Trajectory in the Synoptic Gospels and the Pauline Writings" (1987),
shows well this interconnection. The contributions of Eller (1981)
and McCurley (1983) are also very helpful. Both Lind (1980) and
Ollenburger (1987) develop major OT perspectives to an understanding
of Yahweh's warfare.
23. The same development of thought is reflected when the Septuagint translates the OT term, "man of war" (Exod 15:3), by the
phrase "The Lord destroys war" (kurios suntriben polemous) (Klassen,
ms. 6). Another connection between the OT holy war practices and
the NT may be found in Rebecca Yoder's article in which she shows a
trajectory between the ban (herem) of the OT and church discipline
practiced in the NT. In both cases the aim was to eliminate evil
from the community.
24. We have decided to handle Jesus and the Synoptic Gospels
together, although one could make the case that Matthew, Mark and
Luke have distinctive theological emphases of their own and should
be handled separately. For example, what is the significance of
Mark's gospel giving major emphasis to exorcisms in an A.D. 65-70
context when it was written? Does this reflect the practice of the
churches to which Mark wrote? Is it an effort to connect with the
prevailing understandings in the Greco-Roman world concerning
"divine men"? Or is it basically a representation of Jesus' ministry
in this way to accent the inauguration of God's reign? The latter

is the opinion of James Robinson in *The Problem of History in Mark*. Further research needs to be done to answer these questions.

25. William Klassen also treats the relationship of Jesus to the OT imagery of warfare. Citing many texts from intertestamental writings and the time contemporary to Jesus, he concludes, "Jesus embraced the Messianic war idea but followed those of his Jewish colleagues who saw it as a struggle in which suffering love even to the point of dying for one's enemies could bring liberation" (1987: 175).

26. Kallas argues that in the Gospels Jesus' triumph over demons is just as important as the theme of eschatology. Most scholars have emphasized the latter considerably, but have given very little attention to the former.

27. The texts in which this concept is found are Zech 14:3,5; Deut 33:2; Ps 89:6-8.

28. Luke's Gospel emphasizes this latter point by announcing that Jesus' coming is "Peace on earth; good will for humanity" (2:14) Jesus' public ministry is consummated with the antiphonal response from Jesus' disciples, "peace in heaven, and glory in the highest" (19:38). Luke uses the word peace (*eirene*) 14 times, thus showing special effort to connect the establishment of God's shalom with "healing all those who were oppressed" (Acts 10:38).

29. A verbal form of the same occurs again in verse 22 with a similar form in 25:19. While in the OT the trend was to identify foreign gods with demons, especially in the LXX, the trend in English translations of the NT is to render a text which uses the term demons by the term foreign gods.

30 For sustained description of this process see Daniel Patte's exposition of Paul's faith convictions in Romans 1-8 (261,284-85).

31. One learning for me (WMS) in this consultation, triggered by discussions on whether demons are real, was the thought that the word *real* occurs rarely in the Bible. It is rather at home in Greek thought. A check in concordances confirmed my hunch that no Hebrew or Greek word is readily translated *real*. Translators introduced it here in the RSV.

32. For what follows, see Finger, Vol. II, ch. 7.

33. While John seldom emphasizes the kingdom, he makes it very clear that this was the issue over which Jesus was crucified. When Jesus tells Pilate that his kingdom is "not of this world," he is not referring to a purely spiritual kingdom. He goes on to explain that if it were, "my servants would fight, that I might not be handed over to the Jews..." (John 18:36). Here Jesus contrasts the way of his kingdom, the way of *agape*, with the way of "the world" as carried out by both the religious leaders and Pilate.

34. Hamm cites ten reasons why the church today should not take exorcism as normative for its practice and then seven reasons why it should (49-52). After assessing the arguments, he leans toward employing it in the church's ministry today, but with caution and care.

35. On the matter of ancestral influence, we note the principle
enumerated numerous times in the OT that the punishment of one's
sins may extend into the third and fourth generation, in contrast to
God's love extending to thousands of generations. But Ezekiel 18
speaks against using this principle to explain the plight of the
exiles i.e., blaming their situation on the sins of their forebearers.
Rather, Ezekiel holds that "the soul that sins shall die," thus
affirming personal accountability. Going beyond the scope of biblical exegesis *per se*, we may want to examine the interrelationship
between a family systems approach to human problems, as used in
psychology today, and the earlier biblical principle of sin affecting
the third or fourth generation.

36. 1 Corinthians 10 is addressed to believers. Schlier then
mentions the warning against demonical power in Revelation:

The rest of humankind, who were not killed by these plagues,
did not repent of the works of their hands nor give up worshiping demons of idols of gold and silver and bronze and
stone and wood, which cannot either see or hear or walk; nor
did they repent of their murders or their sorceries or their
immorality or their thefts (9:20).

In our judgment this text does not speak of believers, but of the
part of humankind under the power of the beast.

37. We are not suggesting diagnostic signs for the demonic in
the socio-cultural corporate sphere, since this is not the focus of
the consultation. Both Berkhof and Wink speak to this. It does
raise the question whether our witness to the structures of Christ's
victory over the powers should include some form of social exorcism.
One conference participant told of such experiences, in which exorcistic declaration was part of a liturgy used in witness against
socio-political evil.

38 We have the right to pray for God's angels to protect us.
References to angels appear almost half again as often as that to
devil(s), Satan, and evil spirits, in the Bible according to Young's
Concordance. In J. B. Smith's *Greek-English Concordance*, angels
occurs 186 times, while devil occurs 38 times; demon(s) (noun and
verb), 78 times; and Satan, 37 times. While "evil spirit," appears 47
times, the (my)Spirit/Holy Spirit/Spirit of God/Lord/Christ/Truth
occurs 226 times.

39. We recommend the book by Robert E. Webber, *Celebrating Our
Faith* in which the worship of the believing community is described
both historically and contemporarily as the resource for triumph
over demonic powers.

Bibliography

Bender, Philip D.   "The Holy War Trajectory in the Synoptic Gospels and the Pauline Writings." M.A. Thesis: AMBS, 1987.

Betz, Hans Dieter, ed.   *The Greek Magical Papyri in Translation, including the Demotic Spells.* Chicago and London: University of Chicago Press, 1986.

Böcher, Otto.   *Das Neue Testament und die dämonischen Mächte* (Stuttgarten Bibel-Studien 58).   Stuttgart: Katholisches Bibelwerk, 1972.

Brown, Peter.   "Sorcery, Demons and the Rise of Christianity: From Late Antiquity into the Middle Ages." In *Religion and Society in the Age of Saint Augustine.* New York: Harper and Row, 1972. Pp. 118-146.

Brownlee, William H.   "From Holy War to Holy Martyrdom." In *The Quest for the Kingdom of God.* Ed. by H. B. Huffman, F. A. Spina, A. R. W. Green. Winona Lake, IN: Eisenbrauns, 1983. Pp. 281-292.

Dunn, James D. G. and Graham H. Twelftree.   "Demon-Possession and Exorcism in the New Testament," *Churchman* 94, 3 (1980), 210-25.

Eller, Vernard.   *War and Peace from Genesis To Revelation.* Scottdale, PA/Kitchener, Ont.: Herald, 1981.

Ferguson, Everett.   *Demonology of the Early Christian World.* New York/Toronto: Edwin Mellen Press, 1984.

Finger, Thomas N.   *Christian Theology: An Eschatological Approach,* Vol. 1; Thomas Nelson, 1985/Herald, 1987. Vol. II; Herald, 1989.

Gerbrandt, Gerald.   *Kingship According to the Deuteronomic History* (SBL Diss. Series No. 87). Atlanta, GA: Scholars Press, 1986.

Hamm, Dennis.   "The Ministry of Deliverance and the Biblical Data: A Preliminary Report."   In *Deliverance Prayer: Experiential, Psychological and Theological Approaches.*   New York/Ramsey: Paulist Press, 1981.

Hay, David M.   *Glory at the Right Hand: Psalm 110 in Early Christianity* (SBL Monograph Series 18).   Nashville/New York: Abingdon, 1973.

Kallas, James G.   *The Significance of the Synoptic Miracles.* Philadelphia: Westminster, 1961.

Kamps, Timothy James.   "The Biblical Forms and Elements of Power Encounter." M.A. Thesis: The Columbia Graduate School of Bible and Missions (SC), 1985.

Klassen, William.   "Jesus and the Messianic War." In *Early Jewish and Christian Experience: Studies in Memory of William Hugh Brownlee,* eds. C. A. Evans and W. F. Stinespring.   Atlanta: Scholars Press, 1987.

Klassen, William.   "The God of Peace: New Testament Perspectives on God." Ms., 1987.

Langton, Edward.   *Essentials of Demonology: A Study of Jewish and Christian Doctrine, Its Origin and Development.* London: The Epworth Press, 1949.

Lind, Millard.   *Yahweh Is A Warrior.*   Scottdale, PA/Kitchener, Ont.: Herald, 1980.

Mbon, Friday M.   "Deliverance in the Complaint Psalms: Religious Claim or Religious Experience."   *Stud.Bib.Theol* 12.1 (April, 1982), 3-15.

McCurley, Foster R.   *Ancient Myths and Biblical Faith: Scriptural Transformations.*   Philadelphia: Fortress Press, 1983.

Miller, Paul M.   *The Devil Did Not Make Me Do It.*   Scottdale, PA/Kitchener, Ont.:   Herald, 1977.

Ollenburger, Ben C.   *Zion the City of the Great King: A Theological Symbol of the Jerusalem Cult* (JSOT Supp. Series 41).   Sheffield Academic Press, 1987.

Patte, Daniel.   *Paul's Faith and the Power of the Gospel: A Structural Introduction to the Pauline Letters.*   Philadelphia: Fortress Press, 1983.   Pp. 256-295.

Robinson, James M.   *The Problem of History in Mark.*   London: SCM Press, 1957.

Schlier, Heinrich.   *Principalities and Powers in the New Testament.* New York: Herder and Herder, 1961.

Smith, Jonathan.   "Towards Interpreting Demonic Powers in Hellenistic and Roman Antiquity."   In *Aufstieg und Niedergang der romischen Welt* II. 16.1 (ed. W. Haase).   Berlin/New York: Walter de Gruyter, 1978.

Swartley, Willard M.   "Worship Resource on Revelation."   Mennonite Board of Congregational Ministries, 1987.

Twelftree, Graham H.   "The Place of Exorcism in Contemporary Ministry," *St. Mark's Review* 127 (Sept 1986), 25-39.

-----.   *Christ Triumphant: Exorcism Then and Now.*   London *et al.*: Hodder & Stoughton, 1985.

Webber, Robert E.   *Celebrating Our Faith: Evangelism Through Worship.*   San Francisco *et al.*:   Harper & Row, 1986.

Wink, Walter.   *Unmasking the Powers: The Invisible Forces that Determine Human Existence.*   Philadelphia: Fortress, 1986.

Yoder, Rebecca.   "From *'Herem* to Anathema':   The Participation of God's People in His Judgment."   AMBS Library, 1980, and in *OccPapers* No 1 (IMS) under altered title.

Response to Thomas Finger and Willard Swartley

Josephine Massynbaerde Ford

I should like to say that this was an interesting paper and covered the material in a very comprehensive way. In this response I should like to take three approaches:

(a) a reflection on the material in pages 10-17, perhaps bridging the deuterocanonical books and the New Testament by reference to Qumran and to further details from the *Pseudepigrapha;*
(b) some reflections on the New Testament materials;
(c) brief suggestions for pastoral application.

Palestinian Jewish Background of the First Century CE

Among the *Pseudepigrapha* newly translated under the editorship of James H. Charlesworth[1] is a document as fascinating as it is astounding, namely, *The Testament of Solomon*, translated by D. C. Duling.[2] This is a folktale about Solomon building the Temple. He subdues the demonic world (male and female) to assist him in building the Temple. From this document we learn of the names, physical appearance and functions of many demons, and we are told how we can overcome them, usually by the invocation of an angelic name or the name of God *per se* or, sometimes, by a kind of spell rather similar to the exorcisms in the Book of Tobit.[3] *The Testament of Solomon* is an excellent example of the influence of magic, astrology, angelology, demonology and primitive medicine practiced by people in the ancient world. It was most probably written in Koine Greek[4] and is usually dated during the first to the third century C.E. In an old but still useful article Conybeare[5] argues that it was a Christian redaction of a Jewish document "the very collection of incantations which, according to Josephus, was composed and bequeathed by Solomon." Conybeare[6] argues for a first century CE date. He also compares the demonology common to Paul, the apostles, and that of the Essenes (he is writing prior to the discovery of the Qumran documents). Duling[7] states that the general agreement is that it reflects first century Judaism. The author appears to have been a Greek-speaking Jew; later a Christian redacted the material. Duling[8] argues that the material has an "international quality" but may come from Babylonia, Asia Minor or Egypt: it is, of course, a composite work as we have the text now.

The importance of the *Testament of Solomon* for the modern Christian, particularly the scholarly Christian, is that it represents a part of the world-view of the Second Commonwealth for the Jew and of the early church for Christians. It is an attempt to meet human needs whether these be physical ailments, psychological problems or interpersonal conflicts, either domestic or in a wider sphere. It also gives us an insight into the Jewish and/or Christian view of Solomon which might well be behind Jesus' statement during the Beelzebub controversy:

39

...for she (the Queen of Sheba) came from the ends of the earth to hear the wisdom of Solomon, and behold, something greater than Solomon is here (Matt 12:42).

What I wish to do now is to compare a few examples from this ancient text with Jesus' exorcisms as recorded in the canonical Gospels.

(1) The binding of the Lion-shaped Demon (*T.Sol.* 11:1-7). The demon comes to Solomon "roaring like a stately lion" (cf. 1 Pet 5:8). He tells Solomon that he is associated with terminal illnesses but he also says:

I have another activity. I involve the legions of demons subject to me...The name of all demons which are under me is legion."

We may compare the incident of the Gadarene demoniac (Mark 5:1-20 and par). Solomon asks for his name and also how he can be thwarted. The demon replies in words which surely show Christian redaction:

By the name of the one who at one time submitted to suffer many things (at the hands) of men, whose name is Emmanouel, but now he has bound us and will come to torture us (by driving us) into the water of the cliff....

(2) Another interesting example is that of Kunopegos, the sea-horse demon. He tells Solomon:

King Solomon, I am a cruel spirit of the sea. I rise up and come on the open seas...and I trip up the greater number of men (who sail) on it. I raise myself up like a wave and, being transformed, I come in against the ships, for this is my activity: to receive beneath the sea treasures and men. For I raise myself up, take men, and hurl them under the sea (*T.Sol.* 16:1-5)

We may compare Jesus rebuking of the sea: *epetimēsen tō anemō kai eipen tē thalassē: siōpa, pephimōso* (he *rebuked* the wind and said to the sea, Peace! be still. Mark 4:35-42 and par). This demon is thwarted by Iameth but Solomon deals with him as follows:

Then I ordered him to be cast into a broad, flat bowl, and ten receptacles of seawater to be poured over (it). I fortified the top side all around with marble and I unfolded and spread asphalt, pitch, and hemp rope around over the mouth of the vessel. When I had sealed with the ring (the magical ring of Solomon), I ordered (it) to be stored away in the *Temple of God* (T.Sol. 16:6-7).

We may also compare this to the angels with bowls who come from the temple in Revelation 16. We must not let too many demons retain us! However, I wish to make some reference to the thirty-six heavenly bodies which (who), according to the *Testament of Solomon*, are purported to have evil effects on humankind. These thirty-six are as follows:

Disorder	Demon	Thwarted by
throbbing headache	Ruax	Michael
migraine	Barsfael	Gabriel
eye disorder	Artosael	Quriel
sore throats	Oropel	Raphael
ear disorders	Kairoxanondalon	Uriel
tumours of the parotid gland and tetanic recurvation	Sphendonael	Sabael
paralysis	Sphandor	Arael
perversion of heart and mind	Belbel	Karael
colic	Kourtael	Iaoth
nephritic conditions	Metathiax	Adonael
domestic fights and feud	Katanikotael	Those wishing to make peace must 'write on seven laurel leaves the names of those who thwart me: Angel, Eae, Ieo, Sabaoth, imprison Katanikotael.
dissensions in human minds	Saphthorael	Write down these words "Iae Ieo, sons of Sabaoth," wear around neck.
loosenings of the tendons	Pheobothel	Adonai
chills with shivering and sore throats	Leorel	Recite "Iax, do not stand fast, do not be fervent, because Solomon is fairer than eleven fathers.
shivering and numbness	Soubelti	Rizoel
incurable fevers	Katrax	Pulverize coriander, rub on patient's lips, say "I adjure you by Zeus, retreat from the image of God."
convulsions, falling to ground	Ieropa	Say into right ear of patient, "Iouda Zizabou." (3x)
separates wife from husband	Modebel	Write names of the eight fathers and place in door ways
incurable fevers	Mardero	Write his name in house.
knee disorders	Rhyx Nathotho	Write Phounebiel on piece of papyrus.
croup in infants	Rhyx Alath	Write Rarideris and carry it.
heart pain	Rhyx	Write Audameoth "Raiouoth."
nephritis	Rhyx Manthado	Write "Iaoth, Ouriel"
pain in ribs	Rhyx Aktonme	Write on piece of wood from ship which has run aground, "Marmaraoth of mist."
indigestion	Rhyx Anatreth	If he hears "Arara, Arare" will retreat.

"I make off with minds and alter hearts"	Rhyx, the Enautha	Write "Kalazael."
diarrhea and hemorrhoids	Rhyx Axesbuth	"If anyone adjures me in pure wine and gives it to the one who is suffering. I retreat immediately."
insomnia	Rhyx Hapax	Write "Kok; Phedismos" and wear on temples.
hysteria, pains in bladder.	Rhyx Anoster	Mash seeds of laurel into pure oil, massage patient's body, say, "I adjure you by Marmaraoth."
longterm illnesses	Rhyx Physikoreth	Put salt in (Olive) oil, massage, say "Cherubim, seraphim, help (me)."
swallowing fish bones	Rhyx Aleureth	Put bone from fish into breasts of patient.
detached tendons	Rhyx Ichthuon	If he hears "Adonai, malthe" will retreat
tonsilitis	Rhyx Achoneoth heap.	Write on ivy leaves "Leikourgos," place them in
jealousy and squabbles between those who love each other	Rhyx Autoth	Write down Alpha and Beta
evil eye on people	Rhyx Phtheneoth	Thwarted by the much suffering eye, when inscribed.
holds grudge against body; demolish houses; cause flesh to rot	Rhyx Mianeth	Write on front entrance of house "Melto Ardad Anaath."

This long section, summarized from Duling, can be illuminating for our study of demonology in the New Testament in a concrete way and particularly it is useful as a contrast to Jesus' manner of deliverance.

Reflections on New Testament Materials, with Pastoral Aspects

In general we note concerning Jesus' exorcisms:

(a) Except for the case of the Gadarene swine, which contains some unique and incongruous details, which in all likelihood do not go back to the historical Jesus, the Lord does not parley with the demon(s), ask their names or use magical devices;

(b) Jesus touches physically ill patients but does not touch demoniacs (cf. Vermes)[9]

(c) Jesus' exorcisms do not seem to be associated with angels, but only with the Name of God. (Subsequently the disciples use only the name of Jesus, not names of angels).

(d) When considering Jesus' healing miracles it is sometimes difficult to discern whether a case is one of demonic possession[10] or obsession.[11] For example, in the cure of the boy with epilepsy there seems to be a fusion of two stories (Mark 9:14-29 and par) and in Mark 4:39 Jesus "rebukes" the demonic in the physical sea. We can ask here whether Jesus, or the evangelist, is using contemporary language or whether Jesus himself believed that physical illness and natural disasters were caused by the demonic. The latter seems unlikely.

Revelation of John and the "demonic"

I should like to make a few remarks about the Revelation of John and the "demonic." Strange as it may seem, "demons" *per se* and "unclean spirits" are not prominent in the Apocalypse. It is curious that a highly developed angelology should not also reveal a comparably developed demonology. Or have we, as Finger and Swartley suggest, the mediation of both good and evil or blessing and curse through the angelic beings? I would suggest that there is a cryptic demonology at play, at least on the literary level, in the Revelation of John.

Firstly, we have the idea of seals and unsealing. Now, although the seals with which we are concerned here are the seals on the scroll which the Lion of Judah unleased,[12] yet the whole idea of "sealing" for protection or unsealing followed by calamity would provoke a sensitive reaction on the part of those who heard or read the Apocalypse. God is called "The Lord of Sealing."[13] A person can be sealed "with the g[re]at seal of the Lord of the Universe whose knot cannot be united and whose seal cannot be broken" or "sealed with the three signet-rings and doubly sealed with the seven seals..." By sealing one was protected against cosmic and other catastrophes. I will give one example, again from the *Testament of Solomon*,[14] although many other examples can be found. This text (22:9-15) describes how the Arabian wind demon was trapped in a leather flask. The following instructions were given:

"Load your camel, take a leather flask and seal, and go off to Arabia to the place where the spirit is blowing. Then take hold of the wineskin and (place) the ring in front of the neck of the flask (against the wind). As the flask is being filled with air, you will discover that it is the demon who is filling it up. Carefully, then, tie up the flask tightly and when you have sealed (it) with the ring, load up the camel and come back here. Be off, now, with blessing" (22:9-11).

I suggest that the breaking of the seals means the unleashing of cosmic catastrophies just as demons were loosed from bottles.

A closer influence of magic on our text, I believe, is found in the section on the bowls, the third septet (Rev 16). One notes that the bowls appear to be in the heavenly Temple, for the angels bearing them proceed from there. The word *phiale* is used of a liturgical bowl. The angels are robed as priests. When the bowls are poured out calamities occur. About one hundred Aramaic incantation bowls have been found with the charm written inside the bowl. This appears to be quite a feat for an artist. Writing may have been regarded as quasi sacred. The bowls were charms against evil spirits. They have been found in pairs fastened rim to rim. Some were sealed with bitumen, some tied together. In Text 15 of Isbell[15] we have a bowl which is deposited and sunk down in the earth. They are often found either in pairs or turned upside down in foundations of houses. In the Apocalypse the angels pour out the contents of

the bowl and various calamities occur: many of these are reflected
in the texts quoted and translated by Isbell.[16]

I must add that archaeologists date the bowls which have been
found only from the sixth century, but literary evidence is earlier
than this.

However, the message of Revelation is one of "peace" because God
is represented as the controller of all events both good and evil.
God's kingdom triumphs in the end.

I end by noting the "demonology" at Qumran. This is, of course,
found most clearly in the *The Rule of the Community*. As in the *War
Scroll*, there is, of course, a sharp dualism; but in no ways does it
appear magical. The section on the Two Spirits, the Spirit of Truth
and the Spirit of Perversity is found in I QS 3:13-4:26. The point
which is of interest to us is that the teaching on the repudiation of
the Spirit of Perversity is an integral part of the initiation of
members through which they enter into the *New Covenant* and which
requires purification rites through water. Thus we might tentatively
say that the Qumran initiation rite forms an interesting antecedent
to Christian baptism which, at least from the third century, contained exorcism rites.

The fruits of the Perverse Spirit comprise cupidity, neglect of
righteousness, impiety, falsehood, pride, haughtiness, falsity, deceit,
cruelty, abundant wickedness, impatience, much folly, burning
insolence, abominable deeds committed in the spirit of lust,
blaspheming tongue, etc. The fruits of the Spirit of Truth include
humility, forbearance, abundant mercy and eternal goodness, understanding and intelligence, wisdom with faith, etc. (1 QS 4:2-14).

If there is one main point which Qumran can teach us, it is the
importance of angelology. It is curious how people become obsessed
with deliverance but seem almost to overlook the commitment which
must follow, a commitment to God but also to the company of holy and
pure spirits whom we usually term "angels." For the Qumran people
these were healing messengers from God.

I should conclude, therefore, that we have concrete evidence for
popular demonology in the time of the New Testament, but that Jesus'
exorcisms stand out as unique. They are devoid of magic, incantation, parley with the demonic, and long and repeated ceremonies.
That Jesus came as the Messiah who conquered all demons is no
insignificant part of his ministry. It brought to the people of his
time a freedom from real bondage, from fear and superstition; but it
offered more than this. It offered a radical discipleship which
would bring the bruised of the world into union with the Wounded
Healer and make them resplendent with the gifts and fruits of the
Spirit.

Notes

1. J. H. Charlesworth, *The Old Testament Pseudepigrapha* (hereafter *OTP*), vol. I & II. Garden City, N.Y.: Doubleday, 1983, 1985.

2. *OTP*, vol. I, 935-987.

3. See, for example, Tobit 6:6-8 (demons can be driven away by smoke from the heart and liver of a fish). "As he went he remembered the words of Raphael, and he took the live ashes of incense and put the heart and liver of the fish upon them and made a smoke. And when the demon smelled the odour he fled to the remotest parts of Egypt, and the angel bound him," (Tobit 8:2-3).

4. For a discussion of the original language see C. C. McCown, *The Testament of Solomon*, Leipzig, 1922 (an indispensable critical edition).

5. F. F. Conybeare, "The Testament of Solomon," *JQR* 11 (1889), 14. See also further reference cited by Duling, *op. cit.*, 940-941.

6. Conybeare, *JQR* 11 (1898), 12.

7. Duling, "Testament of Solomon" (*OTP*, I), 1983, 942.

8. "Testament of Solomon" (*OTP*, I), 1983, 943.

9. Geza Vermès, *Jesus the Jew* (London: Collins, 1973), 66.

10. For examples of possession and obsession see, for example, R. P. Aug. Poulain *The Graces of Interior Prayer*, 1959, 428ff. (This is a very helpful discussion, also of exorcism practice, ed.).

11. The Roman Catholic church makes a clear distinction between possession (where the patient is taken over by the demonic and has no control--a case unlikely if a person is a practicing Christian--and obsession which is an attack by the demonic (e.g. purported to be experienced by the Curé d'Ars and other saints) where a person is conscious and can take means to control the situation.

12. As E. Vischer, *Die Offenbarung des Johannes,* 1895, points out, it is really the Lion of Judah, not the Lamb, who is worthy to open the seals.

13. Charles D. Isbell, *Corpus of the Aramaic Incantation Bowls,* Missoula, 1975 (Text 4).

14. Duling, "Testament of Solomon" (*OTP*, I), 984.

15. Isbell, *Bowls,* 1975.

16. Isbell, *Bowls,* 1975, (see text 1,3,4,17,28,37,38 and 39).

RESISTING THE DEVIL IN THE PATRISTIC, MEDIEVAL, AND REFORMATION CHURCH

Dennis Martin

It is impossible to survey this question over nearly two millennia of church history in a single paper. This essay will select a number of focal points that, its author believes, are sufficiently illustrative to shed light and advance our understanding of the issues involved. The essay's point of departure is the observation that the points at which there is serious, crisis-type preoccupation with the devil and demon possession are the first two centuries of conversion and Christianization[1] --anywhere from the first to the twelfth to the twentieth century--depending where the frontier of conversion and Christianization happens to be--and the centuries of upheaval and secularization--the sixteenth-seventeenth centuries, and, increasingly, the twentieth century. These are all periods of first-generation Christianity. During the second generation, ca. third to fifteenth centuries, resistance to the devil emphasized prophylaxis and preventive medicine, rather than crisis intervention. One of the reasons we find ourselves increasingly in a pagan, first-generation situation is that we have not taken good enough care of second-generation institutions, indeed, have pilloried them as legalistic, formalistic, and therefore inauthentic.

The most fruitful understandings of the subject came at the transition point from first- to second-generation Christianity: during the third and fourth centuries. Problems emerged in the later Middle Ages when scholastic theologians tried to define and specify too much about the demonic. This is what lies behind the witch craze of the later Middle Ages and Reformation period. In much the same way that the dialectical mystery of Christ's presence in the Eucharist found in the writings of the first four centuries gives way to the iron-clad doctrine of transubstantiation in the thirteenth century, with dire consequences for lay people at worship, so the effort to overdefine demonology (in response, it must be added, to the overtly dualistic and anti-sacramental theologies of the Albigenses and others), when combined with a new rigor in canon law, led to the excesses and the panic of the early modern witch crazes.

This essay will describe four types of responses to the activity of the devil.

1. In metaphysics and theology an attempt was made to understand evil and sin, to engage the "problem of evil." By refusing to take the devil overly seriously, by insisting both on freedom as the origin of evil[2] and on the providence and total goodness of God, a theological defense was developed.

2. In the area of liturgical and sacramental life, by developing a ritual and sacramental spirituality for the laity, an effective preventive defense against the Devil was developed that grew from the same theological and metaphysical assumptions described under section I but which, precisely because it was actualized and embedded in the church's worship life, could speak to non-theologians.

3. In the area that we would now call "spirituality," by developing the contemplative life, at least for a monastic core of the church, a powerful counterforce against the demonic was developed, a method of resisting the Devil that not all Christians were in a position to pursue but that developed more intensely the same sacramental and liturgical assumptions described in section II.

4. In the area of crisis intervention, apart from the exorcism ritual at baptism, a variety of exorcism rituals and prophylactic blessings of all aspects of daily life were developed and eventually systematized in the early seventeenth-century *Rituale Romanum*. In this way the church developed methods of dealing with demon possession and distinguishing it from witchcraft.

This paper will focus on the patristic and medieval periods, with a brief look at what happened in the sixteenth and seventeenth century among the mainline reformers, counterreformation Catholics, and Anabaptists.

I. Metaphysics and Theology:
the Problem of Evil, Sin and the Devil.

Jeffrey Burton Russell outlines four possible positions on the problem of evil:[3] (a) atheism; (b) absolute dualism--the belief that there are two independent powers, one good and the other evil, struggling against each other in the cosmos; (c) coincidence of opposites--in some mysterious, paradoxical way, good and evil are part of the same one Principle--a form of more or less consistent (if only by way of paradox) monism; (d) mitigated dualism/mitigated monism --the assertion that evil is privation of good and has no being of itself. There is only one (monistic) reality or source of being, and evil is not its opposite, even though its power is evident. Rather, evil has no being; evil is nonbeing.[4] This last position is not all that distant from (c).[5]

The last position (d) is the most prominent one for Christians both in the Eastern Orthodox and Latin traditions. The struggle against dualism dominates the first fifteen centuries of the Church's response to the demonic. This is because of the holistic attitude toward creation that was part of the Jewish tradition and because Christians defended that attitude against the Gnostics, buttressing it with Neoplatonic metaphysics.

Common to the writings of the Fathers is the belief that the Devil was a being created by God, rather than an independent evil force. Because God is the source of all being and because God by definition produces no evil, the Devil, although created good by God, cannot be evil in his being. Rather, the evil of Satan is a continual choice to deny his own being, to choose nonbeing, nothingness, and chaos. Of course, one can still say that God is somehow responsible for evil because God permits free choice of evil on the part of Satan. But the Fathers were more concerned about the dangers of dualism or of any claim that God causes evil. Thus they chose the route of asserting a created cosmos distinct from yet participating in its omnipotent Creator who nonetheless gives creatures freedom to defy him. I find none of the alternative metaphysical systems to be superior. There is no easy solution to the problem of evil but the solution chosen after long and difficult struggle with Gnosticism and other forms of dualism, is not to be quickly dismissed. It is based in the assumption of the goodness of creation as redeemed in the incarnation, and it permits a very nuanced Christian humanism in which none of God's creation, human society, or institutions is totally evil or depraved. It is in this metaphysics of evil as nonbeing, as the privation of good rather than dualism that the basis for the Augustinian view of the church, of sacraments, and of society is grounded.[6]

This point requires emphasis because it is in the rejection of this metaphysics that the radical Protestant Reformers, including the Anabaptists, rendered themselves incapable of maintaining a sacramental view of the world and the church and thereby slid unwittingly into the dualism that has characterized most of modern philosophy and theology.[7]

What is of concern here is that patristic and early medieval writers (to the twelfth century) understood the "problem of the Devil" to be intimately connected with the problem of sin. Their understanding of sin was grounded metaphysically in the problem of evil, and their response to sin was just as much metaphysically grounded in a sacramental world view and sacramental ecclesiology, which asserted the reformation and redemption of creation, above all, of the human person created in the image of God but twisted and tarnished by sin.[8] One could not deal with sin without addressing the role of Satan. In contrast, our modern churches have explained sin away, weakened or abandoned sacramental structures for dealing with it (baptism, confession-penance, the Eucharist) and then, when cases of overt evil meet their attention, can only respond in a crisis intervention manner. The patristic and medieval writers understood sin and salvation as a great continuum stretching from, at the one extreme, overt demonic possession, to, at the other extreme, contemplative ecstasy in a foretaste of heavenly wholeness and salvation. In between were the various degrees of bondage to sin, of freedom and salvation in the sacraments, of intensified growth in spirituality. This might be illustrated by the following chiastic outline, with its center found under C:

    A. [for some, bodily possession by Satan and the demonic]
    B. sin, sinful nature, characteristic of all humans

C. sacramental rebirth, new creation in baptism, nourishment in the Eucharist for the wayfarer between heaven and earth, repeated sin (of whatever intensity), repeated rebirth and renewal in repentance and sacramental confession

B'. Complete salvation, shalom, wholeness, beatific vision in heaven--for all Christians

A'. [for some--for those who have ears to hear--the intensified spiritual life of a second baptism in martyrdom or in monastic asceticism, leading for some to a foretaste of heavenly shalom]

Thus early Christian demonology, whether in the writings of the Desert Fathers, John Cassian (d. ca. 435), Augustine (354-430), or others, is inseparable from early Christian teaching on sin and salvation. Modern Christians tend to see demonic possession--if they accept its reality at all--as something qualitatively different from "normal" sin, just as our tendency is to see the monastic life and mystical ecstasy as qualitatively different from the path of Christian living and salvation experienced by all Christians. Before the Protestant Reformation, however, the monastic life was perceived as a quantitative intensification of the same sacramental path of salvation followed by all Christians. The goal for all was the same: shalom, salvation, Sabbath rest, the heavenly banquet that perfects the Eucharist we know on earth. The difference between monastics and lay Christians was that the monk or nun *might* have a foretaste of the heavenly banquet while yet in this life. In a similar fashion, the existence of the demonic was part and parcel of the struggle with sin. In a certain sense all temptation, all sinfulness was the result of Satanic activity.[9] The remedies against sin were not qualitatively different for cases of overt demonic possession than they were for the struggle against sin and vice that each Christian was to be engaged in. We will return to this subject in our summary of John Cassian's views on sin and the demonic under section III below.

Because of this broad metaphysical spectrum, patristic and medieval writers at times seem to take the Devil for granted, to see him active in things that we would consider "normal" sin. To us it might seem like they take the Devil too seriously. We are suspicious of their "familiarity" with the demonic. At the same time, we might think these writers do not take the Devil seriously enough. They don't have elaborate strategies for crisis intervention. Their treatises on discerning spirits all too often degenerate (in our eyes) into works on vices and virtues and on the contemplative life.

First we will look in a bit more detail at the general late antique context and then at the metaphysical diabology of Augustine.

In Peter Brown's work we currently have the best analysis of the general late antique context.[10] Brown argues that late antique society entered a period of disequilibrium in the late second century (the end of the reign of Marcus Aurelius in 180 and the lifetime of Aelius Aristides [118-180] offer convenient reference points). Formerly a society for whom religion was embedded in civic ritual and conformity, a society in which one tried not to stand out against one's fellow citizens, the Graeco-Roman world slowly became fascinated with those whose dreams and visions, whose connections to the demi-monde of sorcery and miracles, made them stand out from their fellow citizens. The Christian bishop, Christian martyrs, and Christian ascetics were examples of these "holy men"; and the fascination of their society with people who claimed to have contact, even leverage over, the supernatural, was one of the main reasons for Christian success. What John Wimber calls "power evangelism" has always been powerful--whether the first five centuries in the Mediterranean world, the eighth century in northeastern Europe, or the nineteenth and twentieth centuries around the world. The ability of Christian leaders to cast out demons and cast down pagan shrines was a mainstay of Christian evangelism in the late antique world. For this reason, Christian thinkers from Justin Martyr (d. ca. 160) to Augustine devoted much attention to the metaphysics of the divine and the demonic.[11]

We turn our attention now to Augustine's views on evil, the Devil, demons, and angels.[12] There are two main points to make in regard to Augustine's understanding of evil: (1) evil is the result of free choice. It does not have a cause, because the cause would have to be God or an independent evil, both of which Augustine chose to reject. It was his abandonment of the latter option--the independent existence of evil-- that marked his shift from Manichaeanism to Neo-Platonism on his way to embracing the Catholic faith.[13] Yet, (2) God is in charge even though God is not the cause of evil. God's "inchargeness" includes human freedom but this inchargeness or providence is so great that it can handle free choice (and thus the possibility of evil).[14] This by no means exhausts Augustine's views on the subject, nor is his system watertight. There is no shortage of critics willing to point to inconsistencies.[15] Precisely in his refusal to seek a watertight answer to the Great Question, the problem of evil, precisely in the ambiguity of his system lies his superiority over later scholastic approaches.[16] In much the same way as later theologians tried to resolve the paradoxes and ambiguities in his sacramental theology and ended up with high scholastic transubstantiation doctrine which in turn became the first step in the breakdown of Catholic sacramental theology, so later scholastics tried to work out the details of the problem of evil and set in motion the process that led to eventual disbelief in the demonic.

For the sake of brevity we will omit a detailed summary of books 8-9 of *The City of God.* In them Augustine asserts (contrary to the Neo-Platonist view which insisted that there were some good demons) that all demons are evil; that demons do not mediate between God (the gods) and humans; and that only Christ can mediate in this manner. In other words, Augustine's understanding of salvation, like that of the Greek fathers of the fourth century (Gregory of Nyssa, Basil the Great etc.), was based on a mediated monism or mitigated dualism. There is a clear distinction between Creator and creature and the creature was created good, in the image of God (unlike Manichaeanism and Gnosticism) yet fallen, warped, and stained by sin. But that distinction has been bridged, mediated, in the incarnate Christ. Thus the image of God can be, indeed, from God's eschatological viewpoint, has been restored, cleaned up, reformed. Both the distinction (asymmetry) and the mediation are crucial. If either one is weakened, the other is affected. The church, as Christ's body, and her sacraments are the dynamic symbols (in the ancient meaning of symbol) of Christ's mediation. It is thus via the sacraments of the church (based on the Sacrament of sacraments, the incarnation) that the relationship between creature and Creator is restored. Demons have no part in that mediation and their efforts to seduce the creatures from this path of restoration must be resisted.

The basic outlines of Augustine's theology dominated the Middle Ages. At the same time, on the periphery a seesaw battle between absolute monism[17] and extreme dualism took place during these centuries. The dualism entered Latin Christendom during the tenth and eleventh centuries and reached its high point in the twelfth and thirteenth centuries in the Albigensian movement. We cannot examine this movement here.[18] Instead, we merely note that the rise of the mendicant orders and their scholastic theology was, in part, a response to Albigensian dualism. Particularly the "Order of Preachers" or Dominican order, to which Thomas Aquinas (1225-74) belonged, concerned itself with developing a systematic, rational theology that could deal with the difficult theological, scientific, and metaphysical problems raised by the heresies. Aquinas' views on the demonic and on the problem of evil are within the classic Christian tradition.[19] But the seeds of a breakdown of the sacramental, mediated asymmetry that undergirded the patristic and early medieval synthesis were being sown. Ironically, it was in the quest for too great a unity between creature and Creator that the mitigated dualism or mediated asymmetry was first weakened--in the writings of Meister Eckhart (ca. 1260 - ca. 1329), who himself came out of the Paris scholastic milieu.[20] At the same time the ontological and sacramental linkage between sign and thing signified, between Creator and creature that classic Christian theology had grounded in the incarnation, was being undermined by the growing empiricism and covenantal theology of the via moderna or nominalists.[21] It is no accident that this is also the time of the systematizing of the church's bureaucracy, its canon law, and the time of the Inquisition.[22] Before we criticize the church and the papacy too much for these developments, we need to realize that it was not only the church that was systematizing and bureaucratizing. The temporal rulers were consolidating their control in France, Sicily, and England. There was a very real conflict between popes and the powers claimed by the emperors; the church legitimately recognized a need to resist those claims. That the papacy over-reacted and overreached itself, is one of history's tragedies. Yet the popes were not unprovoked. It takes two to quarrel.

The threat from the dualistic heresies should also not be underestimated. We live in the wreckage of these struggles, a world in which concepts and thoughts are dismissed as unimportant in comparison with actions and empirical observations. For that reason, we see Albigensian dualism as harmless metaphysical variation and cannot begin to perceive why the church resisted it so strenuously. What was at stake, however, was whether God really does control this universe or not. What was at stake was the question of Christ's victory over the powers. What was at stake was faith in the incarnation as victory over the demonic, and the sacramental, churchly life as a life lived within that victory. We will never understand the late medieval and early modern obsession with witchcraft and the demonic unless we realize that a battle for the cosmos was underway in the high Middle Ages and that the theological leadership of the church, in its effort to deal a death blow to non-Christian cosmologies, unwittingly destroyed the marvelous ambiguity that made the patristic metaphysics so powerful.

This is part of a larger general change in world-views. As the role of the human free will was accentuated more and more in the twelfth and following centuries, the cosmic, omnipotent, providential Creator and the sacramental theology based in it receded. R. W. Southern has talked about a shift from epic to romance that one can observe in the art and literature of the twelfth and thirteenth centuries,[23] but the same thing is happening in theology from Abelard through Ockham. We will return to this set of overall philosophical, theological, sociological changes in section III.

If Karl Morrison is correct, a variety of changes in how people perceived the universe in the late Middle Ages had created a situation where it was impossible for the leading Protestant Reformers to maintain a classic Christian understanding of the reformation of the image of God in the incarnation of Christ. The mediated asymmetry necessary to it had been weakened. John Calvin's understanding of both sacramental theology and of evil is, of the major Reformers, closest to Augustine in its willingness to live with ambiguity and paradox. Unfortunately, even within the Reformed wing of Protestantism, a more radical dualism was powerfully active in the form of Zwinglian antisacramentalism. On paper, Calvin attempted to preserve both the providence of God and the non-existence of evil in an Augustinian tension. In practice, the Reformed tradition dismantled the sacramental worship and world-view that made it possible for God to be revealed to humans in Christ, in Scripture, and in the Eucharistic elements. Scripture became both a scholastic textbook and a holy, almost magical idol, but it could not function as a mediating icon. The bread and wine were reduced to mere symbols rather than dynamic *symbols*. Christ and his incarnation, death and resurrection were reduced to a historic event with which we come in contact by mental processes. Unable actually to appropriate in worship Calvin's generally excellent metaphysical and theological framework for the problem of evil and the demonic, the Reformed

tradition entered the modern world vulnerable to extremism. Calvinists were not alone: the shift from "differentiated dualism" of
the Augustinian type to the various dualisms of the modern world
affected Catholics and Protestants alike. (Even modern empirical
scientism is one half of a dualism—after separating too sharply the
noumenal and the phenomenal, we concentrated on the phenomenal for a
century or two, trying to convince ourselves that that is all there
is. But the noumenal would not disappear and, as it has reasserted
itself with force in the late nineteenth and twentieth centuries,
most people can only explain it dualistically, leading to the obsession with the occult found both within and without the church in the
late twentieth century.)

In the section that follows we will attempt to clarify what has
been presented abstractly here by looking at worship, specifically at
the baptismal exorcism. It is important, however, once more to
emphasize that abstract ideas are important, as Thomas Oden reminds
us.[24] One of the main reasons we are skeptical about the reality of
sacramental power, about the dynamism of symbols, is that we have
abandoned a metaphysics of wonder. For several centuries we tried
to deny that the observable world is the tip of an unseen iceberg.
Symbolic and sacramental worship rests on basic assumptions about
the cosmos.

II. Liturgical and Sacramental Defenses.

The earliest descriptions of Christian baptismal rituals incorporate exorcisms both during the prebaptismal fasting period and at
the ceremony itself during the Easter vigil. Henry Ansgar Kelly has
investigated these dramatic ceremonies thoroughly and the texts of
four important fourth-century baptismal homilies, including descriptions of the rituals, are conveniently assembled by Edward Yarnold.[25]
The ceremonies included fasting, exorcisms in the strict sense (the
expulsion of Satan by adjuration), deliberate renunciation of Satan
(in the fourth-century liturgies this took place with the baptizand
facing the west), a pledge of oneself to serve Christ alone (in the
fourth century this took place with the baptizand facing east), blowing away Satan (exsufflation) and breathing in the Holy Spirit
(insufflation), a rubdown with oil in the manner of an athlete
preparing for a wrestling match, anointing with the chrism oil for
confirmation (strengthening for future resistance against temptation), and signing the ears and nostrils with the cross.

On the basis of the argument from silence, Kelly has suggested
that these ceremonies owe something to Gnostic rituals. While it is
true that there is no positive evidence that Christians included
exorcisms and antidemonic rites in their baptismal liturgies before
the early third century, neither is there positive evidence that they
did not.[26] The argument from silence is risky and should be used
with caution.

Apart from the question whether exorcisms in baptism were a
later import into Christian baptismal ritual deriving from Gnostic
sources, the question that has vexed much of Christian history is in
what sense they are applicable when infants are being baptized.
Kelly argues that the church was able to retain the exorcistic and
anti-demonic rites only by giving them symbolic and figurative meanings, since the alternative was to argue that newborn children were
possessed by demons. Kelly misses the point here: figurative meaning is an essential part of ritual whether for adults or children
and the shift from adult to infant baptism was a natural development
for a premodern society that assumed real linkage between generations and between orders within society. If infant baptism makes
sense, and if exorcism makes sense at adult baptism, then exorcism
also makes sense at infant baptism. Everyone knew that the child
couldn't answer for himself or herself, that parents accepted
responsibility for the nurture and upbringing of the child, and that
parents were mediators of everything from food to education to faith
for their children. That they should serve as stand-ins, mediators,
in the exorcism rites was part of the package. If sin is all-
pervasive, if it is in some mysterious sense an inheritance along
with all the rest of our humanness, and if sin is in some mysterious
sense intimately connected with the activity of Satan and his demons,
and, if baptism is a cleansing from sin and entry into the new life
of Christ, then the whole package applies.[27]

The issue of mediation is crucial here. In a first-generation
setting, new converts answer for themselves because they are the
first generation to convert. There is no preceding generation to
answer for them (leaving aside the issue of child baptism or
household baptism in the New Testament period). In a second-
generation context, two generations are present. That parents take
responsibility for and exert authority over their children in matters
of education, marriage, etc. simply was not challenged any more than
the assumption that the aristocracy exercises authority over and
represents the peasants and plebians in government. This mediation
does not mean that parents take total and permanent responsibility
for the next generation. It simply means that mediation from generation to generation is part of the way the cosmos runs, part of the
way the new generation acquires genuine, personal faith, which in
turn it passes on to the next generation. This is what we call a
"traditional" society--a 'handing down' society.

The shift from a society that assumed vicarious mediation, a
society in which monks prayed for all, peasants worked for all, and
knights fought for all, to a society in which everyone prayed,
worked, and fought, is one of the overriding themes of the emergence
of the modern world. It took several centuries for this to be completed. Interestingly enough, whereas the "magisterial Reformers"
championed priesthood of all believers (only to replace a sacramental elitism with a scholastic elitism) for adults but retained the
vicarious role of parents and baptismal sponsors as faith-givers to

their children, the Anabaptists retained mediation and accountability among adults (the "Anabaptist community" that we make so much of)[28] but denied that parents could be accountable for their children's faith. In other words, Anabaptists denied mediation across the generations even while they accepted it within a generation, within their adult community of faith. Not wishing to belabor the point, a quotation from Pilgram Marpeck (actually from Bernhard Rothmann) must suffice:

> What should we say about those who call themselves godfathers, who run and become sponsors for the child, as mentioned above, and, on behalf of the child, confess the faith, abjure the Devil, and whatever other blasphemy they may commit? Is this not presumptuous nonsense? What do the godfathers or patrons know about the eventual intentions of a child? As soon as he grows up and thinks for himself, even though they do not now know him and indeed cannot know him, for God alone knows him, why do they run and promise good and deny the evil for the child?
>
> Two kinds of nonsense originate from this action. First, God is mocked when, as it often happens, the godfathers themselves, as patrons, do not believe or know anything about faith. Indeed, they do not even know or consider what they are doing, nor do they understand that to which they are answering, what they are promising, contradicting, or rejecting. They reject only with the mouth, and it happens very often that these very same people are God's enemies in their hearts, that they are friends of the Devil and the world. How, then, can they stand in the place of a child before God?" (*Admonition* (1542) in CRR 2: 217-18)

The very use of the term "age of accountability" indicates that the rejection of infant baptism forced Anabaptists to deny mediation across generations. A term that is commonly used in a positive sense by present-day neo-Anabaptists to represent the essence of their ecclesiology is denied applicability to the relationship between parents-godparents and children. Children are *accountable* for themselves, and their parents cannot be accountable for them in matters of faith. (Of course parents remain accountable in matters of discipline, clothing, food, education, etc.).

Often the entire question of infant baptism and the related issue of the exorcism ritual in baptism, is reduced to a question of original sin. G. M. Lukken has examined early Christian assumptions about the dominion of Satan over the cosmos since the fall of Adam and Eve:[29]

> The New Testament thus clearly expresses the idea that the Devil exercises dominion over unredeemed humanity. Satan's rule is behind all physical and moral evil, behind sickness, death and sin.... According to the New Testament Satan exercises his dominion particularly when man sins. Whoever sins is called not only the slave (doulos) of sin (John 8:34), but

also a son of the Devil who sins from the beginning (1 John
3:8). (159)
Satan has, by right, dominion over the world, but he holds it in
a relative sense, subject to God's complete sovereignty.[30] Not only
does he have dominion, but also in a certain sense, the Church
Fathers believed that he indwells human beings. This developed out
of baptismal theology: if Christ indwells those who have been buried
with him in baptism, so Satan, in some sense indwells those who have
not submitted to Christ and thereby have submitted to the Devil.
This applies to the early Fathers, writing in a first-generation setting in which most if not all converts were conscious, responsible
adults. What happened when Christians began to baptize infants?[31]
Lukken argues that the practice of infant and child baptism predated
the theology of original sin. In the period before child or infant
baptism became common (most of the second century), children are
considered personally innocent, but the Fathers equally emphasize
the general corruption, the "structural evil" in our terms, that
affects all of humanity. There is neither a formal affirmation nor a
formal denial of original sin. It was the practice of baptizing
infants "for the remission of sin" that raised questions about how
one harmonizes personal innocence with the general sinfulness of
human beings, eventually leading to the classic doctrine of original
sin in Cyprian, Augustine, and others.[32] As is the case with every
major doctrine of the church, practice preceded dogma. Lex orandi,
lex credendi (the rule of prayer, i.e., pattern of worship, is the
rule of belief). This is why Tertullian (ca. 160-220), perched on the
watershed between first and second generations, says, Why baptize
children who are tainted with this general fallenness? Why not wait
until this fallenness manifests itself in personal, deliberate sin?[33]
Seen against this background, Tertullian can not be used as a
prooftext for believer's baptism, as he so often has been. Origen
(ca. 185 - 254) agrees that children are tainted by fallenness
(nullus mundus a sorde--no one is free of taints) and speaks of the
"taint of birth" (nativitatis sordes), elsewhere noting that the real
stains of sin (genuinae sordes peccati) are present in all. Unlike
Tertullian, he believes it good to baptize infants in order to remove
this fallenness. These two men, a half-generation apart, illustrate
the transition from first to second generation.
    The entire question is closely related to attitudes toward the
sacraments. The concept of mediation is basic to sacramental theology. By entering into the created order, Christ, the God-Man,
restored fallen creation and humanity to its original dignity, win-
ning the victory over original sin. It is that mystery that is
celebrated in the Eucharist and in baptism, in which created things
serve as real, dynamic symbols of this already-but-not-yet victory
over pervasive, original sin. For a variety of reasons, this understanding of the linking of heaven and earth, of Creator and creation
in the incarnate Christ, in his body the Church, and in her sacraments, was under attack during the Reformation. It is precisely the

most radically anti-sacramental groups that atack most vehemently
the practice of baptismal exorcism.   Anabaptists rejected infant baptism and transubstantiation because they insisted on the presence of
personal and individual faith.[34] In matters of faith there could be
no vicariousness (which ultimately produced the Mennonite struggle
with accepting extrinsic, vicarious atonement and mercy from God--
our attack on infant baptism lies at the heart of our inability to
find grace and our bondage to perfectionism). My own hunch is that
they first rejected infant baptism and transubstantiation for a variety of "common sense" reasons and the rest of their anti-mediation,
anti-sacramental theology followed from this choice.   Yet, were we
able to probe this more deeply, we would find that their "common
sense" inability to accept infant baptism and transubstantiation was
grounded in subtle metaphysical shifts of the type outlined by Morrison.[35] In any case, the Anabaptist rejection of baptismal exorcism
is not surprising[36]--it is part of their dualistic rejection of
sacrament and mediation.[37]

Corroboration of this hunch is found in the quarrel between
Lutherans and Calvinists over whether to retain the exorcistic rites
in baptism.   Luther himself insisted on retaining them, but already
during his lifetime, his followers were indifferent.   Only in the
later sixteenth century, as competition between Reformed and
Lutherans heated up in Germany, did Lutherans insist on retention of
exorcism in infant baptism.   The anti-sacramental character of the
Reformed movement, especially the Zwinglian legacy, was a threat to
Lutheran faith in the real presence of Christ in the Eucharist, and
the fact that the Reformed could see nothing but superstition in the
exorcism rite only strengthened Lutherans in their resolve to retain
it.[38]

Sacrament and liturgy are extremely difficult to maintain. They
rest on assumptions about how God relates to creation that are
balanced tenuously between dualism and pantheism.   Any really
sacramental understanding of the created world runs the risk of
turning into idolatry and superstition.   A sacramental system
requires a costly investment in leadership and teaching if people
are to continue to live in the presence of mystery without turning
it into magic.   The modern world has been at a distinct disadvantage
in this regard because it has assumed that every person should be
able to understand matters of faith for himself or herself.   (Matters
of science are a different question, apparently--there we still
permit a priesthood to tend to the mysteries of the laboratory.)   As
a result, theology, metaphysics, and thinking in general have
steadily declined in favor.   This is of great significance in the
question of demonology.   The groups most interested in the subject
today tend to be the most suspicious of sacrament and priesthood, of
theology and metaphysics.   The scholars of our churches dismiss the
subject as superstition unfit for a modern scientific age, thereby
insuring that it will become superstitious in the hands of at least
some of those who remain interested in it.   Any attempt to deal with

the Devil and his legions today must begin by restoring respect and
confidence in the guardians of the liturgy and sacraments together
with the theology and metaphysics of mediation that undergird them.
For Mennonites, who retain very little in the way of sacraments,
liturgy, or priesthood, and who have scant respect for conceptual
answers to existential questions, the path toward a full-orbed
response to the demonic is even harder. Mennonites, other
Protestants, and Catholics alike would do well to heed Cardinal
Suenens' warnings about the need to respect the church's traditional
teaching authority, the restriction of exorcism to the bishop or his
representative, and the need for caution in lay activity.[39] At the
same time, the problem has emerged because priests and theologians
have for too long neglected or dismissed the topic as unimportant.
They must hear the voices of lay people calling for attention to the
subject and respond with theological, liturgical, and sacramental
answers (which are but three sides of the same reality).

III. Spirituality: The Discernment of Spirits.

Backing up and taking another longitudinal survey through
church history, we will look this time at writings on contemplative
spirituality and the place they assign to the demonic. This survey
will illustrate the way in which a sane and restrained demonology
was developed during the patristic and early medieval periods.
The desert fathers are known for their intense struggles against
demons and temptation. We will not look at this early period of
Christian contemplative spirituality, except to recall Peter Brown's
efforts to place these "holy men" and women into the general late
antique preoccupation with dreams and demons.[40] What we will give
our attention to is the more mature and moderate spiritual director's manual written by John Cassian as a compendium of the wisdom
of the East. We will note the careful limits he places on the power
of demons yet the way in which the struggle against demons is
intimately integrated into his spiritual teaching. One cannot make
progress toward contemplation without dealing with the demonic.
Space will not permit us to give detailed attention to a similar
spiritual director's manual from the end of the Middle Ages, which
illustrates the same principle: a sizeable portion of Denys the
Carthusian's treatise, *De discretione et examinatione spirituum* is
devoted to what we would call "mystical theology."[41] In this he is
typical of his contemporaries, several of whose treatises on similar
topics he refers to.[42]
Similarly, John Cassian's conferences dealing specifically with
evil and with demons and their powers and limits are sandwiched
between his conferences on the active life of struggle against vices
(Conference V of Abbot Serapion on the eight cardinal sins) and his
two conferences on prayer (Conferences IX and X of Abbot Isaac, in
which he deals with what we would call mystical union or pure
prayer—his term is "purity of heart").[43] Conferences V and IX-X are

among the most important of John Cassian's immense legacy to medieval spirituality. This demonology, in Conferences VII and VIII, is fully integrated with what we find to be his much more palatable "positive" spirituality. John Cassian's influence was immense for more than a millennium, but he is shamefully unknown in Protestant circles.[44]

Among the salient features of John Cassian's discussion in Conference VII are the following:[45]

1. God's providence is ultimately triumphant and sin is the result of free choice, not of determinism:

> For greater is He who is in us than he who is in this world and His aid fights on our side with much greater power than their hosts fight against us; for God is not only the suggester of what is good, but the maintainer and insister of it, so that sometimes He draws us towards salvation even against our will and without our knowing it. It follows then that no one can be deceived by the Devil but one who has chosen to yield to him the consent of his own will: ... (NPNF, vol. 11:365).

2. Demons can only take possession of people's bodies,[46] not of their souls (spirit). Only God, the Holy Trinity, after whose image the soul (spirit) was created, can take possession of our spirits (what we could call contemplative union). Of course, since what happens to the human body affects the spirit (the essence of all ascetic theology--that body and soul [spirit] are intimately interconnected),[47] demonic possession of the body is a serious matter-- demons can have an effect on the spirit but only via the senses, not directly and immediately. Thus the powers of demons are clearly circumscribed. (ch. 9-14, NPNF, 366-67). The reason the demons cannot unite themselves to the human spirit is that they are not incorporal--only God is incorporal. (ch. 13). Demons are clever and adept at reading the external signs of what is going on inside one's soul (spirit) but they have no direct access to the spirit. This became the consistent position of medieval theologians.[48]

3. Certain demons have the ability to tempt us with certain sins. (This is the parallel to Cassian's systematic treatment of the eight cardinal sins in Conference V.) But even though there is this semblance of hierarchy among them, there is no true concord and team spirit among the demons. Rather, they only manage to work together on certain occasions. Concord, harmony, hierarchy in its true sense belongs to God and the good angels alone. (ch. 17-18, NPNF, 11:368).

4. Beginners in the spiritual life are assailed by weaker demons. The stronger one is in spiritual growth, the more vigorous attacks one can expect. Ths demonic attacks are a sign of progress in spiritual warfare. (ch. 20; 11:368).

5. Demons can inflict injury on humans only by the permissive will of God (here, of course, the Book of Job offers the prooftext). (ch. 22, NPNF, 11:370).

6. The power of the demons has weakened since the heroic days

of the Desert Fathers. Cassian is not sure why this is true --
either the demons have been beaten back by the power of the cross
penetrating more and more of the world, even to the desert wastes,
or, because Christian warriors have grown careless, the demons no
longer need to mass their attacks against them, since Christians are
sinning of their own accord through complacency. (ch. 23, NPNF,
11:370).

7. It is far more wretched to be possessed by sins than by
demons. Sins affect the soul (spirit); demons can only affect the
body and tempt the soul (spirit). (ch. 25, NPNF, 11:371).

8. We ought not to despise those delivered up to demonic possession or to temptations. This is because, in the first place, no one
can be tempted without God's permission and secondly, because all
that happens to us is under God's fatherly providence and works
ultimately to our good. Instead of despising those afflicted by
demonic temptation or possession, we should pray for them without
ceasing as if they were part of our own bodies, which, of course,
they are. For, "we know that we cannot possibly be perfected without
them, inasmuch as they are members of us, just as we read that our
predecessors [the Desert Fathers] could not attain the fulness of
promise without us, as the Apostle speaks." [Hebr. 11:39-40 follows].
Note how the sense of community works forwards and backwards across
generations but also in the present day across all levels of victory
or temptation. Here is the monastic tradition of community at its
best. To reinforce his point, Cassian insists that the Eucharist
should not be denied to those under demonic persecution--indeed, the
bread and wine is a purification of body and soul, for "when it is
received by a man it, so to speak, burns out and puts to flight the
spirit which has its seat in his members or is trying to lurk in
them. . . . For the enemy will more and more abuse the man who is
possessed, if he sees him cut off from the heavenly medicine, and
will tempt him more often and more fearfully, as he sees him removed
the further from this spiritual remedy." (ch. 28-30, NPNF, 11:372-
73).[49] This also remained the dominant position in the Middle
Ages.[50]

9. Instead, the people worthy of being despised are those who
"defile themselves with all kinds of sins and wickedness, yet not
only is there no visible sign of the Devil's possession shown in
them, nor is any temptation proportionate to their actions, nor any
scourge of punishment brought to bear [by the demons, with God's
permission] upon them"--in other words, those who seem to be coast-
ing along in their sins are the ones worthy of being despised, if
anyone is. (ch. 31, NPNF 11:373).

IV. Crisis Intervention: Demon Possession and Exorcism.

Our look at crisis intervention responses to the demonic must be
very brief, with references to the voluminous literature on the subject. The peak of the witchcraft craze came in the seventeenth

century, during the "age of reason." It was the outgrowth of systematized approach to heresy and demonology that posited the existence of a pact between humans and the Devil.[51] This was exacerbated by the Protestant and Catholic Reformations, in which exorcism and demon possession became tools with which to attack the opposition. For centuries the Catholic portrait of Luther was dominated by assertions that he was demon-possessed; both Catholics and Protestants used exorcisms to proclaim the superiority of their theology.[52] Keith Thomas, in his book, *Religion and the Decline of Magic*,[53] has argued that a popular system of "protective ecclesiastical magic" had grown up around the sacraments, indeed the church had encouraged this, in part unwittingly. When Protestantism purged Christian religion of this magic (and, I would add, eliminated much that was healthy about the sacraments in the process), while at the same time emphasizing human depravity and the Devil, the result was an explosion of logic outside the church rather than sacraments inside the church: the witchcraft craze. At issue, of course, is the exact relationship between superstition and sacrament, a relationship that was confused on all sides, with the unfortunate effect that any healthy view of the sacraments has been clouded beyond recognition both in the sixteenth century and in the eyes of many today.

In addition to these ecclesiastical and theological changes, there were sociological changes taking place. The twelfth and thirteenth centuries saw the emergence of the urban (not yet industrialized) commercial society that dominated until the Industrial Revolution of the eighteenth and nineteenth centuries.[54] Spirituality moved out of the monasteries and onto the streets, while theology moved out of the monastery and into the lecture hall. The mendicant orders (Franciscans, Dominicans) were involved in both moves.[55] In the process spirituality became more and more eccentric.[56] The situation was ripe for spiritual excesses, both saintly and diabolical. A priest- and monk-led society of vicarious and ordered spirituality gave way to a lay spirituality.[57] The liturgical regularity of the monastery, the steady rounds of intercessory prayer, the spirituality of presence atrophied, giving way to the mass pilgrimages to venerate miraculously bleeding communion wafers.[58]

It is striking how little is made of crisis exorcisms during the Middle Ages and how matter-of-fact are the descriptions of those that do pepper the pages of the more eccentric collections of tales, like Caesarius of Heisterbach's (fl. 1220-50) *Dialogue on Miracles*.[59] Crisis exorcisms scarcely figure in Russell's volume on the Devil in the Middle Ages--indeed, the Devil becomes a comic figure in medieval folklore, someone who can be outwitted even by humans because he has already been vanquished by Christ.[60] Christopher Nugent summarizes this aptly: "To be sure, residual paganism, popular superstition, and the magical arts survived, but the malign powers had been effectively 'de-fanged.' Even St. Anthony of the Desert finally dismissed the Devil as 'that old rogue.'"[61] In the history of the diabolic, the Dark Age is not the Middle Ages but the Renaissance and early modern period, even more so, the twentieth century.

This is not to say that crisis intervention exorcisms were
unknown. All the great saints cast out demons--for examples, one
can turn to Franz's stories of Euphrasia (d. after 410), Bernard of
Clairvaux (1090-1153), and Hildegard of Bingen (1098-1179).[62] The
procedures for churchly exorcisms are outlined by Franz, including
the actual texts culled from a variety of monastic manuscripts.[63]
The culmination of these developments is found in the *Rituale
Romanum* of 1614. It strikes me, although I lack any real experience
in the matter, as a mature and defensible approach. Exorcism is
reserved to the bishop or his deputy.[64] The priest must be prepared
for this task by living a holy life and by study of exorcism.[65] It
is not a procedure to be approached casually (points 1-2, p. 169).
He should be skeptical and cautious--not overly credulous (point 3,
p. 169). The three signs of demon possession are ability to speak or
understand a language otherwise unknown to the person; ability to
divulge future and hidden events and a display of powers beyond the
subject's age and natural condition (point 3, p. 169). The priest
should learn from each experience so that he can be better prepared
the next time (point 4). He must beware of the wiles of the Devil
(points 5, 7, pp. 169, 171). He must use a commanding voice, observe
which words in particular cause the evil spirits to tremble and then
repeat these words (points 16-17, p. 171). He should be careful not
to give medicine to the patient but leave that to physicians (point
18, p. 171). He should use words from Holy Scripture in preference
to his own words or those of other people (point 20, p. 171).[66]
Walker has pointed out the care taken by exorcists in the sixteenth
and seventeenth to distinguish between illness and demon possession
and between demon possession and witchcraft.[67]

V. Suggestions for Mennonites

What lessons does this exploration of some of the corners of
this immense topic offer to twentieth-century Mennonites? I will
make a few very simple and practical suggestions.

a. We should, after a careful study of the matter and careful
teaching in our schools and congregations, restore the weekly observance of the Eucharist. This was the universal practice of the early
church and of the earliest Anabaptists. Apparently the only reason
that communion became infrequent among Mennonites was an exag-
gerated awe growing out a desire to have complete concord and
reconciliation within the congregation. These are similar to the
reasons that led to infrequent communicating by lay people in the
late Middle Ages (awe before the holiness of the sacrament and dis-
comfort with the sacramental confession that was required before
communicating) and this development was no less disastrous then. We
would do well to recall John Cassian's (point 8 above) and Theodore
of Mopsuestia's (d. 428) insistence that the Eucharist strengthens
against temptation and heals the wounds of "minor" sins. (If one is
a habitual or deliberate sinner, then confession and reconciliation

should precede the Eucharist, but for the day-to-day struggles with temptation and sin, the Eucharist is a source of healing and power.)[68] In our own day, Cardinal Suenens has reminded us that the Eucharist is the main weapon in our combat with Satan.[69]

b. We must restore the renunciation of Satan and confirmation (strengthening for combat) to our baptismal liturgy.[70] Confirmation could take a low church form such as that practiced traditionally by the Church of the Brethren (laying on of hands and invocation of the Holy Spirit)[71] or it could include anointing with oil, which would be a restoration of the practice of the early church. Along with the reintroduction of these rites must come proper teaching about baptism as in itself exorcistic[72] and about the spiritual combat one can expect to face as a result of baptism and commitment to Christ. We should give serious thought to restoration of the Easter vigil service with its dramatic celebration of Christ's victory over evil and renewal of baptismal commitments.[73]

c. We should encourage the practice of dedication of infants and include in the ritual prayers for protection of both the infant and the parents from the Devil's wiles. We should consider developing some form of "co-parents" or godparents to make even more explicit the role of the congregation in nurturing children.[74] Among other things, infant dedication ceremonies could include some recognition of the presence of demonic bondage in family systems and claim the power of Christ to break that bondage.

d. Prayers for protection from evil should be prominent parts of our worship services. More frequent use of the Lord's prayer would be one step in this direction; explicit prayers for protection as part of the conclusion of worship services would be helpful. Again, this must be accompanied by careful teaching to avoid both extremes: taking the Devil too seriously and not taking him seriously enough.[75]

e. We must give serious attention to orders within the church: the equivalent of the role played by monastic orders in the past. This will not occur overnight, but the first step is to recognize how much we Protestants have suffered as a result of rejecting the monastic option, how much we have missed the presence of professional pray-ers. The incense of unceasing prayer needs to rise once more from our midst. As was true in the early church, this is a ministry and vocation accessible especially to "widows" and "virgins"--the elderly, single adults.

These and similar measures should be taken even as we work at questions of crisis intervention from the theological, scriptural, and psychological perspectives. If there is one lesson to be learned from the history of the church's combat with Satan and his demons, it is that the primary weapons she has employed have always been embedded in the regular worship life of the church, which has always been the center of the life of the mystical body of Christ.[76] *Lex orandi, lex credendi, etiamque lex exorcizandi*: The rule of worship is the rule of belief, and, indeed, the rule of exorcism.

Dennis D. Martin

Feast of SS. Peter and Paul, Apostles, 1987

Notes

1. Sociologists and anthropologists have argued that Europe was never completely Christianized until the sixteenth century or later. For an effective and convincing response see John Van Engen, "The Christian Middle Ages as a Historiographical Problem," *American Historical Review* 91 (1986), 9-52.

2. Hence evil is nonbeing, privation of good; it is not caused by anything, i.e., it is the result of nothing except free, disobedient choice.

3. *Lucifer: The Devil in the Middle Ages* (Ithaca: Cornell, 1984), p. 187 and elsewhere.

4. Cf. Col 1:16.

5. The term "mitigated dualism" is Russell's. Later we will encounter Karl F. Morrison's discussion of mediated asymmetry as another way of reminding us that classic Christian theology has always avoided both the extreme of dualism and that of thoroughgoing monism. Much of the criticism of Christian ascetics as "dualists" is misleading, if by dualism one has in mind absolute dualism of the Manichaean type.

6. I find it reassuring that one of the best, pastorally informed, discussions of the demonic coming out of contemporary Roman Catholic charismatic circles does not neglect to establish this metaphysical basis at the outset. See Leon-Joseph Cardinal Suenens, *Renewal and the Powers of Darkness*, Malines Document, 4, trans. Olga Prendergast (Ann Arbor: Servant Books, 1983), 6-7, 17.

7. I cannot demonstrate this assertion here in detail. I have attempted to compile some relevant texts from Menno in an unpublished essay written on the occasion of the 1600th anniversary of Augustine's conversion to the Catholic faith and baptism into the Catholic Church (386-87) and Menno's aversion from Catholicism and conversion to Anabaptism (1536). Even modern monistic philosophies, for example, Hegelian idealism, are possible only because they were preceded by a dualism that rejected the possibility of mediation between the Creator and creation. As God faded from the picture in the Enlightenment, being put on part-time work as the great clockmaker and in Kantian dualism, and then given a pink slip as no longer needed at all in the aftermath of Darwinian evolution, an immanentist monism of the Hegelian type was possible. See also Karl F. Morrison, *The Mimetic Tradition of Reform in the West* (Princeton: Princeton University Press, 1982).

8. The best book on this subject and one that no theologically literate person can afford not to be familiar with is Gerhart B. Ladner, *The Idea of Reform: Its Impact on Christian Thought and Action in the Age of the Fathers* (Cambridge, Mass.: Harvard University Press, 1959).

9. Again, I am gratified to see this point made contemporaneously by Suenens, *Renewal,* p. 31-46.

10. See, for example, *The Making of Late Antiquity* (Chicago: University of Chicago Press, 1978) and "The Rise and Function of the Holy Man in Late Antiquity," *Journal of Roman Studies* 61 (1971) 80-101, reprinted in Brown, *Society and the Holy in Late Antiquity* (University of California Press, 1982), 103-52; *The World of Late Antiquity* (New York: Harcourt, Brace, Jovanovich, 1971); and "Sorcery, Demons, and the Rise of Christianity: from Late Antiquity into the Middle Ages," in *Witchcraft Confessions and Accusations*, ed. M. Douglas (1970; reprinted in *Society and the Holy* [see above], 119-46. More recently, see Brown's contribution to *A History of Private Life*, vol. 1: *From Pagan Rome to Byzantium*, ed. Paul Veyne, trans. Arthur Goldhammer, (Cambridge, Mass.: Harvard-Belknap, 1987), 235-311.

11. An essay of this sort necessarily must omit large blocks of the Christian tradition, in this case, the teaching of Pseudo-Dionysius (ca. 500) on the celestial hierarchies and the divine names, which sets forth an angelology and demonology that was quite influential in both East and West during the Middle Ages. Fortunately, Russell has summarized this succinctly in *Lucifer*, ch. 2, as an illustration of Eastern Orthodox understandings.

12. My basic sources are *The City of God*, Bks. 8-10 and *On the Divination of Demons*, trans. Ruth Wentworth Brown, Fathers of the Church series, 27 (New York: Fathers of the Church, 1955) 417-40; Robert M. Cooper, "Saint Augustine's Doctrine of Evil," *Scottish Journal of Theology* 16 (1963) 256-76; and Jeffrey Burton Russell, *Satan: The Early Christian Tradition* (Ithaca: Cornell, 1981), 195-218. In addition, one might consult *City of God*, Bk. 5, ch. 9; Bk. 11, ch. 9, 13-15, 17, 18, 20-22; Bk. 12, ch. 2-3, 5-7; Bk. 14, ch. 11; Bk. 19, ch. 13 on the question of evil and the goodness of creation. On demons and angels, in addition to Bks. 8-10, see Bk. 11, ch. 13, and Bk. 18, ch. 18. For Augustine's rejection of the possibility of "good magic" see Bk. 10, ch. 9 and 26. On exorcism and crisis intervention, see Bk. 22, ch. 8, 21-22 (Augustine's discussion of miracles, in the course of which he gives several examples of exorcisms).

13. One of the best discussions of this process is found in John J. O'Meara, *The Young Augustine: The Growth of St. Augustine's Mind up to His Conversion* (New York: Alba House, 1965), ch. 6-7, 9-11. See also, Peter Brown, *Augustine of Hippo* (University of California Press, 1967), ch. 5, 9.

14. On God's ability to adapt to human choice yet remain immutable, see, for example, *City of God*, Bk. 22, ch. 2.

15. Russell, *Satan*, ch. 7.

16. R. R. Brown, "The First Evil Will Must Be Incomprehensible: A Critique of Augustine," *Journal of the American Academy of Religion*, 46 (1978), 315-30, on the other hand thinks Augustine's error was to seek too much consistency which, in the problem of evil, is a mistake and impossibility.

17. Eckhart, perhaps John Scotus Eriugena [ca. 810-77], although Russell says he was basically true to Augustine's "differentiated monism." See *Lucifer*, 114ff, esp. 121-23.

66   Martin

18.   See R. I. Moore, *The Origins of European Dissent* (Oxford: Basil Blackwell, 1977, 1985), 139–240; Russell, *Lucifer* 185–91; Edward Peters, ed., *Heresy and Authority in Medieval Europe: Documents in Translation* (Philadelphia: University of Pennsylvania Press, 1980) 103–37.

19.   Some excerpts are found in Alan C. Kors and Edward Peters, eds., *Witchcraft in Europe, 1100–1700: A Documentary History* (Philadelphia: University of Pennsylvania Press, 1972),   53–73, esp. 65–71. The basic discussion is found in the *Summa contra gentiles*, Bk. III, pt. I, ch. 4ff, ch. 71, etc., rather than in the *Summa theologiae*. See the discussion in Russell, *Lucifer*, 160ff, 183, 297, 194.   Another systematic treatise on demonology was written by William of Paris (also known as William of Auvergne, 1180–1249) as part of his *De universo*, which in turn was part of a larger encyclopedic work titled *Magisterium divinale*.   See Adolf Franz, *Die kirchliche Benediktionen im Mittelalter*, 2 vols. (Freiburg i. Br.: Herder, 1909; reprinted Graz: Akademischer Verlagsanstalt, 1960), 2:524–26 and Willem Cornelis van Dam, *Dämonen und Besessene: Die Dämonen in Geschichte und Gegenwart und ihre Austreibung* (Aschaffenburg: Paul Pattloch Verlag, 1970, 1975), 101.

20.   Morrison, *Mimetic Tradition of Reform*, esp. 202–10.

21.   See William J. Courtenay, "The King and the Leaden Coin: The Economic Background of Sine Qua non Causality," *Traditio* 28 (1972) 185–209; and Steven Ozment, *The Age of Reform, 1250–1550: An Intellectual and Religious History of Late Medieval and Reformation Europe* (New Haven: Yale, 1980), 22–42.

22.   John W. Baldwin, *The Scholastic Culture of the Middle Ages, 1000–1300* (Lexington, Mass.: D. C. Heath, 1971); Friedrich Heer, *The Medieval World: Europe, 1100–1350* (London: Weidenfeld and Nicolson, 1961; New York: World, 1961); and Francis Oakley, *The Western Church in the Later Middle Ages* (Ithaca: Cornell, 1979), 162–70.

23.   Richard W. Southern, *The Making of the Middle Ages* (New Haven: Yale, 1953), 219–57.

24.   *The Living God: Systematic Theology*, vol. 1 (San Francisco: Harper and Row, 1987), p. 1, on the joy of studying the doctrine of God.

25.   Kelly, *The Devil at Baptism: Ritual, Theology, and Drama* (Ithaca: Cornell, 1985); Yarnold, ed., *The Awe-Inspiring Rites of Initiation: Baptismal Homilies of the Fourth Century* (Middlegreen, Slough: St. Paul Publications, 1972).   A useful cross section in the high Middle Ages is offered by Arnold Angenendt, "Der Taufexorzismus und seine Kritik in der Theologie des 12. und 13. Jahrhunderts," in *Die Mächte des Guten und Bösen: Vorstellungen im XII. und XIII. Jahrhundert über ihr Wirken in der Heilsgeschichte*, ed. Albert Zimmermann (Berlin: De Gruyter, 1977), 388–409.   Roger Beraudy, "Scrutinies and Exorcisms," in *Adult Baptism and the Catechumenate*, Concilium, 22 (New York: Paulist, 1967), 57–61, has given us a brief overview of the early medieval sacramentaries on this subject.

26.   F. J. Dölger, *Der Exorzismus im altchristlichen Taufritual: Eine religionsgeschichtliche Studie* (Paderborn, 1909), 9-10, agrees that there was no exorcism ritual before the early third century, but that it was in process of formation during the late second century. Van Dam, *Dämonen*, 97-98 notes that the baptismal exorcisms were merely part of, indeed the conclusion of, the prebaptismal catechism. In the late second and early third century this process was developing and expanding, as was the baptismal liturgy itself. Given the exorcistic nature of baptism itself, the simple process of liturgical development may be adequate explanation for the appearance of the baptismal exorcism.

27.   Wilhelm Nagel, "Exorzismus II: Liturgiegeschichtlich" in *Theologische Realenzyklopaedie*, vol. 10, ed. Gerhard Krause and Gerhard Müller (Berlin: De Gruyter, 1982), 750-52, at 751, argues that exorcism was first applied to pagan converts, rather than Jewish converts, out of the assumption that pagans were tainted by the demonic and in need of cleansing more than Jews, but that this distinction gradually faded.   Dölger, *Exorzismus*, 38-39, is more cautious about this distinction.

28.   Even here, when it comes down to it, faith is an individual matter for Rothmann/Marpeck.   See the *Admonition* as translated in Pilgram Marpeck, *The Writings of Pilgram Marpeck*, trans. William Klassen and Walter Klaassen, Classics of the Radical Reformation, 2 (Scottdale: Herald, 1978), 291-92: "The bread and wine are nothing more than an external signal.   However, the power and the might of that which counts rests alone in the heart of the individual who, girded with genuine faith and love, and thus in the church of Christ, can partake of the bread and wine."

29.   Lukken, *Original Sin in the Roman Liturgy: Research into the Theology of Original Sin in the Roman Sacramentaria and the Early Baptismal Liturgy* (Leiden: E. J. Brill, 1973), 156-265.

30.   Lukken, *Original Sin*, 173.

31.   Origen, of course, says that infant baptism went back to apostolic times.   I will not review the literature on that question here.   It is clear that infant baptism was common by Origen's time, indeed by Tertullian's time, the late second century, in other words, at the point at which second and third-generation Christian families were no longer rarities, especially in the larger cities.

32.   Lukken, *Original Sin*, 198.   It is not until the fourth century that "explicit statements to the effect that Satan holds dominion over all the unbaptized, including children" are found. Cf. Van Dam, *Dämonen*, 98.

33.   Lukken, p. 193-94; referring to *De baptismo*, ch.18.

34.   They assumed that there is no other kind of faith--an assumption that a corporative society, accustomed to trusting leaders and traditions would express differently.   A corporative society might distinguish between reception and appropriation of traditional faith.   To remain on the level of received or traditional faith is wrong, but that is the only starting point in a transitory, human

society. To wait until individual and personal faith arrives and to
mistrust received faith in the meantime is to risk never reaching
the goal of personal, appropriated faith.
    35. *Mimetic Tradition of Reform*, 202-10, 222-40.
    36. Menno, *Complete Writings*, trans. Leonard Verduin (Scottdale:
Herald, 1956), 252, 570, 700.
    37. Lukken makes the same point with regard to certain eastern,
non-Chalcedonian groups in the 6th century. See *Original Sin*, 200.
    38. This has now been studied in some detail in Bodo Nischan,
"The Exorcism Controversy and Baptism in the Late Reformation," *The
Sixteenth Century Journal* 18 (1987) 31-51; cf. Nagel in *TRE*, 10: 753.
    39. *Renewal*, 24-25, 97.
    40. One of the best summaries is in Brown, *Making of Late
Antiquity*; basic reference sources are given in the article by Jean
Gribomont in *Christian Spirituality: Origins to the Twelfth Century*,
ed. Bernard McGinn and John Meyendorff (New York: Crossroad, 1985),
89-112; cf. Louis Bouyer, *History of Christian Spirituality*, vol. 1:
The Spirituality of the New Testament and the Fathers (London: Burns
and Oates, 1960), has not been surpassed. Note also the extreme form
the desert spirituality takes in later Coptic monasticism as
described by David N. Bell, "Shenoute the Great: The Struggle with
Satan," *Cistercian Studies* 21 (1986) 177-85.
    41. Found in the *Doctoris ecstatici Dionysii Cartusiani Opera
Omnia* (Montreuil, Tournai, Parkminster: Carthusian Order, 1896-1935),
vol. 40, pp. 267-305.
    42. Heinrich of Friemar (d. ca. 1340), *De quatuor instinctibus*
(several printings 1498-1514, excerpts in A. Wittmann, *De discretione
spirituum apud Dionysium Cartusianum* [Rome and Debrecen, 1939], 52-
66, neither of which I have seen). Other treatments of the same subject are by Heinrich of Langenstein (d. 1397), *De discretione
spirituum* (Antwerp, 1648), excerpts in Wittman, 37-46, and Catherine
of Siena (d. 1380) in her *Dialogue*, ch. 9-11, 98-109, trans. Suzanne
Noffke, Classics of Western Spirituality series (New York: Paulist,
1980), pp. 38-45, 184-204. Finally, Jean Gerson, *De probatione
spirituum* in Gerson, *Oeuvres Completes*, vol. 9: *L'oeuvre doctrinale*,
ed. Palémon Glorieux (Paris: Desclée, 1974), pp. 177-85. The best
overall summary is "Discernement des sprits," in *Dictionnaire de
spiritualité ascetique et mystique* (Paris: Beauchesne, 1967), columns
1222-1291. See also D. Catherine Brown, *Pastor and Laity in the
Theology of Jean Gerson* (Cambridge: Cambridge U. Press, 1987), esp.
91-95.
    43. Accessible in the Nicene and Post-Nicene Fathers, series 2,
vol. 11, trans. Edgar C. S. Gibson, pp. 339-409; the conferences on
prayer and other selected conferences were included in translation
by Colm Luibheid in the Classics of Western Spirituality series (New
York: Paulist, 1985), but not the conferences on demonology--not
unlike Vernon Bourke's approach to abridging Augustine's City of
God for "modern readers."
    44. The Rule of St. Benedict recommends Cassian's *Institutes* and

Conferences as "collateral reading" for those who wish to know more about the pursuit of perfection than is contained in the rule. See ch. 73, cf. ch. 42. John Cassian was the one author Thomas Aquinas is said to have kept constantly at his desk.

45. Conference VIII deals with the "problem of evil under the title "On Principalities." It asserts that nothing is created evil by God, discusses the fall of the Devil and the angels and their punishment, the guardian angel and its demonic counterpart who surround each of us, and certain specific questions like the nature of the fallen angels who had intercourse with the daughters of men according to Genesis 6:1-4.

46. For the ancients, "body" may or may not include the animating soul. As it is used here, it generally refers to the living body, the animated body, which would include the "soul," if one distinguishes between soul and spirit.

47. See, for example, Augustine, *De doctrina Christiana*, Bk. 1, esp. ch. 23-25, trans. in Nicene and Post-Nicene Fathers, series 1, vol. 2: 528-29.

48. Franz, *Benediktionen*, II: 524-28, summarizes William of Paris, Rupert of Deutz, Bonaventure, Thomas Aquinas. For Bernard of Clairvaux's articulation of the same position, see Bernard, *Sermons on the Song of Songs*, sermon 5, par. 8; trans. by Kilian Walsh in *Works of Bernard of Clairvaux*, vol. 2: *On the Song of Songs*, vol. 1, Cistercian Fathers Series, 4 (Kalamazoo: Cistercian Publications, 1979), p. 29. Gratian's compilation of canon law in the twelfth century asserts exactly the opposite. See the excerpts in Kors and Peters, *Witchcraft*, 29.

49. Cf. Ignatius of Antioch on the Eucharist as "medicine of immortality" in his letter to the Ephesians, ch. 22.2, in the translation by Cyril C. Richardson, *Early Christian Fathers*, Library of Christian Classics, 1 (New York: Macmillan, 1970), 93. The idea is common in early church writings. See Daniel J. Sheerin, ed., *The Eucharist*, Message of the Fathers of the Church, 7 (Wilmington, DE: Michael Glazier, 1986).

50. Franz, *Benediktionen*, II: 568.

51. Kors and Peters, *Witchcraft*, 5-13.

52. This latter development has been investigated by D. P. Walker, *Unclean Spirits: Possession and Exorcism in France and England in the Late Sixteenth and Early Seventeenth Centuries* (Philadelphia: University of Pennsylvania Press, 1981).

53. (New York: Scribners, 1971), esp. pp. 25-71, 632-40.

54. Lester K. Little, *Religious Poverty and the Profit Economy* (Ithaca: Cornell, 1978); Carlo M. Cipolla, *Before the Industrial Revolution: European Society and Economy, 1000-1700* (New York: W. W. Norton, 1976); Dietrich Gerhard, *Old Europe: A Study in Continuity, 1000-1800* (New York: Academic Press, 1981).

55. Lester K. Little, "Pride Goes before Avarice: Social Changes and the Vices in Latin Christendom," *American Historical Review* 76 (1971) 16-49; John W. Baldwin, *Masters, Princes and Merchants: The*

70   Martin

Social Views of Peter the Chanter and His Circle, 2 vols. (Princeton: Princeton University Press, 1970); Marie-Dominique Chenu, *Nature, Man and Society* (1968).

56. Richard Kieckhefer, *Unquiet Souls: Fourteenth Century Saints and their Religious Milieu* (Chicago: University of Chicago Press, 1984); Leclercq, *Love of Learning*.

57. Georges Duby, *The Age of the Cathedrals: Art and Society, 980-1420*, trans. Eleanor Levieux and Barbara Thompson (Chicago: University of Chicago Press, 1981), as summarized in Günter Zimmermann, "Spätmittelalterliche Frömmigkeit in Deutschland: Eine sozialgeschichtliche Betrachtung," *Zeitschrift für historische Forschung* 13 (1986) 65-81, here 77.

58. See, most recently, Zimmermann, "Frömmigkeit, p. 66-67, 72-73 77-79, with references to earlier literature.

59. *The Dialogue on Miracles*, 2 vols., trans. H. von E. Scott and C. C. Swinton Bland (London: George Routledge and Sons, 1929), esp. Bk. 5, but not absent anywhere in the book.

60. *Lucifer*, esp. 63, 74, 76, 88, 89.

61. Christopher Nugent, *Masks of Satan: The Demonic in History* (London: Sheed and Ward, 1983), 50; this is supported by Franz's treatment, *Kirchliche Benediktionen*, vol. II: 519-28.

62. Franz, *Benediktionen*, vol. II:545-46, 551, 553-56. See also Russell, *Lucifer*, 80-92, esp. 82-83, p. 103. See also the illustrations in Kors and Peters, *Witchcraft*, 99-100.

63. See *Benediktionen*, 2: 561-85 for summaries of the development; the texts are found on pp. 586-615. See also Nagel in TRE, 10: 753.

64. Note Suenens, *Renewal*, 97-98, 73-74, on this matter--as far as "solemn exorcism" or "ritual exorcism" is concerned--as well as Suenens' critique of the Rituale and call for reform of it, pp. 73-81, 86-87, 91-92, 94, critique that by no means is a rejection of its basic approach.

65. I have used the convenient Latin/English text, *Roman Ritual in Latin and English*, vol. 2: *Christian Burial, Exorcism, reserved Blessings, Etc.*, trans. and ed. Philip T. Weller (Milwaukee: Bruce, 1952). The exorcism rites take up pp. 160-229.

66. Robert Petitpierre, ed., *Exorcism: The Findings of a Commission Convened by the Bishop of Exeter* (London: S.P.C.K., 1972), offers an Anglican parallel to the *Rituale Romanum*.

67. Walker, *Unclean Spirits*, 9-12.

68. See Yarnold, ed., *The Awe-Inspiring Rites*, esp. 256-58.

69. *Renewal*. p. 17, 21-26, 105-9. See also Van Dam, *Dämonen*, 96.

70. We might even consider restoring the catechumenate along the lines of the new Roman Catholic *Rite of Christian Initiation of Adults* or along the lines suggested by Geoffrey Wainwright, *Doxology: The Praise of God in Worship, Doctrine, and Life: A Systematic Theology* (Oxford: Oxford U. Press, 1980), 141. The *Rite of Christian Initiation of Adults* is found in *The Rites of the Catholic Church* as Revised by Decree of the Second Vatican Ecumenical Council, Study

Edition, English translation by the International Commission on English in the Liturgy (New York: Pueblo Publishing Company, 1976), 13-182. See the commentary by Robert E. Webber, *Celebrating Our Faith: Worship as Evangelism* (San Francisco: Harper and Row, 1986).

71. See *The Brethren Encyclopedia* (Philadelphia and Oak Brook: Brethren Encyclopedia, Inc., 1983), 333-34 for bibliographic reference and a brief description of the practice.

72. Van Dam, *Dämonen*, 97-98; Lukken, *Original Sin*, 255-65; Dölger, *Exorzismus*, 4-8.

73. See Lukken, *Original Sin*, 211-14. Robert E. Webber, *Celebrating Our Faith*, is relevant to all these points.

74. Joseph H. Lynch, *Godparents and Kinship in Early Medieval Europe* (Princeton: Princeton University Press, 1986), offers an excellent overview and points to the standard literature on the subject.

75. Examples from the Book of Common Prayer are compiled in Petitpierre, *Exorcism*, 29-30.

76. See Webber, *Celebrating*, pp. 3-5, 50, 70-83.

Response to Dennis Martin

Thomas Finger

The primary value of Dennis Martin's paper, as I see it, lies in its suggestion of an overall, cosmic understanding of good and evil, and therefore of salvation and sin and of the healing role of the Church. Although his paper abounds with interesting historical information, in this consultation our main concern must be not with events and chronology, but with the broader insights that past ages can grant us.

We Mennonites tend to have great pride in our historical awareness, for we generally know far more about the period of our origins than most other groups know about theirs. To be candid, however, we often know very little about the rest of church history. We usually have little appreciation for the positive values of those traditions from which our ancestors departed. And we are seldom adequately aware of those larger socio-cultural trends in which our own history has played a part. For these reasons, someone who dates his paper on the "Feast of SS. Peter and Paul, Apostles" provides an invaluable contribution to the Mennonite church. Although I question some of Dennis' assertions, I want to express gratitude for his raising such important issues in such a challenging way.

Let me begin by attempting to sketch that cosmic perspective of good and evil which permeates Martin's paper. If my summary is hazy or incorrect at points, these can hopefully be remedied in our ensuing discussion.

Martin's Sacramental Metaphysics

Dennis calls his view of the cosmos "sacramental." All things originate from a God who is wholly spiritual, but who chooses to communicate to us through a world which is material. This spiritual God remains distinct from the material creation. Yet at the same time God permeates and indwells it. Human beings, like God, are spiritual beings; yet they are also physical creatures who express their spiritual and personal intentions through the medium of matter. God created humans to express their inner reality through symbols—through physical words, pictures, gestures, etc.—which represent, and thus communicate the reality of, what they signify. God also created humans to express the significance of physical facts through mental concepts which appropriately express them. Moreover, in the world as God created it, persons and other beings become more fully what they were intended to be by following those processes and rhythms which God imbedded in life. These include relationships of continuity and harmony with all other persons and things, by which the entire creation becomes more real, or whole.

In such a creation, how could evil ever arise? Martin, as I understand him, says that this occurs when creatures turn aside from

those processes and relationships through which they become more
fully real. Evil results when creatures turn towards that which
makes them less alive. Evil, then, is not really an active force or
principle. It is simply "non-being." "The evil of Satan," Dennis
says, "is a continual choice to deny his own being, to choose non-
being, nothingness, and chaos" (p. 48). Yet this choice of non-being
has very real consequences. It turns creatures away from the goals
for which they were created, and out of harmony with other beings.
It brings dissonance and fragmentation into the world.

The worst consequence of this fragmentation, as I understand
Martin, is what he calls dualism. Spiritual and personal reality are
torn away from matter, concepts from facts, symbols from things. The
modern world arose through an outbreak, as it were, of dualism. It
was launched when, with the help of the Protestant Reformation, faith
became an individual matter and individuals were torn loose from
traditional social and ecclesiastical communities; when, with the
help of the scientific revolution, the physical world came to be seen
as dead matter, so that it could be reshaped and manipulated by the
human mind and spirit. Through this process, however, individuals
became increasingly homeless, isolated and lonely. People fell ever
further out of the sacramental harmonies which God created. Evil
became ever more disruptive and often had to be handled through
crisis intervention.

What is the remedy for this dualistic rupturing? The essential
remedy was bestowed 2,000 years ago in the incarnation, which Martin
calls "the Sacrament of sacraments" (p. 51). God entered the
material world in a decisive, personal way and began reuniting this
estranged, distorted creation to himself. Christ did not create a
new humanity from scratch, for the "image" of God in human nature,
though it had been "twisted and tarnished" (p. 48), had not been
totally lost. Christ began the "reformation of the image of God"
and of nature (p. 51), but not their total re-creation. Jesus continued this restoration of "the ontological and sacramental linkage
between sign and the thing signified, between creator and creature"
(p. 51) by establishing the church, a physical institution through
which spiritual grace is bestowed, especially through sacraments—
material signs and actions which communicate what they signify.

The Reformation, however, tore the focal points of Christian
faith out of their overall sacramental context. Christ's incarnation,
death and resurrection, rather than being acts through which God
reunited himself with creation, "were reduced to a historic event
with which we come in contact by mental processes." Bread and wine
"were reduced to mere symbols" of this event (p. 52). The Anabaptists, by insisting on individual faith for baptism, tore this rite
out of the context which had mediated the invitation to faith through
the generations. Through the holes which the Reformation rent in
this sacramental fabric, evil began to spurt in drastic ways like
witchcraft and demonic bondage.

Martin's main solution for the problem of bondage today is
mainly one of "prophylaxis and preventive medicine, rather than

crisis intervention" (pp. 60-61). It "must begin by restoring respect
and confidence in the guardians of the liturgy and sacraments"--I
assume that means clergy--"together with the metaphysics of mediation that undergird them" (p. 58). This will require much teaching,
and thus a higher status for theologians, and possibly the establishing of monastic orders. Essentially, though, it is the church's worship life which must be restored, for this "has always been the center of the life of the mystical body of Christ" (p. 63).

Comments and Critique

I find much beauty and truth in this sacramental view of the
cosmos. I regard the proclamation and actualization of such a
vision as central to the church's mission, especially in its healing
ministry. Yet I want to raise three kinds of questions.

First, is it really true that evil is non-being? Despite
Martin's criticism of the Reformation, he praises Calvin for affirming "the non-existence of evil" (p. 52). Yet Calvin, like other
reformers, criticized the traditional definition of original sin as
"the lack of the original righteousness" because it did not express
"effectively enough" sin's "power and energy." (Institutes: 251-252).
Calvin called original sin a "contagion," a "corruption" which has
"infected" us, which is "diffused into all parts of the soul..."
(249,252). Whatever else we may think of these concepts, they hardly
represent sin as nothingness. In our modern world too, scourges
like systemic injustice, dictatorship, and nuclear escalation seem
far more like active, intentional forces. And evil is experienced as
actively and pitilessly volitional in demonic bondage. Perhaps the
Reformation, rather than simply allowing evil to erupt more actively,
rediscovered its dynamism, which had lain hidden--and thereby worked
more effectively--under the static hierarchical medieval system.

I wonder, then, if Martin's brand of sacramentalism can take
evil's active power seriously enough. Dennis apparently approves of
two assertions of John Cassian which I would question (p. 59). Cassian says that while God can draw us towards salvation "even against
our will and without our knowing it," the devil can only deceive
those who have intentionally yielded to him. While this probably
overstates the extent to which God will work through what we call
the subconscious, it vastly underestimates the devil's tendency to do
so. Second, Cassian says that demons can directly affect only our
bodies, but not our souls. But demons seem to work most effectively
through the subtle but terrible oppression and depression they wreak
upon the psyche. Martin seems to assume that if we can put life
back into its proper sacramental context, many of the disruptive
phenomena of bondage will subside. But to what extent is he
underestimating the active power of the demonic?

Second, Martin often says that evil was overcome through
Christ's incarnation. Yet as I read Scripture, Jesus' conflict with
the Powers was a long-term struggle. While the incarnation marked
God's irreversible entrance into the battle, it was waged throughout

Jesus' struggle with Satan in the wilderness; his continuing encounters with demonic, religious, and political opposition; and finally the terrible depths of Gethsemane and Golgotha, and his triumphant emergence from the tomb. Evil was decisively defeated only by Jesus' continued adherence to the way of servanthood and of God's Kingdom amid opposition, and even unto death. To speak of evil as vanquished simply by the incarnation seems once again to minimize its active power. It also seems to overlook the active power which guided and sustained Jesus and raised him from the dead--the Holy Spirit.

Third, I agree with Martin that the Anabaptists, in reremphasizing the dynamism of evil and of God's transforming work, sometimes divorced the latter too far from its context in the continuities of material creation. For instance, most Anabaptists regarded salvation as the bestowal of a brand new nature. Because this transformation was so radical, those who experienced it were expected to live quite soon on a much higher plane. But while this expectation expressed admirable confidence in God's power, it often supposed that this transformation would bypass some normal processes of human development. It eventually led to unrealistic expectations which could only be enforced in legalistic ways. Similarly, Anabaptists often supposed that God created new churches instantaneously. True Christianity seemed to have disappeared from the current Catholic, Lutheran and Reformed communions. Overlooking what continuity their movement might have with these streams, Anabaptists sometimes supposed that God had suddenly raised them up to restore something that had disappeared. Seeing themselves as largely detached from history and society, Mennonites later separated geographically. Seeing little continuity between what they and the rest of the world were doing, they often lost their sense of mission.

But although Anabaptists did rupture creation's material continuities in these ways, they restored them in others. To be sure, the invitation to faith was no longer mediated through the generations by baptism. But as Mennonites became ethnic communities knit together by distinctive behaviors and oft-rehearsed traditions, the invitation to faith was mediated more vividly than it usually was in Catholicism. To be sure, aesthetic joy in God's creation was largely eliminated from worship. But the Mennonites' expression of their inner faith and love for God through agriculture, crafts, cooking, and quilting--these could hardly be more "sacramental" in the broader sense. Mennonites, in fact, were far more embedded in the continuities of material creation than was most of the increasingly individualized, industrialized western culture; and therefore they were often less vulnerable to eruptions of the demonic.

What overall implications can be drawn? First, let's celebrate the positive ways in which our tradition has been broadly "sacramental." But, as Martin urges, let's see if some of this can be restored to our worship. We often celebrate communion infrequently or irregularily and as a mere reminder of past events. But are there

ways, rooted in Scripture, in which we can begin to experience
Jesus' active, gracious presence through it? I think so. Let's
begin exploring this. And while we are at it, let's begin experiencing and expressing God's presence more fully through our eyes,
gestures, and bodies in general in worship. Similarly, let us learn
from those traditions which relate spirituality to personal and
psychological development. In these and other ways, let us integrate
our spiritual lives with the rest of our lives and, as Martin suggests, provide a "prophylaxis" against demonic eruption.

At the same time, however, let us not suppose that either evil or
the Holy Spirit can be wholly domesticated within "sacramental"
structures. Until the consummation, evil will remain virulent and
destructive, and the Spirit will challenge and guide the church in
ways that we cannot wholly manage or predict. Our lives, however
rooted sacramentally, must be open to the Spirit's reshaping. And
we desperately need those who are able to confront the challenge of
the demonic directly on this level.

AN EVANGELICAL POSITION
ON BONDAGE AND EXORCISM

Timothy M. Warner

Since many groups would identify with the label "evangelical" and since within those groups there would be widely varying positions on this subject, I can speak only for myself. However, from my knowledge of the people involved in "deliverance" ministry and of the literature on the subject, I believe I represent a fairly middle-of-the-road position in the segment of the church usually designated as "evangelical."

The World View Problem

Dealing with Satan and beings called demons has become increasingly difficult as our culture has gone through the process known as the "mystification of religion" and "the secularization of science." This process has resulted in a world view with two discrete realms--the supernatural and the natural, the realm of religion and the realm of science. It relegates spirits and spirit activity largely to the supernatural realm. It assumes that for any phenomenon in human life or in the physical world there is a cause in the same realm. Seldom, if ever, are spirits thought to invade human experience, if, indeed, such spirits are even thought to exist. It results in the asking of either-or types of questions: Is it religious or is it scientific? Is it a spiritual problem or a psychological problem? Is the cause supernatural or natural?

This is a world view entirely foreign to that held by most of the cultures of the world and one that is foreign to that of our Lord as reflected in the Gospels. It is a world view in which spirits of any kind, and especially evil spirits, have little place. While we may give lip service to a belief in spirits both good and evil in our formal statements of theology, such spirits are not functional realities in everyday life for most Christians--even for most theologians.

We assume that we can send missionaries to evangelize peoples holding animistic beliefs in which spirits are seen as involved with all aspects of life and give them theological answers to the ultimate questions of life, death, and eternity and scientific answers to the events of everyday life. Then we wonder why the people we evangelize end up with syncretism in their expression of Christianity. They know the evil spirits are real, and no scientific explanation is going to make them go away. If we don't show them how the power of Christ applies in the spirit realm, they will resort to the practices they know from their past.

The real problem is that we are syncretistic also, but our syncretism is from the secular end of the animism-materialism continuum. We have been taken in by the assumption that belief in
spirits, and spirit causation especially, is not compatible with our
technologically advanced society. We have assumed that if we posit
God as Creator, we have a Christian world-view. It is not thoroughly
Christian, however, until it includes a functional belief in the
existence and activity of angels and demons.

The fact is that world-views are held largely at a subconscious
level. It is as one of my college professors was fond of saying,
"People may not practice what they profess, but they will always
practice what they believe." Our world-view is what we really
believe. So, even though our profession includes spirits, our lives
are lived as though they did not exist because they are nonfunc-
tional in our world-view. This, unfortunately, is true even of the
Holy Spirit. Just ask yourself, for example, in a domestic argument
when tempers get involved, when do you control your emotions
better--when an important person is present whom you wish to
impress, or when the Holy Spirit is present?

So, our world-views need careful scrutiny to determine to what
extent we have allowed the world to pour us into its mold (Rom 8:2,
Phillips)--to what extent we have become the victims of the
secularizing drift of our society.

Spiritual Warfare--A Reality

Spiritual warfare has been a part of the human scene ever since
Satan practiced his deception on Eve. Satan's character and tactics
have not changed significantly from that time to this. He is, to be
sure, very adept at adjusting his methods to where people are at any
given time, but his desperation to achieve his diabolical purposes
has not changed. Jesus himself indicated that Satan would be active
throughout the time between his first and second comings and that
his activity would become more intense as the time of the eschaton
neared (Matt 24, esp. vss. 24,25).

Satan's Origin and Motive
The Bible does not tell us clearly where Satan came from. It
does tell us many things about him, however. Without taking time to
build a case for my position, I assume that Satan was originally one
of the highest angels--perhaps a "guardian cherub" (Ezek 28:14) with
a position in heaven pictured on earth by the guardian cherubs
covering the mercy seat in the tabernacle. His perception of the
glory of God was as clear as that of a created being could be. But,
for whatever reason, he became jealous of that glory and coveted it
for himself. So we find him playing the role of a god in the
institution of idolatry (1 Cor 10:20). We find him tempting Jesus to
bow down and worship him (Matt 4:9). And at the end of the age we
find him coming in the man of sin to set himself up in the temple of
God "proclaiming himself to be God" (2 Thess 2:4).

The irony of all this is that instead of becoming a glorious being like Yahweh, he has become the fiend who epitomizes all that is unholy and evil. The significant lesson to be learned, however, is that the fundamental issue at stake in the world is the glory of God. Satan's jealousy has reached that stage where he knows he will never rise to the level of God and will never share God's glory; so he is determined to deprive God of all the glory he can. It is, of course, not possible to deprive God of glory in the realm of heaven. Such a frontal attack is an impossibility. He therefore concentrates his attack on God's children--children by creation and children by redemption.

The Glory of God versus Self

Paul tells us that we are to live our lives to the glory of God (1 Cor 10:31; Eph 1:6,14). If Satan can get us to live our lives at such a mediocre level that we do not reflect the glory of God, he has accomplished his purpose in us. The fact that we are preoccupied, at worst, with our right to personal fulfillment and, at best, with the salvation of people is evidence of how successful Satan has been in getting the focus on ourselves instead of on God and His glory. Personal salvation and fulfillment are legitimate objectives, but they are ultimately by-products of a prior concern with the glory of God.

The problem is that we fail to recognize that this is also part of spiritual warfare. We recognize Satan's work only when it takes on more obvious manifestations; and one of the reasons we are so slow to deal with the more overt activity of the powers of darkness is that we do not recognize it in the affairs of everyday life. We have become so accustomed to living powerless lives that we do not recognize what we are missing, and we therefore are not in touch with the power which makes Satan flee.

A doctoral student of mine said to me recently: "I have been teaching the Gospel of Mark in Indonesia for many years, and I just discovered that I have completely missed one of the primary emphases of that book--the demonstration of power over the work of the enemy; and yet power is a key concept in Indonesian culture."

Glory versus Power

Power has become the issue because Satan knows he can not compete on the level of glory. Because he has supernatural power, however, he can use that power to impress and intimidate God's people. Our lack of experience with the reality of the incomparably great spiritual power available to us (Eph 1:19) causes us to back off in the face of Satan's intimidation rather than resisting him and causing him to run from us as James says we should (Jas 4:7).

Satan, of course, is a limited being, even though he tries to create the impression that he is the eternal counterpart of God. Satan is a powerful being, however, and while that power must be respected, we must not ascribe to him more than is his due. He is not omnipresent. He can not be everywhere at once doing his work. He must therefore depend on his corps of demons to carry out his mission. Because they were angels by creation, they were God's agents to carry out God's purposes in the created world, they now use their powers to pervert God's creation--both the human creation and the material creation. This is why Jesus treated disease and storms in much the same manner that he treated demons. (See James Kallas, *The Significance of the Synoptic Miracles* for development of this concept.)

The point is that demons are very much involved in the events of this life. That is not to say that we control the affairs of life by controlling demons. It is to say that spiritual warfare is a factor that must be considered when analyzing and dealing with the events of our lives.

The Christian Position of Victory

Early in the consideration of this subject it is imperative to establish the fact that the work of Christ on the cross disarmed Satan (Col 2:15), destroyed his works (1 John 3:8), and ultimately destroyed Satan himself (Heb 2:14,15); and that the person who is "in Christ" is at the place of certain victory.

When the seventy returned from their field work assignment given to them by Jesus as part of their training, they said, "Lord, even the demons submit to us in your name." I think they emphasized the "us" because they were surprised at their authority. Jesus responded by telling them that they did indeed have "authority to trample on snakes and scorpions and to overcome all the power of the enemy; [and] nothing will harm you." He quickly added, however, "Do not rejoice that the spirits submit to you, but rejoice that your names are written in heaven" (Luke 10:17-20). I understand Jesus to be saying that authority over demons is not some special gift given to a few believers over which those believers could gloat. On the contrary, it is the privilege of every believer to "resist the devil" and make him flee (Jas 4:7); and they should focus on their relationship to God, not on evil spirits.

This does not mean that every believer should be involved in a "deliverance" ministry. It does mean that Christians do not need to live in fear of the activity of demons. With proper instruction, an obedient walk, and a functioning faith, the believer can stand against all the devil's schemes (Eph 6:11) and can demolish his strongholds (2 Cor 10:4).

Paul's prayer for the believers in Ephesus (Eph 1:15-23) involves some foundational truths concerning the position of one who is "in Christ." He prays first that they may have "a spirit of wisdom and revelation" in order to know God better, because everything begins with a right view of God.

Based on that knowledge of God and the relationship such knowing involves, Paul prays for three special perspectives for the

Christian. First he prays that they may know "the hope to which he has called you"; that is to say that they may have the "long view" of things and not be trapped by the immediate circumstances of life.

Then he prays that they may know "the riches of his glorious inheritance in the saints." This goes back to the figure of adoption which he used in 1:5. Because God has adopted us into God's family, we have now become joint heirs with the Son Jesus Christ (Rom 8:17) of all the resources of God. This is an incredible fact seldom perceived or acted on by God's people.

As if to reinforce the impact of this, Paul goes on to pray that the believers may know "his incomparably great power *for us* who believe." To make certain that the point is not missed, Paul says that the power he is speaking of is the power which raised Christ from the dead and "seated him at his right hand in the heavenly realms, far above all rule and authority, power and dominion, and every title that can be given, not only in the present age but also in the one to come."

This passage gives as clear a statement of the supremacy of Christ over Satan and demons and of the resources available t the believer for spiritual combat as is to be found in the New Testament. But to make certain that the point is not missed, in chapter two Paul proceeds to apply it to the Christians in Ephesus. After establishing the hopelessness of the person without Christ (2:1-3), he says, "But because of his great love for us, God, who is rich in mercy, made us alive with Christ . . . and seated us with him in the heavenly realms in Christ Jesus" (2:4-6).

Paul establishes the fact that it is the believer's identification with Christ through the work of the cross which gives him or her the basis for authority over the principalities and powers. This is illustrated by the experience of a well-known missionary leader.

Dick Hillis was a young missionary in China when a young Chinese soldier came to his door and said, "Missionary, is your Christ all powerful?"

Without hesitation Hillis replied, "Of course he is!"

"My wife is in the courtyard," the soldier said, "and she is demon possessed. Twice the demon has ordered her to kill herself, . . . but I was able to rescue her. However, I do not know what to do now . . . so I have brought her to you."

Hillis had had no training in theological school about how to deal with demons, but he had to do something; so he and his wife and some Bible women began to pray with the woman. For three days they prayed with no results. Hillis and his wife were reading at that time in Ephesians one and two. The impact of being "in Christ" dawned on them; and this time, instead of asking God to deliver the woman, he commanded the demon to leave, and the woman was instantly delivered. (*Demon Experiences in Many Lands*, Moody Press, 1960, pp. 37-39)

It appears that, at least at times, God will not allow us to delegate things back to him through prayer but requires us to use the authority which has been delegated to us. Any parent should understand that delegation of authority and responsibility to children and adolescents at appropriate levels is essential preparation for adulthood. The principle of not allowing delegation up is also well known to successful administrators.

Coming back to the biblical basis for this authority, however, we find a clear statement of it in Rev 12:11. After an account of the defeat of Satan and his angels by Michael and his angels and of Satan's expulsion from heaven, we are told that the people on earth were able to overcome the attacks of Satan "by the blood of the Lamb and by the word of their testimony; they did not love their lives so much as to shrink from death."

The first element in the basis for victory is the blood of Christ which takes care of the sin problem. The blood removes the impediment between humans and God, it removes the guilt with which Satan makes his case against us, and effectively destroys Satan's power over us. As Barclay puts it, "On his Cross and through his Resurrection Jesus conquered and overcame forever the worst that sin and evil could do to him. He met the full assault of evil and overcame it. And those who have entrusted their lives to him share in that victory." (William Barclay, *The Revelation of John*, Vol. 2, p. 103)

The second basis for victory is death to the dominance of self— "they did not love their lives so much as to shrink from death." This principle is a recurring theme in the Gospels, and it is like saying to Satan, "You can't threaten me with the loss of my life because I have already died. My reputation, my fulfillment, even my physical life is not the issue. It is the glory of the One who has become my Lord." To quote Barclay again, "It is a matter of setting loyalty to Jesus Christ before safety and security and the comfortable way." (*Ibid.*, p. 104) The blood of the cross and the giving up of personal rights—even the right to live—remove the ground Satan depends on to accuse and to tempt us.

I believe this is what Paul had in view when he wrote to the Colossians, "And having disarmed the powers and authorities, he made a public spectacle of them, triumphing over them by the cross" (Col 2:15). Our identification with Christ at the cross in forgiveness for sin, and death to our old natures effectively takes the weapons which Satan has used against us out of his hands.

This does not mean that there are no battles, however. It only means that we have the necessary resources to win the battles. God promised Israel the promised land, and that promise was as good as the character of God; but they still had to fight every battle as it came along in the conquest of Canaan. So it is with us; we have the assurance of victory but not the assurance that there will never be any battles.

While the position of victory is assured for the believer, not all are believers; so we need to take a brief look at the place of the unbeliever in this spiritual warfare.

Satan, Demons, and the Unbeliever

Derek Prince makes a key point when he says, "Human beings are like walled cities. Certain natural defenses protect us against the entrance of demons. Basically, these are provided by sound, healthy minds, emotions, and wills." (Christian Life, June 1984, pp. 30,31). The point is, demons can not do whatever they please. They operate under the limits established for them by God. They have to devise a perversion of God's plan and induce a person to act on that perversion in order to gain control over the person.

Those who have not placed their faith in the sacrifice of Christ to cover the guilt and the penalty of their sin, and especially those who live in parts of the world where the church has not been planted, are more apt to provide ground for demonic invasion than persons who confess Christ as Savior and Lord. In any case, however, one will find many degrees of relationship with evil spirits. It is not a simple matter of possessed or not possessed.

Casting demons out of an unbeliever should always be done in connection with leading that person to personal faith in Christ. One does not go around casting out demons, or attempting to do so, apart from the whole of the Christian evangel. To do so would be to ignore the serious warning of Jesus in Matthew 12:43-45. In the experience of Dick Hillis cited above, God also led him to have the soldier destroy the idols the couple had in their home. One can not be giving open ground to the demons through idolatry and still expect the demons to leave.

Satan, Demons, and the Believer

The Bible frequently pictures the Christian life as a warfare. For many of us this figure is repulsive because of our convictions about participation in war. Participation in spiritual combat, however, is not optional. To practice nonresistance against our spiritual enemy is to disobey the clear commands of Scripture. All of the biblical warnings about spiritual attacks and about our responsibility to resist are addressed to believers.

Special objects of attack
Christians are the special objects of Satan's wrath for a number of reasons. First of all, Satan hates us simply because we are God's children, and he attacks the child to get at the Parent. A part of being a child of God is being created in God's image with the potential for glorification—a sharing of God's glory. As staggering as the thought is, that is the destiny of the believer (Rom 8:30; 9:23). Satan coveted such a position for himself, and his jealousy over our having it is now directed at us.

Another amazing statement about our relation to God is that God has made us "heirs of God and co-heirs with Christ" (Rom 8:17). Satan would love to have such a position. He has frequently tried to pawn himself off as the equal of Christ. A good example of this is found in Mormonism which makes Jesus and Lucifer brothers. It is not only "glory by and by," however. We have the privilege and responsibility of living now to "the praise of his glory" (Eph 1:14). So desperate is Satan to try to deprive God of His glory that he will do whatever he can to keep us from living at a level of victory which will be commensurate with the glory of God. His primary objective for you and me, therefore, is just to keep us spiritually ineffective.

Finally, Satan makes us the special objects of his attack because we are the foot soldiers of our Lord sent out to retake the territory usurped by Satan at the fall. We are commissioned to bring people "from darkness to light and from the power of Satan to God" (Acts 26:18). This gives him further reason for rendering us spiritually ineffective. It is important to note that at this stage it is no longer simply a matter of resisting Satan's attacks. The Church is now on the attack against Satan with the combat becoming more intense, and counterattack is also a certainty.

The Old Testament model

I believe the conquest of Canaan by Israel is a type of this spiritual warfare. The whole campaign was under the ultimate control of the Lord himself. It was under God's authority that the invasion took place at all. Strategy at every point was provided by the Lord, and victory came only through God's power. It was never the clever tactics or the military superiority of Israel which won the battles. It was always the power of God. God planned it so that each battle required new battle plans. Israel could never assume that they could reuse the battle plan for the previous town. So in our spiritual warfare, we can never assume that we have the secret formula for victory. The basis for victory is in our relationship to the Lord, not in a ritual for dealing with demons. (This is one of the reason I prefer not to use the term exorcism. It is not a biblical term to begin with, being used only of non-Christian exorcists, and it has come to connote a special ritual or formula for removing demons.)

Possessed versus Demonized

Numerous passages in the New Testament indicate that Christians are not automatically protected from demonic attacks (e.g., Eph 4:27; 6:10-18, Jas 4:7, 1 Pet 5:8-9). If that is true, the question is, how far can a demon go in its attacks on a believer? The question is often framed, "Can a Christian be demon possessed?" I would suggest that "possessed" is not an accurate term to describe the relationship between a demon and a human being. It is not a required translation, and perhaps not even a correct translation, of the words in the Greek New Testament used to depict this relationship.

Many who are working in this area of ministry are now using the more general term "demonized." It is virtually a transliteration of the Greek term *daimonizo* which the King James translators chose to translate "demon possessed." The term "possessed" is too strong a term to use for the relationship usually encountered in Christian people.

The more accurate concept is that suggested by Paul in Ephesians 4:27 when he says, "Don't give the devil a foothold (literally, a place)." The figure here is that of an enemy which is not strong enough to conquer (to possess) a country but which establishes a small beachhead from which guerilla raids can be carried out. Such raids can keep a country in a considerable turmoil, but it would not be correct to say that the rebel group possessed the country.

To put it in more theological terms, I assume that we are body (*soma*) with which we have world consciousness, soul (*psuche*) with which we have self consciousness, and spirit (*pneuma*) with which we have God consciousness. I also assume that my spirit is so uniquely Godlike in its quality, having been created in image, that Satan has no access to it. If the Holy Spirit resides within my spirit, I have spiritual life. If not, I am in spiritual death.

This means that Satan is limited in his activity to the soul (*psyche*) and to the body of human beings. This is what John means when he writes in 1 John 5:18, "We know that any one born of God does not sin, but He who was born of God keeps him, and the evil one does not touch (*haptetai*) him" (RSV). This cannot mean that Satan does not tempt or attack the Christian. There are too many warnings of such attacks to make that a possible meaning. I believe that the person which the devil cannot touch is the new person I become in spirit when the Holy Spirit takes up residence in me. That new life is not co-terminus with my psyche or my body. They are all interrelated, to be sure; but Satan may do things to my body and my soul without touching my spirit. On that basis the Lord sent messages to the churches in the Book of the Revelation saying that they would suffer various things and that Satan would put some of them in prison (Rev 2:10).

Recognizing the limitations of spatial diagrams for non-spatial things, I suggest the following diagram to picture what I have been saying.

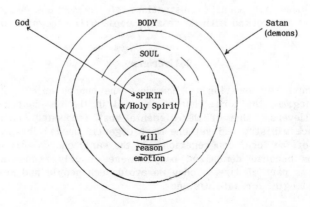

The following chart is an attempt to indicate the varying
degrees of relationship which demons may have to people. Our
Western penchant for creating neat categories for everything leads
us to this type of analysis, but in reality the boxes are not as discrete as the chart would seem to indicate. The use of dotted lines
in places is some recognition of this. The quotation marks around
"inside" and "outside" are a further attempt to indicate that these
terms may not be entirely appropriate when talking about beings
which do not occupy space. The terms "oppression," "obsession,"
"inhabitation," and "possession" are certainly not absolutes--only
attempts to indicate a progression in the relationship.

Given these limitations, I still offer the diagram as an aid to
understanding the various stages in the relationship of demons to
humans, and I acknowledge my indebtedness to other people for some
of the concepts and terms employed.

DEGREES OF DEMONIZATION

"OUTSIDE"		"INSIDE"	
Temptation	Activity affecting the function of the person	Foothold or "ground" held in person's life	Demons in control
Attack			
"Hassle"			
OPPRESSION	OBSESSION	INHABITATION	POSSESSION
Christians involved at these levels			Non-Christians only
Handled through normal Christian disciplines		Assistance usually needed from the Church (counselors)	

Time does not permit illustrations of the various stages, but
anyone who has worked with demonized people will recognize the progression.

Deliverance

The next key question is "How does the church help?" As used
on the diagram, the term "church" is used in the broadest sense of
other believers. One of the elements most frequently lacking in
deliverance ministry and yet one most urgently needed is the participation of the local congregation. In the early church this was not
a problem because demonized people were readily recognized and
accepted as part of life. Today we avoid such people and keep them
at arm's length, for safe distance.

The church ought to be a healing community in which persons who have been through the emotional traumas of life find acceptance and healing and in which those under special demonic attack find deliverance and support. Our arms ought to be around them in encouragement and healing. One of my older brothers who is a psychiatrist says that there are some people he will almost refuse to see unless he is assured that they have a Christian support group to whom they can relate on an ongoing basis.

The church also ought to be involved in providing assistance to its members or to others who seek its help in dealing with demonic attacks of any type. It ought also to be a source of encouragement and support to its members who are involved in direct ministry to demonized persons. The church, finally, ought also to provide a line of accountability to those in such ministry. The best way to avoid excesses and to maintain a biblical balance in such ministry is to have a line of accountability to the church. The problem is that this must be an informed accountability, and few congregations are prepared to handle such an assignment. Indeed, few ministerial fellowships are prepared to provide such informed accountability for their members.

Deliverance ministry ought, then, to be carried on in the context of the church. And it ought to be done in cooperation with other healing ministries. Physical, emotional, and mental components are almost always involved in some way.

While we cannot formulate a how-to-do-it manual which just anyone can pick up and use in order to do deliverance, there are some key elements which are always present. First of all, Satan always works on the basis of deceit, which is simply clever lying. The antidote to that is truth. Biblical teaching is always needed as a base for countering Satan's lies and for laying a foundation for deliverance and future victory.

Since demonic footholds almost always involve a root in sin, the footholds must be reclaimed by confession (saying about the situation what God says about it), repentance and/or renunciation (where the sin of parents or ancestors may be involved), and cleansing (application of the merits of the blood of Christ). In some cases the demonic activity ceases when these steps are taken. In some cases this will need to be followed by open commands to demons to leave.

Again, however, it must be stated that persons needing deliverance will also frequently need other types of spiritual and emotional healing in a thoroughly Christian context. This must always be kept in view when ministering to a demonized person.

Conclusion

The great need today is for a return to a worldview in which spirits are functional beings and in which the spiritual power of Christ is a functional reality in the Church. The Church needs to be carefully instructed in their privileges and responsibilities as the

children of God so that they may live life to God's glory and may
provide a place of healing and strength to the hurting and the
demonized among them. A communist is said to have made the accusation against the Church that "it is the only army which shoots its
own wounded." To the extent that this has been true we need to make
certain that it does not continue.

Response to Timothy M. Warner

Gayle Gerber Koontz

Timothy Warner and Jacob Loewen pose a question which we must face squarely in our continuing discussion. Is it critical for contemporary Christians to have a fairly literal "functional view of angels and demons" (Warner) or is it acceptable or preferable to interpret evil "keeping 'both feet' in the psychomechanical model of Western science" (Loewen)?

Warner is concerned about contemporary accommodation of Christian faith to a secular world-view, about the extent to which "we have allowed the world to pour us into its mold." "The great need today," he writes, "is for a return to a world-view in which spirits are functional beings and in which the spiritual power of Christ is a functional reality in the Church." His hope is that through such a return the children of God may "provide a place of healing and strength to the hurting and the demonized among them."

Loewen agrees with Warner that in "everyday life North American Christians are firmly rooted in and practically operating on the premise of a material universe." But he differs in his analysis of the problem and the solution. The problem is a kind of Christian schizophrenia--the church "believes" in the New Testament spirit world even though in practice Christians do not experience either evil spirits or much of the Spirit of God. Loewen's resolution of the tension is not an eschewing of the Western scientific world-view in favor of a return to a New Testament world-view, but a call to develop models for understanding experiences of the demonic and of spiritual growth "which are solidly anchored in the Western scientific world-view." Rather than assuming the opposition of scientific and Christian views of the demonic which Warner's theological approach does, Loewen assumes that science and religion might be compatible.

Warner warns against uncritical accommodation of faith to culture; Loewen is concerned that Christian faith be articulated with relevance and integrity in relation to modern physical and social sciences. As a theologian in the church I share both concerns, for a foundational theological task is to faithfully connect the remembered revelations of God in the past to present experience. Such connection-making requires interpretation and judgment. What does it mean to claim that the God of Abraham and Sarah is also the God of Jesus and the God of Menno and the God of Mother Teresa? In what way is the Apostle Paul's understanding of God connected to Thomas Aquinas', Martin Luther King's, Paul Tillich's and Jim and Tammi Baker's? Theologians seek to develop discerning judgment and to provide theological argumentation which indicates why certain understandings of God and the world are essential and what difference faith in such a God makes for the present. It is also certainly true that in speaking about God Christian theologians have

throughout history run the risk of making statements that seem or
are irrelevant to the present experience of some, or which distort
or limit perceptions of God because of uncritical accommodation to
the perceptions or values of their particular cultural context.
The task of answering the question "what do we believe about the
demonic?" is not one for theologians alone, but for communities of
Christians to work at together. We need the information and various
interpretations of biblical, historical and contemporary experience
we can offer each other in deciding what God's intention and Spirit
are saying to us regarding bondage and deliverance in our time. I
am grateful for the way in which this conference was designed to
embody a process of theological reflection that takes seriously a
community-based model of discernment which includes a variety of
Christians from different academic disciplines and practical ministries connected to and interested in understanding the demonic. In
response to Warner's paper I would like to make several comments to
add to our ongoing conversation as a community of Christians.

Like Warner I am concerned about the accommodation of Christian
faith to a secular world-view insofar as that pervades North
American society. I too lament the loss of the sense even among
Christians of the presence and transcendence of God, and agree that
we need to critically judge from a Christian perspective the thought
categories assumed by the cultures in which we live. With Warner I
assume that Scripture testifies to God's will for our lives, that
Jesus reveals God to us and saves us from the powers of darkness,
that we are called to remain unswerving in our loyalty to Christ and
to claim the power of Christ as we face evil.

I am troubled, however, by the assumption that Warner seems to
be making that there is only one acceptable or "thoroughly
Christian" way for Christians to define, explain and respond to the
demonic. This troubles me because as I read the biblical story, God
is one who chooses to be present with, to confront and to love
humans in the thick of changing historical realities. God related to
us, called, judged and forgave us--that is, communicated Holy character and will to us--in different ways in different cultural, historical, social and personal situations. In current missiological language, one might say that God, being a missionary God, was concerned
about contextualization long before we had any conception of its
importance in communication. It is true that we need to be faithful
to the God of Jesus Christ, which means affirming spiritual as well
as material reality; but I do not think the biblical story indicates
that we must assume that only one set of cultural-linguistic
categories is adequate or necessary in order to express Christian
faith and all others to be eschewed. The good news of the gospel
can be articulated and lived within a variety of cultural-linguistic
world-views.

What faithfulness to Jesus meant for New Testament Christians in
their setting and means for us in "secularized" cultural contexts
involves theological and ethical judgments about what is *essential*

for Christians to believe and do, given the character and will of God
(central issues on which it is important for all of us to have unan-
imity), and what is *permissible* but not necessary for Christians to
believe and do given the character and will of God (issues on which
we can have acceptable diversity). Such judgments characterized the
discernment of the early church in relation to attitudes and practices among Jewish-Gentile Christians.

It seems to me that it is *essential* for Christians to recognize
the seriousness of evil on earth, to trust in God's power over evil,
and to follow Christ in confronting evil. Therefore I agree with
Warner that the powers of darkness are present and real, and that it
is "the believer's identification with Christ through the work of the
cross which gives him or her the basis for authority over the principalities and powers." But precisely how Christians *explain* evil
and specifically how we explain what we call "demonic," is secondary.
I would argue that some diversity in our explanations of what causes
profound evil on earth is to be expected given the historical and
cultural dimensions of our humanity, and is not by itself a mark of
unfaithfulness if the various explanations can be seen to be compatible with faith in the God revealed through Jesus Christ.

To develop this line of thinking more fully, it is helpful to
look more closely at several slippery terms we have been using in
our conversations--"evil" and the "demonic"--to see where Christians
(and I suspect this group as well) differ in understandings. How we
define and therefore experience evil and the demonic has implications for how we explain it and how we believe Christians should
respond to it.

The Demonic Defined

Christian ethicists usually use the word "evil" to encompass both
moral and nonmoral evil. Moral evil is evil which results from
some measure of human freedom or choice. Nonmoral evil is suffering
which does not seem to be attributable to human choice--disease,
earthquakes, drought. The discussion at this consultation indicates
that we seem to be confused about the relation of evil and the
demonic. Not all evil is demonic...or is it?

Our waffling and potential disagreement on this is related in
part, I suspect, to the way in which we choose to define "demonic."
The dominant functioning definition in our conversation so far is
outlined by Warner. When some phenomenon or event is understood to
be caused by transhuman evil spirit beings (tempting humans to sin
and/or causing nonmoral evil or human suffering) it is properly
named "demonic." All of us face the attacks of the demonic through
temptation and hassle although only a few can be appropriately
designated as "demonized," that is, seriously and intensely under the
influence of evil spirit beings or demons. Denial of the existence
of such spirit realities, Warner continues, stems from a limited
scientific perspective which, because it does not take seriously

demonic powers, cannot claim the power of God in the face of such evil.

It is my judgment that we would be helped in our communication and in our common stand against anti-Christian principalities and powers, if we would define the demonic in a way that would include Warner's definition as appropriate or permissible for Christians, but which could also be potentially meaningful to Jacob Loewen and other Christians who share his perspective. In this respect I have found helpful the late theologian Arthur McGill's essay "Structures of Inhumanity" and his extension of some of these ideas in *Suffering: A Test of Theological Method* helpful.[1] McGill suggests that while all evil stands in opposition to the serving, nourishing will and way of God as witnessed to in Christ, we might call "demonic" that destructive power which seems to come from "beyond all human agency"(1975: 116) Demonic power releases destruction, or cuts through to a depth, or ruthlessly dominates the lives of people, or involves finality that seems beyond individual or corporate human agency, that cannot be attributed clearly to moral self-conscious decision.

A sense of demonic powerfulness, he continues, is not as foreign to contemporary society as we might initially conclude if we were to focus solely on experiences of "demonization" or occult involvements. Contemporary folk-views of disease, for example, depict disease as an event of destructive transhuman power, as an invasion from the outside into a strikingly vulnerable body. Many people, McGill notes, show "extraordinary pessimism" about their own God-given human resources in the face of sickness.   In addition he points to accidents (events detached from significant purpose), to the irrationality but very real possibility of nuclear war, and to the sense of the inhuman and inflexible powerfulness of complex bureaucracies which seem too great to be controlled by human resources and which seem essentially destructive of God's will and way for humans.

Such contemporary experience of the demonic may not be self-conscious.   Instead of taking form as dragons (St. Anthony in the desert) or fallen angels (Jesus and the tempter), these lurking demonic forces have no form and no name. The demonic appears rather "as a formless and impersonal dynamism that seizes upon us unexpectedly in the cancer cell, in the auto accident, in the cascade of napalm bombs, or more subtly in the impersonality of bureaucratic systems on which we depend" (1975: 124). What, after all, McGill notes, "is a mere dragon compared to the hydrogen bomb? What is devastating about the experience of the demonic *in whatever form we encounter it* is how it profoundly colors people's attitudes about the universe as a whole. As McGill concludes:

> what appears often today is the belief that if we extend our gaze beyond the human sphere we will find no meaning, no value and no life. We will find only the kingdom of the demonic. In other words death as the violation and

extermination of life becomes the sign of all final realities
(1975: 125).

Bondage whether to occult practices, to demonic voices or to
death and despair as ruling powers is serious and real in the world
God calls us to love. However we differ in delineating the stages
of bondage to these demonic powers, there seems to be a mixture of
human willing and transpersonal elements at work. Bondage or
demonization describes situations when the intensification of evil in
individual lives or in social institutions and practices is so great
that it does not seem that individuals alone or humans in macro-
groups have the freedom to will or to act to change things.

In Christian perspective it seems to me both *permissible* and
helpful to accept the broader definition McGill offers us as ground
for our continuing conversation. This definition does not dilute the
incredible power and reality of the demonic, a consideration which
legitimately concerns Warner, but it does extend our vision to
include expressions of the demonic which many more contemporary
Christians experience and to which we and they need to respond. The
definition can encompass the forms of evil Warner identifies, which
are primarily individualistic in focus, but it also incorporates
principalities and powers which take institutional or structural
systemic forms. It helps us lift up those latter elements in contemporary experience and provides a clearer connection to that
emphasis in the biblical story.

Perhaps most important in my view is that the broader definition
helps build up Christ's church so we are formed into a stronger body
for combating demonic powers. How we define demonic makes a difference in who we identify as having or lacking experience with the
demonic, who of us we think has or lacks spiritual power in the face
of the demonic, how we see and articulate how Christ has liberated
us from bondage, and who of us are "thoroughly" and who "partially"
Christian. What do we gain by specifying or narrowing our definition of the demonic as Warner does if it excludes, ignores, or undercuts as "unbiblical" those contemporary Christians who do not hold to
the "more or less literal functional reality of angels and demons"
but who have given their lives in service to God, resisting with
courage and power the ultimate rule of death and despair? What do
we gain by specifying or narrowing our definition of spiritual power
in a way that breeds self-doubt and uncertainty in those Christians
who are deeply committed to sharing in God's redeeming work in the
face of contemporary "formless" demonic power but who do not speak
the language of angels and demons? Should we not rather pray that
God would form us together into one body whose head is Christ, a
body not weakened by divisions resulting from carelessly narrow
theological definitions, but one which can stand together strong in
faith, hope and love in the face of demonic powers.

The Demonic Explained

Assuming we agree to accept the broader or more inclusive definition of "demonic," finding therefore that the experience of the demonic is more common in more of our lives than we might have first supposed, we are still faced with the question, how can we *explain* evil, especially this intense transhuman powerfulness we call "demonic." As Martin pointed out, Christians have provided over time a variety of responses, all offered within the context of belief that evil confronts us within a good world created and sustained by a God of justice and love. Human sin and human freedom has been the primary explanation for evil. While most doctrines of original sin locate sin in the human self rather than in social institutions and practices, developments in social scientific analysis and their impact (family systems theory, liberation and political theologies, etc.) have heightened Christian awareness of how social institutions and practices can radically affect the extent and type of sin even if social reformation will not erase sin.[2] The "fallenness" of some social structures, and the perversion of family systems which affect individuals at subconscious levels, become explanations for evil that are due to human sin but which go far beyond the choices of particular individuals.

Nonmoral evil has been even harder for Christians to rationally explain, given affirmation of the goodness and power of God. If one presses the arguments hard enough, human suffering defies full rational explanation. Is human freedom and the world itself worth *so much suffering*, from both moral and nonmoral evil? Is God truly good and/or truly powerful? One response in the history of Christian theology has been that the mystery of creation and God's goodness is beyond human comprehension. We cannot and need not understand it. But many Christians who have not been satisfied with either sin as partial explanation or the "we can't explain it but God is good" approach to evil, have attributed evil in general, and particular manifestations of destructive transhuman powerfulness considered "demonic," to the influence of spirit beings which oppose God--the devil, Satan or demonic spirits.

As contemporary Christians we are here engaged in a family debate about the significance of demonic spirit beings as an explanation for human suffering. There are those who argue against explaining the reality of evil in such terms or at least against stressing such explanation. They fear that too much emphasis on evil spirit beings undercuts human and individual responsibility--the "devil made me do it" phenomenon. Others are concerned that Christians will begin looking for a demon behind every bush, increasing the fear of children and new believers and heightening the level of suspicion among believers toward one another and toward outsiders. Such attitudes break down rather than build up the Christian community and hamper mission and service. Some regard belief in evil spirits as superstitious or mythological, holding that there are other satisfactory explanations for most of the phenomena attributed to evil spirits over the centuries. They point out, for example, that within the world-views available to Christians there were no psychological categories to describe mental illness.

Others of us in the family argue that we shouldn't rule out evil spirits because their reality is assumed in the Bible and because modern cultural categories may be prejudiced and wrong. Some remind us that we can't *fully* explain demonic suffering according to scientific or social scientific categories either; others that psychological explanations and religious explanations are different but not mutually exclusive. Besides, some continue, if we rule out the existence of evil spirits, don't we have to rule out the existence of good spirits (i.e. God)? Others emphasize like Warner that the task of Christians to combat evil will not be taken seriously enough if we don't assume the functional reality of angels and demons.

I would again suggest that thinking in terms of what is essential and what is permissible for Christian family members to believe and do might be helpful in our continuing conversation. It *is* necessary for all Christians to take demonic evil seriously and to respond to such evil in ways that are consistent with the character and will of God revealed through Jesus Christ. Warner helps to sharpen our commitments here. But I would hold that it is *not* necessary for Christians to agree on one explanation for demonic evil.

The reality of demonic evil is *meaningfully* expressed for Christians in our cultural context with reference to a more than human tempter or to a personal devil. But it is not *necessary* for Christians to believe in a more than human evil spirit being in order to have a profound sense of the reality of demonic evil. In biblical and Christian history there have been many different cultural categories, many languages, and many different word pictures that have meaningfully expressed the power and reality of evil (as well as of God's goodness). One important explanation of the pervasiveness and intensity of evil is a personal devil-tempter. But it is also possible to have a profound sense of the enormity and reality of demonic evil without such explanation.

I suspect that in part the debate has to do with what might be called propensities toward conservative and liberal uses of the imagination in our theological speech, specifically as concerns us, in relation to God and the devil. On the one hand, we should respect and celebrate our imaginative powers for they are God-given, it is the visionaries, the ones who dream dreams, who frequently "see" God's face and path in the midst of this creation more clearly than many of the rest of us. It is holy imagination that rings through the Psalms, that engages the prophets, that calls Peter to confess "Thou art the Christ," and Paul to claim that Jews and Gentiles have been made members of one household, that enriches and feeds worship, that draws us to God right in the midst of the ordinariness of everyday life.

On the other hand, we need to discipline our imaginative speculations with reference to the character and will of God as revealed through Jesus Christ in the New Testament witness. As we explain reality to be "shot through with spirit" we need to take care that the interpretations and explanations we give of everyday events are faithful to the God of Jesus Christ, i.e. are ones which undergird rather than undercut human responsibility for sinful behavior, which take seriously the demonic elements of evil, which avoid "God of the gaps" or "devil of the gaps" explanations, which present God as truly powerful in the face of evil.

As far as demonic evil is concerned, I believe we have an inordinately strong desire to *explain* it, for if we can explain or name evil, we have some small measure of control over it. "Power encounters" with spirit beings fascinate us in part, I would suggest, because of our sense that God may work through us in a dramatic way to fight/control the demonic. It is not only exciting, but it is possible to do something concrete about the powerlessness we feel in the face of the demonic. If we can explain the source of demonic evil we might be able also to learn what words to say, how to make demons identify themselves, and how to authoritatively help release suffering individuals from bondage. Explanation or naming is itself a kind of power.

The desire to explain the demonic is perhaps both a gift and a temptation. It is a gift insofar as it fires our holy imaginations in ways that break us open to God's spirit so that through us God can bring healing to others. We have seen and heard of how God brings deliverances from demonic evil through Christian healers. But a freely expressed religious imagination in relation to the demonic may also heighten fearfulness and tempt us with the promise of personal power--a kind of "magical" control over demonic evil which can buttress our own sense of powerlessness in the face of suffering. The line between our desire to be open to the power of God working in us in "power encounters" and our own desire for control and personal affirmation as healers is a fine line indeed.

I suspect that it is for reasons such as these that some contemporary Christians give free reign to holy imagination in relation to the presence and reality of God as personal spirit but opt for a restrained use of the imagination in relation to demonic spirit-beings, leaving the problem of demonic evil unexplained. It is true that such a choice limits the religious language and categories one has available or feels comfortable using when relating to others whose explanations of evil in terms of demonic spirit-beings is fully developed, both those in other cultural settings and in our own. But such Christians may develop theological language which better communicates the essence of the gospel to people in cultural settings who are not familiar with or comfortable with speaking of evil in terms of spirit-beings. Perhaps *both* approaches are needed in Christian ministry and mission.

It is my conviction that whether evil is explained as the work of personal evil spirits and of willful human sin or whether it is simply accepted as a reality that cannot be fully explained is not a significant test of Christian faithfulness. Of central import is faith in the goodness and power of God in the face of evil and the sense of God's presence with us as we suffer. I would suggest that we can and should accept pluralism in our *explanations* of evil, recognizing that both the active imagination and the restrained imagination have their strengths and weaknesses. While as different members of Christ's body we may have different contributions to make and different correctives to offer one another as we seek to explain demonic evil, we are bound together on essential matters-- recognizing the reality of demonic evil, affirming our dependence on the redeeming love and power of God disclosed in the biblical story, and responding with courage and faith to the demonic powers which sorely test us.

The Demonic Resisted

I agree with both Warner and McGill that most educated post- Enlightenment people are ill prepared to deal with the demonic. While Warner stresses the disempowerment that comes from secular skepticism about angels and demons, McGill stresses that our cultural tradition is problematic because of its optimistic humanism. We assume that because we are creatures of reason, the world is rational, that if something cannot be explained it doesn't exist or it will eventually be explained. We assume that because we are creatures of creative projects, that nature is made for our human projects. We assume that because we are creatures made for loving and being loved, there is no fundamental destructiveness, aggression and fear in humans. The experience of the demonic stands in opposi- tion to this (1985: 125-26).

Historically Christian response to the demonic has not sought escape from it by denying its reality, nor recommended a stoic "indifference," nor adopted a pessimistic outlook. Christians have emphasized two duties in response to evil in general which apply also to demonic evil: to combat evil by every means, and to believe that God will triumph over evil.[3] These two duties, it seems to me, are essential for Christians; but exactly *how* we resist evil is is a matter on which I believe we can accept some measure of pluralism. The ways in which we seek to break the power of demonic evil are "faithful" insofar as both the specific ends and the methods employed are compatible with the character and will of God revealed through Jesus Christ.

As Warner outlines his understanding of our call as Christians to resist evil, he refers to the work of Christ in disarming Satan, exposing idolatrous powers for what they are. Ultimately Jesus brought death to the idolatrous dominance of the self. Jesus met and overcame evil, freeing us through his blood which removed the guilt with which Satan makes his case against humans. While the demonic no longer has ultimate power, there is continuing spiritual warfare. In developing his view of the struggle between good and evil spirit beings, Warner adopts warfare imagery drawing heavily on imagery from OT and Pauline texts. He warns Mennonites wryly that "to practice nonresistance against our spiritual enemy is to disobey the clear commands of Scripture." While he does not assume that all Christians will engage in deliverance ministries, he notes NT precedent for claiming the authority to cast out demons in the manner of Jesus.

In contrast to Warner, McGill suggests that there are *two* fundamental biblical patterns in Christian tradition for dealing with the demonic. One is exorcism or what we have chosen here to call "deliverance ministry" in which God may rule by removing dreadful forces through the ministry of believers. This he concludes is a minor pattern. The other, which is primary and dominant in the NT in his view (and in much Mennonite thought) is the way of the cross.

While it is easy to see how God rules when demonic powers seem to be broken in the casting forth of evil spirits or in more gradual processes of healing, it is another thing to claim that God rules when demonic power seems to be in full force--that is, when Jesus is on the cross. How does God vindicate holy power or holy rule on or through the cross? McGill holds that Jesus' taking up of the cross was not an act of nonresistance but of resistance to evil. Jesus did not submit to the demonic, that is he did not act as if it, rather than God, were the master of his destiny. Indeed he refused to fear, to defend himself, to imagine that this dreadful destructivity had any final power over him. Even in the face of death, Jesus was sustained in his confidence in God, in his compassion and care for those around him. God vindicated holy rule not by removing the powers and destruction of death from him, but by maintaining in Jesus trust and love even while these powers worked their fullest.

Unlike Warner, McGill holds that "taking up the cross" is the *primary* way Christians are called to face the demonic. Taking up the cross means entering into areas of demonic suffering. It means opening our eyes and hearts not only to demonized individuals but also resisting formless demonic powerfulness which negates the will and way of God and leads to despair. McGill's testimony, based on the history of Christian witness, is that when demonic powerfulness tests faith, perhaps especially when victimization is imposed on those we love, we most deeply discover God's power to sustain us in trust and love while the demonic is at work. When we are most tempted to despair of God, to let anger or panic possess us, to turn away from those persons who suffer in order to preserve our own sanity, God's own suffering presence upholds us. Jesus disarmed the claims to ultimacy of the powers of might and of death.

But the Christian story does not end with the cross. God raised up Jesus! God transformed Jesus' death, the cross into new life, and Jesus' friends into a new body. Long after Roman powers of state have dissipated, the power of God's Holy Spirit and the Christian movement remains. Taking up the cross in the face of demonic evil

means committing our lives fully to God, giving our spirit into
God's hands and trusting that what we cannot explain or fully control is in the hands of a good and trustworthy creator.   For followers of Jesus the resistance of the cross is a last step, a final
step in a life dedicated to fighting evil fiercely with love.   As
McGill writes:

> To companion another who is dying without withdrawal, to
> continue working with the poor after all the resources have
> failed, to maintain one's trusting and one's loving when the
> forces of demonic inhumanity seem to be in full control--as
> I see it, that is what it means to take up Jesus' cross....
> This dimension of service, however, only begins when one is
> willing to endure the impact of demonic enormities (133).

In *Suffering: A Test of Theological Method*, McGill reminds us
that our discussions of the demonic need to include conscious
reference to other Christian affirmations we make.   How much
priority we give to the demonic rather than to sin in defining,
explaining and resisting evil may have something to do with how
much we want to emphasize or minimize human responsibility for evil.
How much we focus on the power of the demonic may affect the degree
to which we appreciate the goodness of the present world and the
likelihood of our developing a spirituality of grateful praise for
being.   In spite of this caution to see and speak of the demonic in
proper perspective, he calls us to take on demonic suffering as an
essential part of the love of neighbor and of the knowledge of the
power of God.   Contemporary experience of the demonic in all its
forms and formlessness points us--all of us--to this need for
extraordinary faith and courage.

Notes

1.   In *Disguises of the Demonic*, ed. Alan M. Olson (New York:
Association Press, 1975), 116-133; *Suffering: A Test of Theological
Method.* Philadelphia: Westminster, 1982.
2.   *The Westminster Dictionary of Christian Ethics*, ed. James F.
Childress and John Macquarrie (Philadelphia: Westminster Press,
1986), 585.
3.   *Ibid.*, 215.

A CATHOLIC VIEW OF EXORCISM AND DELIVERANCE

Robert T. Sears, S.J.

The Roman Catholic Church has always had a ministry of exorcism and of deliverance (or "simple exorcism"), but it is the rise of the Charismatic Renewal that has given it increased attention. Movies like *The Exorcist* highlight certain sensational aspects of exorcism, but recent understanding places it as an unsensational but very important adjunct to healing prayer. I personally have used deliverance prayer (though not "solemn exorcisms") in my counseling ministry with important results, and I will illustrate my presentation with some examples. In this paper, I will present first the scriptural and traditional arguments for this ministry, then an interpersonal interpretation of its importance, and finally various areas where we find need for deliverance today.

Scripture

The Old Testament evidence is unclear. Several texts personify evil: "pestilence that stalks in darkness" (Ps 91:5-6), "the torrents of Perdition (*Belial*) assailed me" (Ps 18:4-5), and wicked men are called "sons of Belial" (1 Sam 2:12). "Belial later became the most common name of the Prince of Darkness in the writings of the apocalyptic sect of Qumran; he corresponds in many ways to the Satan of the New Testament."[1] Passions, like the spirit of fornication (Hos 4:12) or the spirit of discord against Abimelech (Judg 9:23) or the spirit of ill will from God on Saul (1 Sam 18:10) are at times personified. Some such texts (like the fall of the Day Star which Isaiah 14:12 applies to a fallen tyrant) form the background of NT imagery. The few texts that speak of Satan are in late (Job, Zech 3:1ff., 1 Chron 21:1), as is the devil (*diabolos*) who brought death into the world (Wis 2:14). 1 Chron 21:1 ("Satan rose up against Israel and enticed David into taking a census of Israel") reflects a desire to differentiate Yahweh from what seemed against his holiness. In earlier texts like Job and Zechariah, Satan is like a prosecuting attorney before Yahweh accusing humans of insincerity or fault; and in 2 Kings 22:19-23 Yahweh himself sends a "lying Spirit" (at the suggestion of an angel) to the prophets of King Ahab. The later view of Satan as hostile to Israel may explain why the serpent in paradise is later identified with "the devil" (Wis 2:24).

Spirits receive increased interest in the intertestimental literature (between 200 BC and 100 AD)--1 Enoch, The Book of Jubilees, The Assumption of Moses, The Books of Adam and Eve, and our canonical Daniel. In 1 Enoch 6 the "sons of heaven" or Watchers were said to take daughters of earth as wives and give birth to giants (inspired by Gen 6:1-4). These children are said to be evil spirits which "oppress, destroy, attack, do battle, and work destruction on the earth" (1 Enoch 16:11ff).[2] In the Book of Jubilees these evil spirits are called demons under the power of Mastema (Satan), and God sends angels to bind them. But at Mastema's request 1/10th are left free to carry out his will against the sons of men. In the Jewish apocalyptic literature the "guardian angels of the nations" become corrupted with their nations through idolatry (see Deut 32:8f.). They are destined for destruction (Isa 24:21ff; 34:2,4); deliverance from their power is *not* in Israel's hands but in the Lord's and his archangels.

The NT evidence is mixed. On the one hand it reflects much of this demonology of the OT without the mythological account of the origin of evil spirits and Satan. The Watchers of Jude 6 and 2 Peter 2:4 simply evoke a strong image of divine punishment. Further, as the NT progresses, there seems to be a decreasing emphasis on a direct deliverance ministry.[3] In John, for example, there is no narrative of Jesus driving out demons, only his total victory over the evil one on the cross. Even the Pauline corpus mentions no case of deliverance. The *daimonia* of 1 Corinthians 10:20ff appear to be pagan gods (from Deut 32:17), but they are not objects of deliverance, and even Ephesians 6:10-17, though aware of demonic principalities and powers in the universe, does not speak of deliverance but of spiritual warfare and its weapons (as also 1 Pet 5:8f.). Many other NT references to Satan or the devil also do not point to a ministry of deliverance but to more indirect forms of resistance. Jesus' temptations in the desert are countered by fidelity to his Father's true call. The implied cure of Satan's power in the sower parable (Mark 4:15ff.) is avoidance of the distractions of the world, receiving the word deeply and being fruitful. The cure of Judas (as seen in the Peter parallel) would have been repentance. In the Synoptic passages on Satan, only the Beelzebul controversy (Mark 3:20-30 par) and the word of Jesus in Luke 10:18f. seem to point to a deliverance ministry. In Acts 5, Ananias and Sapphira are not delivered but punished by death for freely yielding to Satan, the Cypriot magician is cursed by Paul (Acts 13:4-12), and the Philippian slave girl with a soothsaying spirit (Acts 16:16-18) was delivered not for her sake but for Paul's ministry. Paul's references to Satan--like handing over the incestuous man to Satan (1 Cor 5:5), not giving opportunity to the devil through unresolved anger (Eph 4:26f.), lack of sexual control (1 Cor 7:5) or unforgiveness (2 Cor 2:11), etc.--do not refer to the ministry of deliverance. Even the Book of Revelation refers to God as Lord of history, not to a deliverance ministry. In short, in speaking of the ministry of deliverance, we have to keep it in perspective.

On the other hand, there are sufficient texts in the NT to show that exorcism "belongs to the base-rock historicity of the Gospels."[4] In the passage on the power by which Jesus casts out evil, the Q-source (Matt 12:28/Luke 11:20) says "But if it is by the Spirit of God ("finger of God" in Luke) that I cast out demons, then the kingdom of God has come upon you." Jesus here sees himself as coming in the power of God's eschatological Spirit to establish God's kingdom in place of the kingdom of Satan. His power to cast out demons is seen as a sign of this breakthrough of God's rule. Mark's version (3:23-27) adds parables of a house (kingdom, Satan) divided, and sees exorcisms as a moment of battle against Satan. Mark's Gospel traces this idea throughout. Jesus will baptize with the Holy Spirit (1:8), this Spirit drives him into the desert to be tested by Satan (1:12) and when he emerges he delivers a man from an unclean spirit (1:23-27). In sum, "he went throughout all Galilee, preaching in their synagogues and casting out demons" (1:39), and he gave the Twelve authority to cast out demons (3:14f). The narrative of the stilling of the storm (4:35-41) is told in exorcism language as is the healing of the Gerasene demoniac (5:1-20); the commissioning of the Twelve underscores their power over unclean spirits (6:7,13). The cure of the Syro-Phoenician's daughter (7:24-39) and the boy with the dumb spirit (9:14-29) was through deliverance. When Peter balks at Jesus' prediction of suffering, Jesus says "Get behind me, Satan" (8:33) indicating that Peter is joining forces with the enemy. Later, the Pharisees and scribes "test" Jesus (8:11, 10:2, 12:15) as Satan did in the desert, and on the cross Jesus faced demonic mockery, darkness and dereliction. In short, exorcism runs as a thread throughout Mark's Gospel. If the Holy Spirit is taken personally, there is no reason not to take the evil spirit also personally.

Both Matthew and Luke carry on this Markan tradition. Besides this, Matthew includes in his version of the Lord's Prayer "but deliver us from evil (*apo tou ponerou*)" (Matt 6:13) which seems from other uses in Matthew to be masculine, not neuter.[5] Luke adds further cases of deliverance: the women in Jesus entourage "who had been cured of evil spirits and maladies" including Mary Magdalene "from whom seven demons had gone out" (Luke 8:2). Jesus charge to the 72 is only in terms of healing (10:9) but their success is in terms of exorcism and the fall of Satan (10:17-20). Finally, the Lord speaks of his passion as "your hour and the power of darkness" (Luke 22:53). Acts is written in light of Luke showing the disciples' continuing of Jesus ministry. That this included deliverance is shown clearly in Acts 5:16, 8:7, 19:12 and 26:18.

Though the Fourth Gospel does not include an individual ministry of deliverance, it is focused on the overthrow of "the ruler of this world" by the "hour" of Jesus' death/resurrection (see 12:31); similarly, Jesus prays that his disciples will be protected from the evil one (17:15). This is said succinctly in 1 John 3:8: "The Son of God revealed himself to destroy the devil's works," though the victory is only in principle since "the whole world is in the power of the evil one" (1 John 5:19). A similar tension is presented in the Pauline corpus regarding the victory of God in Christ over all the evil forces in the cosmos and the "rulers of this age" (1 Cor 2:6-8), for the final victory will be at the parousia (1 Cor 15:24). While we continue here in this world we battle against the principalities and powers (Eph 6:12) and the "elemental spirits of the world" (Col 2:8,20). The victory, however, is in principle won (Rom 8:38f.). Thus, we have to say a ministry of deliverance from world powers and Satan is solidly grounded in the NT.

Tradition

After the apostolic age, the early Christians continued to exorcise demons (as Mark 16:17 indicated also). Justin Martyr (c. 100–165) affirmed numberless deliverances by Christians in the name of Jesus (2 *Apol* 6), as did Tertullian (*Apol.* 37), Origen (*Contra Celsum* 1.25), Lactantius (*Instit* 4.27) and Cyril of Jerusalem (*Catech* 20.3). All see exorcism as an invocation of God against the harassment of devils.[6]

Toward the beginning of the third century we find rites of exorcism as part of preparation for Baptism. An example of this mentality is found in the Syrian *Clementine Recognitions* probably from early third century.:

> I would have you know for certain, that everyone who has at any time worshipped idols, and has adored those whom the pagans call gods, or has eaten of the things sacrificed to them, is not without an unclean spirit...and therefore needs the purificatino of baptism, that the unclean spirit may go out of him, which has made its abode in the inmost affections of his soul, and what is worse, gives no indication that it lurks within, for fear it should be exposed and expelled. (2,71 ANF)[7]

With this mentality (clearly influenced by 1 Cor 10:20) it soon became the custom to perform a series of exorcisms over catecumens prior to baptism, and to introduce the rite of renunciation of Satan and all practices of idolatry (first evidence in the *Apostolic Tradition* of Hippolytus, early third century).[8] Another feature of the baptismal service as a freeing from demons was the exorcism of the water used in baptism. Consecrated water of this sort gradually came to be used in many ways apart from baptism, and similar prayers and exorcisms were used to bless salt and oil used in baptism. Gradually, the warding off of demons became part of all seven sacraments and numerous sacramentals. "At the time of the Reformation, some of the exorcisms were taken over by Luther and his followers (though not the exorcisms of water, salt, and oil), but they were soon discarded."[9]

Thus, exorcism was practiced liturgically from early times, but also extra-liturgically both by ordained exorcists (an ecclesiastical order from the middle of the third century) and charismatically empowered exorcists (whose validation, Hippolytus affirms, comes from the visible effectiveness of their ministry.)[10] There was an order of exorcists in the Latin church since the third century whose function was gradually taken over by the priests. The books of exorcism which were given priests in the ordination ceremony since the 5th century have not come down to us. At present, the *Roman Ritual*, the priest's manual, specifically limits the office of exorcist to

priests, omitting mention of "other exorcists."   Restrictions on
solemn exorcism were extended to the whole Latin Church in 1917.
The canon reads:

> No one who has the power of exorcism can legitimately exer-
> cise it upon the possessed unless he has obtained the spe-
> cial and explicit permission of his ordinary.
>
> This permission will be granted by the ordinary only to a
> priest endowed with piety and prudence, and of upright life;
> he is not to proceed with the exorcisms until a diligent and
> prudent investigation reveals that the person to be exor-
> cised is really possessed by a demon   (Code of Canon Law,
> 1151 [ed. P. Gasparri], Vatican, 1963).

This directive is continued in the 1983 revised Code (see Can. 1172),
though it omits the directive, "he is not to proceed...by a demon."

This regulation of solemn exorcism (for those confirmed to be
possessed) is not to restrict the use of simple (private) exorcism by
priests in their ordinary ministry and lay persons charismatically
called.   Recognized manuals of moral theology since the time of St.
Alphonsus Ligouri have distinguished between solemn and private
exorcism and encouraged the latter.   St. Alphonsus writes:

> Private exorcism is permissible to all Christians; solemn
> exorcism is permissible only to ministers who are appointed
> to it, and then only with the express permission of the
> bishop.[11]

Private exorcism is when the exorcist acts in his own name, not as
an official representative of the Church.   This tradition of private
exorcism is encouraged for confessors when they suspect the
influence of evil spirits "for when this spirit [of fornication]
infests a person he will not be able to resist temptations."[12]   It is
such "private exorcism" that Catholic Charismatics now call
"deliverance."   It deals with cases of oppression (where the core of
the person's freedom remains intact, while some area is bound), not
with possession (where the evil spirit has totally taken over the
personality).

This is presently the official teaching of the Catholic Church.
Evil spirits exist.   Solemn exorcism is reserved to approved exorcists, while simple deliverance prayer is approved for priests and
gifted lay people.   It must be admitted, however, that in practice
emphasis on personal evil spirits diminished around the time of
Vatican Council II.   The prayer after Mass to St. Michael the
Archangel was omitted with the liturgical renewal, and attention to
unconscious psychological evil made people less sure of evil spirits.
It was the advent of the Catholic Charismatic Renewal in 1968 that
returned attention to personal evil spirits.   Attention to the Holy
Spirit seemed to bring with it a clearer opposition of evil spirits.
Early instruction came from healing ministers (like Francis McNutt,
Healing [Notre Dame, Ind.:   Ave Maria Press, 1974], pp. 208-231),
pastoral guides of covenant communities (see Michael Scanlon and
Randall J. Cirner, *Deliverance from Evil Spirits* [Ann Arbor, Mich.:

Servant Books, 1980]) and ministry to those involved in witchcraft and superstitition (like the work of Fr. Rich Thomas, S.J. with the border Mexicans from Juarez). Not only was there renewed interest in deliverance and healing, but also there was renewed confidence in the power of sacramentals (like Holy Water and Blessed Salt [extensions of Baptism] and anointed music and blessed candles). Those possessed by evil spirits could clearly distinguish blessed articles from those not blessed, and they were helps in driving spirits out. Also, the power of Christian love (like that of the Church of the Redeemer, an Episcopal Charismatic Church in Houston, Texas) was found powerful againt evil spirits.

As the renewal grew, it was found necessary to provide guidelines and instructions. In 1985 the Congregation for the Doctrine of the Faith sent out a directive to Ordinaries that lay people were not to recite the official exorcism prayer of the church (Can. 1172), nor were immature lay people to pray simple deliverance prayers. Actually, the deliverance ministry has been fairly orderly in the Renewal in the United States. The Bishops' Liaison Committee issued a pastoral statement in 1984 which presented the following directives for deliverance ministries:

29. In the biblical witness, deliverance ministries are part of the healing ministry (Luke 9:1) of which the ministry of inner healing is a part. On occasion when prayers for spiritual healing are being offered, deliverance prayer is sometimes needed. Here both wise pastoral guidance and discernment of spirits are absolute requirements. Prayers of deliverance and exorcism should not be confused. Deliverance addresses some form of inordinate control being exercised over a specific aspect of a person's life; it concerns something more than ordinary temptation and less than the total control found in full possession. (The latter is full possession which is the proper object of exorcism.)

30. Silent prayers of deliverance can be offered by every Christian. If there is to be vocal prayer for deliverance, this should be done by a team whose ministry is recognized by the local community and its pastoral authority. Exorcism in the strict sense should be done only by those explicitly appointed by the bishops, as an exercise of the power received through ordination. Excessive preoccupation with the demonic and an indiscriminate exercise of deliverance ministries are based upon a distortion of biblical evidence and are pastorally harmful.

31. As in the ministry commissioned by Jesus, prayer for deliverance is an aspect of the healing minstry (Mark 6:12,13; Matt 10:1). So attention should not be centered merely on deliverance from evil spirits, but, more positively, on total healing (medical, psychological, social, spiritual) and a life in Jesus Christ. Prayer for inner healing is part of that wider ministry. Various approaches

to the deliverance ministries are still evolving and publications are available representing the different perspectives.[13]
Some dioceses (like Brooklyn, N.Y.) have been developing "deliverance
teams" and guidelines.[14]   Others (like Chicago) rely on the Liaison
to the Renewal to oversee the ministry in groups. With deepening
experience in healing, especially growing awareness of the influence
of past generations on illness and bondage, people in the healing
ministry are developing clearer guidelines and directives for the
deliverance ministry. Since I have not yet taken part in a solemn
exorcism, I will direct the remainder of this paper to a consideration of deliverance or private exorcism.

An Interpersonal Interpretation
of Exorcism and Deliverance

The tendency in recent times has been to psychologize evil and
see it as an aspect of mental illness. This perspective does serve
to focus attention on the need for individual conversion rather than
projecting one's evil onto the devil, yet it tends to overlook the
interpersonal nature of being human. From work with family systems
and an interpersonal theology of the Holy Spirit I see stages of
spiritual development in Scripture that correlate with deliverance
and guide its concrete goal.[15] In the early two stages the focus is
on (1) trust and obedience (Initial faith: Yahwist) and (2) keeping
the Law and Tradition (Familial Faith: Elohist/Deuteronomist).   In
these stages the OT formula holds: "I the Lord your God am a jealous God, visiting the iniquity of the fathers upon the children to
the third and fourth generation but showing steadfast love to thousands of those who love me and keep my commandments." (See also
Exod 20:5-6; 34:6-8; Num 14:18; Deut 5:1-10). In these early stages
(not unlike childhood and adolescence) we learn to trust and then to
cooperate by keeping the rules. If our parental system is sinful or
wounded here, then we will also be affected by those sins and
wounds. In the Exile, however, this link to the parents' sins was
broken with the break of the "covenant" made to the fathers (see Jer
31:21). Thus Ezekiel 18 says that the saying "the fathers have eaten
sour grapes and the children's teeth are set on edge" is no longer
to be said in Israel, "for the children are mine as well as the
fathers." In place of this broken covenant Yahweh promises to put
his Spirit in their hearts and "make" them keep his statutes (Ezek
36:27). In other words, because of each one's individual relation to
Yahweh, they are each empowered by God's Spirit to be personally
responsible for what they do with their lives.   I call this third
stage "Individuating Faith," and it is reflected in much post-exilic
literature (Job, later Wisdom Literature, Jonah, Tobit, Maccabees,
etc.). This stage, I would argue, is as far as the OT progressed.
With Jesus we see a new stage of "individuated community" (or "Com-
munitarian Faith") faith based on forgiveness of enemies. This is a

community based not on Law (Familial faith) but on Spirit
(pluralistic, accepting of differences with forgiveness of hurts and
sins). Its novelty is seen in the leaders' and the peoples'
rejection of Jesus' teaching to "love one's enemies," which
ultimately led Jesus to the cross. We must remember that this love
unto death is the ultimate casting out of the evil one (as in John's
Gospel). It gives birth to a spiritual creativity in the community
by the sending of the Spirit at Pentecost (my fifth stage: Mission
Faith). I would argue that much as every human recapitulates stages
of evolution, so we each (and our communities) go through these five
stages (and more) in our spiritual journey. The stages are cyclical
and cumulative. New growth brings crisis and regression to heal
further earlier stages, and each further stage builds on the preceding ones. Though God (who transcends our time) can break through at
any stage, the wounds of the earlier stages will ultimately need
healing if sustained growth is to happen. If sin and evil is seen as
a block to spiritual growth, the work of evil will look different at
different stages. Hence this view (see the appended chart on p. 112)
can help one discern where evil is present. Conversion is an ongoing process of getting free from old patterns and into the pattern
of spiritual growth in Christ.

In the early "Initial and Familial Stages," if one's parental
system (which may also be religious or cultural) is itself influenced
by evil--by its loss of faith, anger at God, distrust in face of
trauma, divisions, etc.--the children of that system will be affected.
That is the basis for the traditional teaching on original sin and
the power of evil which one is under simply by becoming a member of
a fallen human race. Original sin, we learn from healing families,
is particularized in each family and each person of the family. This
power influencing a family system can be looked at as a "spirit" of
the family, group, church, nation, culture. When this "spirit" is
opposed to God, it leaves one open to the influence of Satan or other
evil spirits. Whether or not such evil spirits are actually involved
is a matter for discernment by examing the power exerted (whether
beyond human), the preternatural knowledge (like precognition), the
immoveability of the pattern or the violence or desecration of attitude (like violating the eucharist, priesthood, church, etc.). If
spirits are involved, one is not merely part of an evil system
requiring conversion, one also needs deliverance.

God frees us from bondage to this fallen family system by the
death and resurrection of Jesus and the gift of the spirit. Jesus
died to the negative bondage of family and culture and opened us to
rebirth in God's Spirit. John 19:26-27 ("Woman behold your son..."
etc.) indicates that a new family is given birth through the Spirit
"sent" in Jesus' death/resurrection. Through baptism we are actually
brought into the power of this new family to the extent we are cut
free from the bondage of the previous system. It seems true, as I
experienced myself, that even though one is baptized there can still
be areas of oneself that are in bondage to evil spirits. In my case

it was a spirit of fear that came down through my mother and her
family. In other cases it is due to an unconscious area of a person's or family's life, or a curse put on a family not really broken
in the baptismal rite. Growth into God's family is a gradual
process and areas still not integrated into God may prove to need
deliverance prayer for further liberation and healing. Still, the
principle perspective remains the same. To be freed we are removed
from identifying ourselves in relation to natural family or cultural
patterns in order to identify with the new family born of faith in
the death/resurrection of Jesus. Jesus is given "full authority"
(Matt 28:18ff) to break us free from any evil power, and he has given
this power to the church (the new family) and its representatives.
All deliverance, in this view, is freedom from our fallen family and
culture to the new family in God's Spirit. It is not an individualistic ministry, but a transformation of social systems and one's
participation in them. Once freed, we still have to convert and
bring our life and community into tune with the Spirit, that is, to
be healed. Deliverance must be seen as a part of healing, and healing itself as a help to grow into God's Kingdom (or new family).
This is the perspective I will presuppose in the remarks that follow
on the ministry of deliverance.

Deliverance in Four Areas of Bondage

The social power of evil affects people in several ways--through
hurts, through habits of sin, through occult curses and bondages, and
through family traditions. Each of these ways gives rise to a different sort of deliverance prayer. I will briefly address each of
these types.

1. Ministering Deliverance: According to an experienced minister of deliverance, by far the largest number (about 70 percent) fall
into this category where the evil spirit enters through a traumatic
hurt or series of repeated hurts.[16] The hurt festers like a boil
and can become infected with evil spirits such as rejection, resentment, lack of self-esteem, depression, grief, fear, loneliness. Not
all resentment has an evil spirit infecting it, but if it does, it
will not yield simply to healing prayer. A simple example from my
own experience brought that home to me. I was a consultant for a 30
day retreat, and after a homily on sexuality for the sisters, I began
to be very ill at ease. Had I said the right thing? Had I said too
much? I prayed inner healing prayers for about 45 minutes with no
effect. As I was taking a short run before dinner the thought came
to me, "It is scruples." I thought of my time in the novitiate when I
had scruples, and in my past life. As I was saying grace before
dinner I heard, "you should cast it out." At that many counter arguments came to me, "then you wouldn't be suffering with the
retreatants," etc. I got the idea and uttered a simple command:
"Spirit of scruples, leave in the name of Jesus." It went
immediately. I had prayed healing for 45 minutes with no effect, but

at a simple command it left. I had prayed simple deliverance prayers for the retreatants, but never thought of doing so for myself. The spirit had taken advantage of an old wound not fully healed. In such a case, freedom is gained through deliverance, but healing is needed, sometimes over a long time, if the spirit is not to return. One needs to receive love in place of resentments, fear, etc. Deliverance must be followed by healing love.

2. <u>Cardinal Deliverance</u>: This category refers to spirits that enter because of repeated acts of sin that build patterns of behavior and allow freedom to slip away. In this case, deliverance hinges on repentance and the exercise of will power. As Jesus asked the paralyzed man at the side of the pool: "Do you really *want* to be well?" so also, if a habit of sin or negative choice is discerned, the person is asked to renounce the negative choice and choose good explicitly. One needs to choose to live, to renounce fear, unbridled anger, etc. and open to trust. An example from Randy Cirner might help.[17] Carl had a compulsive habit of masturbation which he couldn't shake by will power or trying to distract himself. Cirner prayed a deliverance prayer and taught Carl how to pray deliverance for himself, and to seek God's authority to overcome the habit. Carl was freed from the compulsion and continued to confront it as taught until there was no more problem. A danger with deliverance prayer is that the person might be expecting magic and freedom without personal struggle. The deliverance frees one *to* struggle with God's grace; until then one's freedom in that area is bound and ineffective.

3. <u>Occult Deliverance</u>: This category is the most difficult and dangerous. Such spirits enter though involvement with the occult-- everything from Satan worship and witchcraft to fortune-telling, astrology, seances, ESP, lucky charms, levitation, astral projection, and games like the Ouija board, Tarot cards and crystal ball gazing. The occult seeks power and/or knowledge outside the kingdom of God. Because of the nature of these cases, it is recommended that a priest or a lay person with a special grace and under proper authority be involved. This is because occult spirits themselves are *sent* by authority and need to be confronted by the greater authority of Christ and the church. As I interpret it, social power needs social power to confront it. McAlear and Brennan have much experience in this area. They advise the following: 1) Warn people about the danger of the occult (especially in today's world where Satan worshippers try to kill those who leave their groups). 2) Make sure there is time to finish the prayer. Otherwise the person will experience more oppression. 3) Require repentance and explicit renunciation of the occult involvement (Tarot cards, etc.) and destruction of all occult objects (books, charms, etc.). 4) Renew baptismal promises--renunciation of Satan and his works and choosing Lordship of Jesus, together with sacramental absolution for the sin involved. 5) Pray an explicit deliverance prayer against the spirit involved. (This is not always needed in the first two categories,

since a healed and repentant person gives no room for the spirit and the spirit may leave spontaneously or at the next reception of the Eucharist.) 6) The inner wound that brought one to seek the occult must be repented of and healed (especially anger and rebellion against God and the church, and needs arising from insecurity). 7) There is need for follow-up to meet the counter attacks of evil. God's kingdom calls for surrender and trust. To enter it we must renounce the manipulation and control of life and accept God's loving design. Thus, the cross/resurrection of Jesus is the final overthrow of Satan's pride and control.

4. Inherited Spirits: Even in the above categories, I have found that generational patterns are involved and need to be addressed. Wounds that invite spirits are often generational and sinful patterns run in families.[18] Occult involvement, in my experience, is often related to superstitious practices in the family history, or curses heedlessly (or intentionally) put on children by parents, grandparents, etc. Occult groups like the Moonies seek the help of dead ancestors to keep people in bondage to the group. Thus, I always investigate the family history of anyone who seems to be in spiritual bondage, and pray to break any curses or to cut free with God's Spirit from any occult practices or dedication.[19] One person was brought for healing who had been helped neither by therapists nor by deliverance. In praying for her with a person who had a spiritual gift of knowledge, we found out that a grandfather had rejected God and all in the family were affected. With the deliverance prayer, we also prayed for the release and healing of the family members involved (some 25 in this case) and she experienced released. It was the combination of deliverance and healing of ancestors that was needed. Another boy of seven who could not get close to his mother and was not helped by counseling, was also not helped by previous deliverance prayer. I asked about the family history and discovered that the first boy in four generations had been mentally ill. We prayed to cut this pattern and that others in the previous generations would be healed and the boy fell asleep in his mother's arms—which he had never before done. The counselor also noted a new freedom to change. Here again, it was a combination of deliverance and ancestral healing that was needed.

5. Sealed Spirits: McAlear and Brennan have found that some spirits are "sealed" in, much as a person is "sealed" by the Spirit in baptism. A seal is a mark of ownership, and can be conferred if the spirit enters in conception, or through occult involvement or dedication (as parents who have sought help from spiritualists for their baby). Satanic groups seal their members with a trinitarian prayer, in mockery of the Trinity, and the seal must be broken three times: "I break the seal in the name of the Lord Jesus" (3 X) or "in the name of the Father, Son and Holy Spirit." For the seven-year-old boy and for myself this prayer of breaking the seal (for the spirit that entered in conception) was a powerful help for healing.

Spiritual Discernment

In this paper I have focused on the extraordinary event of deliverance, but in the tradition there is perhaps an even stronger tradition of discernment. Dennis Martin presented the monastic tradition seen in Cassian. This tradition has been presupposed in all Jesuit training, but it is complemented by the Rules for Discernment, Weeks I and II in St. Ignatius Loyola's *Spiritual Exercises*.[20] Ignatius distinguishes different rules for different stages of spiritual growth. The Rules of the First Week (on sin) are rather like my "Familial Faith" or those conforming their will to God's law. These are quite simply tempted not to pursue spiritual growth because of its difficulty. The Rules of the Second Week pertain to those who have broken through to the Spirit (my "Individuating Faith" stage) and are tempted more subtly under the guise of "light," to exaggerate or distort spiritual growth in such a way that no real progress is made. This would be like the temptations of Jesus that aimed at distorting his call before he really got underway. In the "Two Standards" meditation, Ignatius sees that the key to Jesus' way is humility and the cross ("poverty, humiliations, and humility and from there to every other good"). Satan's way, on the other hand, is power and pride ("riches, honor, pride and from there to every other evil"). Satan moves one to self-love, isolation and pride; the good spirit moves to humble service of God in union with Jesus crucified and communion with the Church. Deliverance seems to deal more with the early stages of spiritual growth; discernment and conversion to Christ, more with advanced stages.

Final Reflections on Deliverance Prayer

When discerned to be needed, prayer for deliverance involves submission to the authority of Jesus and the church. We begin with praise of God and a prayer of protection. We bind off the spirits in the room and pray to bind their communication (lest they gain power from one another). We pray for discernment (after talking with the person and getting the data and issue). Some issues are ancestral, others also involve evil spirits. If evil spirits are discerned, we bind the spirit and cast them out in Jesus' name, and ask the person to renounce them and choose Jesus' truth and way of life. We pray for ancestors who need prayer and cut the person off from negative ancestral patterns or from spirits that have entered from close relationships not according to God's will (affairs, etc., give entry to evil bondage also). Then we pray for infilling with the opposite good spirit (courage to replace fear, love to replace resentment and deprivation, etc.). Finally, we try to be sure the person has a support community or counselor to help him or her grow in God's way. Deliverance is *to* a new way of life, not just *from* bondage. In short, I interpret deliverance prayer as God-given authority to release people from a family or social system governed by evil or worldly spirits to the "new family" in God's Spirit won through Jesus' cross/resurrection. As one grows into this new family, the evil spirit has no more hold from inside, but can deceive through exaggeration or false reasoning. Good spiritual direction protects against this. Spirits can also attack from outside (as we see in the life of the Curé of Ars) and may need to be prayed against through prayers for protection. The ultimate deliverance is when God's kingdom is fully present both within and without, so evil under God's providence motivates us to continue working for the fullness of God's rule.

APPENDED CHART

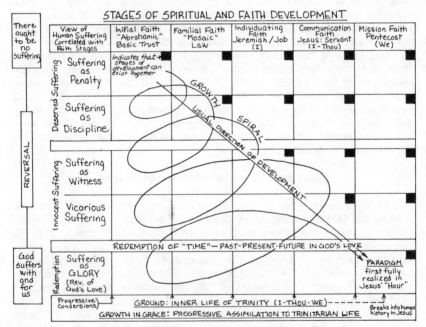

Figure 1. Stages of faith development in relation to view of suffering.

Notes

1. See Henry Ansgar Kelly, *The Devil, Demonology and Witchcraft* (Garden City, N.Y.: Doubleday, 1968) 3.

2. Quoted in Dennis Hamm, S.J., "The Ministry of Deliverance and the Biblical Data: A Preliminary Report" in Matthew and Dennis Linn, ed. *Deliverance Prayer* (N.Y.: Paulist, 1981) 52.

3. So Hamm, "The Ministry of Deliverance," 54ff.

4. See James D. G. Dunn, *Jesus and the Spirit* (Philadelphia: Westminster Press, 1975) 94 (quoted in Hamm, "The Ministry of Deliverance," 60).

5. So John Reumann, *Jesus and the Spirit* (Philadelphia: Westminster Press, 1975) 94 (quoted in Hamm, "The Ministry of Deliverance," 60).

6. See L. J. Elmer, "Exorcism," *New Catholic Encyclopedia,* vol. 5 (N.Y.: McGraw Hill, 167) 748-9.

7. Quoted in H. A. Kelly, *The Devil, Demonology and Witchcraft,* 36-7.

8. *Ibid,* 39.

9. *Ibid,* 41.

10. *Ibid,* 78.

11. *Theologia Moralis,* III, vol. 2, 492 (quoted by James McManus, C.Ss.R. "Exorcism in Catholic Moral Theology," Appendix A in *Deliverance Prayer,* 244).

12. *Ibid,* 245. From St. Alphonsus, *Praxis Confessarii,* n. 113.

13. See *A Pastoral Statement on the Catholic Charismatic Renewal,* A Statement of the Bishops' Liaison Committee with the Catholic Charismatic Renewal, March 1984. Approved by the Administrative Committee, National Conference of Catholic Bishops, pp. 15-16.

14. See Rev. John B. Healey, S.T.L., "The Tradition for Charismatic Deliverance Prayer," in *Deliverance Prayer,* 95f.

15. See R. T. Sears, "Healing and Family Spiritual/Emotional Systems," *Journal of Christian Healing,* 8 (1983) 10-23.

16. See Richard McAlear and Elizabeth Brennan, "Deliverance Ministry: Freedom from Oppression," *Journal of Christian Healing,* vol. 8, No. 2 (1986), 34-37. See also their article "Deliverance: A Perspective From Experience," in *Deliverance Prayer,* 160-173.

17. See Michael Scanlan and Randall J. Cirner, *Deliverance from Evil Spirits: A Weapon for Spiritual Warfare* (Ann Arbor, Mich.: Servant Books, 1980) 42f.

18. See Dr. Kenneth McAll, *Healing the Family Tree* (London: Sheldon Press, 1982) for much data on praying for ancestors in regard to healing the living.

19. See my "Healing and Family Spiritual/Emotional Systems." Also, Kenneth McAll, *Healing the Family Tree,* for many instances of healing through praying for ancestors and thus delivering people from family spirits.

20. See Jules J. Toner, S.J., *A Commentary on Saint Ignatius' Rules for the Discernment of Spirits* (St. Louis: Institute of Jesuit Sources, 1982) for a full explanation of these rules.

Selected Readings

Linn, Matthew and Dennis, ed. *Deliverance Prayer* (New York.: Paulist, 1981). This is the best overall presentation I know.   Several authors.

McNutt, Francis.   *Healing* (Notre Dame, Ind.: Ave Maria Press, 1974) 298-231. A balanced, short presentation.

Scanlan, Michael and Cirner, Randall J.   *Deliverance from Evil Spirits: A Weapon for Spiritual Warfare* (Ann Arbor, Mich.: Servant Books, 1980).   A treatment of deliverance in pastoral care and daily life.

Brennan, Elizabeth and McAlear, Richard, "Deliverance Ministry: Freedom from Oppression," *Journal of Christian Healing*, 8 (1986) 34-37.   Part I of this anticipated book is in *Journal of Christian Healing*, 4:1 (1982).   These presently are the most experienced in the field among Catholics.

Response to Robert T. Sears

Harold E. Bauman

I confine my response to Robert Sears' very helpful paper to two areas: the "law of the generations" and some observations on charismatics and deliverance.

The Law of the Generations.

One of the biblical texts on the relation of sin to generations is Exodus 34:6-7:

> And the Lord passed in front of Moses, proclaiming: "The Lord, the Lord, the compassionate and gracious God, slow to anger, abounding in love and faithfulness, maintaining love to thousands, and forgiving wickedness, rebellion, and sin. Yet he does not leave the guilty unpunished; he punishes children and their children for the sins of the fathers to the third and fourth generation."

A minimum interpretation of this text is that God does not obviate the consequences of sin in a given generation so that the next generation will not be affected. The fruit of sin does carry across the generations.

The medical arts are well aware of the effect of one generation upon the following ones. Witness the medical history forms asking about illnesses in previous generations that one fills out for the family doctor. Witness also the research which is showing the effect of alcohol and tobacco use by pregnant mothers upon the unborn child.

Research is showing as well the tendency of sons of alcoholics to have a weakness toward alcohol. Is it inherited? Is it from the father's modeling? The answer to these questions is not yet clear.

Sears develops an interpersonal interpretation of the family of God with angels given to care for us, and of the realm of evil with Satan and his spirits. He notes that in family systems thought, children learn patterns from parents and pass them on to the next generation. He goes on to say that when deliverance is needed, there is always a wounding or sin in the family system that requires prayer besides the deliverance prayer.

Marilyn Hickey, a current popular teacher, states that it is the weakness toward a given sin that is transmitted between the generations. The devil then tempts the person in that area and leads into sin. Continued practice of the sin can lead to more and more control by the devil. Christians need to know how to bind the devil and resist his powers and to break the generation curse.

Ensign and Howe in *Bothered? Bewildered? Bewitched? Your Guide to Practical Supernatural Healing* state that parental involvement in the occult may make the child much more susceptible to demonic attack and oppression in the future. The children are not

guilty of the sins of their parents, but are suffering the consequences. This may involve the invasion of spirits, the writers say,
which need prayers of deliverance.

In seeking the meaning of the "law of the generations," we
should note that the first occurrence of the biblical statement is in
the giving of the Ten Commandments, Exodus 20:4-6. It is in the context of making and serving idols that the warning is given. Perhaps
this means that the continued family involvement in idolatry or the
occult opens family members to the invasion of the demonic. If the
world view of parents is absorbed by children, the susceptibility to
the powers involved in that world view will certainly be present.
At least many Christian parents pray that this will be true for their
children.

There is much in this question that I cannot explain. I have a
hunch that the primary issue in this consultation will be the same
as in our congregations: what is the relation of the biblical world
view to the rational scientific pragmatic world view of our culture?
Involved in this is the question of the nature of evil: is it only
wrong allegiances followed by wrong choices for which one is
responsible or does it also involve a dynamic power working through
wrong allegiances and wrong choices? I understand Jesus to be
teaching the second view.

Observations on Charismatics and Deliverance.

It is my judgment that the Pentecostal movement and the charismatic movement arose in the midst of a dominant religious culture
which had taken on many of the attitudes of the surrounding rational
scientific culture. While God was worshiped, there was little need
for the supernatural to work in the human scene. The advances of
science and technology would deal with human problems.

The failure of the material and technological culture to meet
human hungers is evident. The hunger of the human spirit led some
to try eastern religions and others to illegal (and legal) drugs.
The absence of the experiential in religious life and of certain
spiritual gifts and the working of the Spirit as seen in the life and
ministry of Jesus and his followers led to the search for these. In
response to human hungers the Spirit can work, even with partial
human understandings of God's will. When areas of no emphasis or
under-emphasis are recovered, the lost areas will tend to be made
larger than life and there will be excesses. Witness the Anabaptist
movement with its multicolored coat.

The recovery of the view that the Holy Spirit is personal and is
to be experienced in one's life, that all the spiritual gifts operating in the New Testament are available to the church for its life
and ministry today, that evil is personal and aggressive, and that
Jesus has given to believers the task of carrying out the same ministry he had is now being witnessed around the world.

The deliverance ministry in the context of healing is one part of this recovery. One example is the work of John Wimber in the Vineyard Ministries in his training of believers to minister. His theology is very akin to the Anabaptist view of the two kingdoms. The fact that there are some things we may call excesses should not cause us to miss his central contribution.

There is a maturing of the deliverance ministry among some groups in Northern Indiana. One group which initially saw a demon behind every headache and problem in life has now moved back from that view, but still has a deliverance ministry. Dean Hochstetler, initially needing to find his way pretty much alone, in recent years has walked with theological, psychiatric, and pastoral counsel, and has been affirmed in his ministry by ordination from his conference. His ordination for deliverance ministry is the first and only one that I know of in the Mennonite Church.

DEMON POSSESSION AND EXORCISM IN AFRICA, IN THE NEW TESTAMENT CONTEXT AND IN NORTH AMERICA

OR: TOWARD A WESTERN SCIENTIFIC MODEL OF DEMON POSSESSION AND EXORCISM

Jacob A. Loewen

This paper is based on several sets of assumptions. First, in regard to the nature of man and the origin of evil, I assume that:

1. Human beings created in the image of God (Gen 1:27) have that of God within them. With Peck (1978: 243-253) and others I would locate this image of God in the person's unconscious.

2. Human beings have been ordained by God to have "dominion" over the created universe (Gen 1:28-30). Thus they have been endowed with all the capacity necessary to "follow God's footsteps" and to fully understand the design God built into the universe, be it material or spiritual. Therefore advancement in human understanding of the natural and social sciences is the God-ordained result of our living out the "divine image" in us and the fulfillment of our assigned task to "master" the laws underlying the universe God created.

3. Good and evil both grow out of divine energy. When disciplined people, obeying God's design, use divine power, they produce good. However, by the same token, when undisciplined people, either willfully or carelessly operating outside of God's design, use it, they produce evil.

4. Human beings have been endowed with the capacity of choice and the ability to distinguish between good and evil. Psychologists, following Freud, call the pull toward the good in a person his/her *superego*, (others, the unconscious) and the pull toward evil his/her *id.*

5. Human beings are notorious for their unwillingness to "own" their evil deeds. They invariably project them: "Not I," says the man, "it was the woman you gave me....;" or "Not I," says the woman, " it was the snake you created who deceived me....;" or, to borrow from Flip Wilson: "the devil made me do it."

Second, in regard to spirit and its place in culture-based worldviews, I assume that:

1. There is no "literal" way of talking about spirits, even in the Bible. Earth-bound human beings can speak of them only in terms of analogies, metaphors or models. The very word for "spirit" in both Hebrew and Greek, *ruach* and *pneuma* respectively, when denoting "spirit," are analogies or metaphors. For both languages the lexicons list the literal meaning of these words as "wind," the extended meaning as "breath," and the figurative meaning as "spirit." In fact, conservative Jews in Jesus' day, like the Sadducees did not believe that such a category of beings even existed.

2. Each culture operates on an unspoken (usually) worldview which functions as a comprehensive model "explaining" the way the universe and human beings in it operate. *Worldviews are not reality,* they merely are functional models of reality; and because humanity still has not mastered all there is to be learned about God's handiwork, all of them are incomplete.

3. It is possible to develop more than one functional model of a given reality. For example, when a crowded fast-travelling bus suddenly leaves the mountain road and hurtles down the mountain side killing all its passengers, both the African and the North American observing the tragedy ask: "What happened?" When the North American, who operates on a materio-mechanical worldview, learns that a front tire blew out or that a steering rod broke, he feels confident that he knows what caused the accident. To the African who operates on a spirit model of reality, however, even these explanatory "facts" which satisfy the North American, are merely a symptom or the means of causing the accident. The African wants to know: "Who caused the blow out or the tie-rod break, and why?" For this reason the African will consult the spirit world (his deceased ancestors) in order to learn the "spiritual" causes of the accident. He will feel satisfied only when the ancestors via a medium tell him that the accident was caused by the soul-of-the-dead of the bus driver's great grandmother who was warning the family that some member had committed a very major offense which needed to be corrected.

4. Culture-bound phenomena, like demon possession, must be studied in their cultural context in order to determine their meaning (Songer: 232). Comparing any African or Chinese case of evil spirit possession and exorcism with any North American case of demon possession and exorcism may be a very dubious enterprise, because we may be comparing, not two apples, but rather an onion and an apple, since each of the cultures operates on a different worldview. Only after we have been able to define the *meaning* of a symptom, trait or action within a specific cultural context, can we compare it with a comparable *meaning* from another culture. It usually is frivolous to compare specific traits apart from their differing meanings.

Outline of the Paper
Based on the above assumptions this paper will now try:
I. To present a functioning model of evil spirit possession and exorcism within an African cultural setting where possession and exorcism form part of the normal routine of life. From this model we will abstract the important aspects and use them as a base line for a comparative listing of models of demon possession and exorcism in other cultures.
II. To show by means of a comparative listing that:
(a) The New Testament culture of Jesus' time operated on a spirit model, very similar to that of modern Africans.

(b) There are very few, if any, points of similarity between the African/NT spirit model of the world and the materio-mechanical universe of Western science, the basis of the North American worldview.

(c) In regard to worldview, most North American Christians are schizophrenic, that is, they habitually operate on the Western materio-mechanical model, except when dealing with matters of the spirit, be it good or evil. Here they try (unsuccessfully by African evaluation) to operate on the spirit model of the New Testament.

III. To evaluate two current Western approaches to demon possession and exorcism, namely:

(a) the Wimber-White model, and

(b) the Peck model.

IV. To attempt a definition of demon possession and mental illness within the categories of the Western scientific worldview.

I. An African Model

The universe, (usually conceived of as fairly local and created by the tribal high god) in which Africans of tribe X^1 live, is alive with spirit. All things—plants, animals, and humans—have their own spirit dimension, if not an actual spirit counterpart. In fact, some plant and animal spirits are considered very closely related to human spirits as in the case of totemism, for the various clans of tribe X have either plant or animal totems.

In this animate universe, elements that are essentially spirit can appear in material form, and essentially material forms like antelopes can change into their spirit dimension and disappear before the viewer's very eyes. As a fundamental generalization one can say that for tribe X the material and the spiritual dimensions of the universe are aspects of a single continuum. Both are equally real, (See figure below).

material ←————————————————→ spiritual

In the realm of spirits there are both good and bad spirits, but all spirits in tribe X's pantheon, regardless of their character, have their origin in deceased human souls. Bad spirits, the equivalent of evil spirits or demons of the Bible, have resulted from improperly treated souls-of-the-dead. Good or friendly ancestral spirits-of-the-dead derive from those who have been properly buried in their home territory and who have experienced the proper series of funerals and other remembrances since they have passed on. Bad spirits are angry souls-of-the-dead, i.e. ancestors who after their death were improperly buried, usually away from their home territory, or ones who have not been properly remembered in the required sequence of funerals. Especially evil and capricious are the souls of foreigners who died in the region and who were buried by non-relatives in alien territory without anyone who would properly remember them. Thus most of the "evil" souls-of-the-dead, which members of tribe X fear, are of foreign origin. These alien souls-of-the-dead/spirits readily lend themselves as tools for evil to any angry person, and especially to sorcerers and witches.

Every illness, mental or physical, likewise has two dimensions--a material and a spiritual one. All social, physical, psychological or spiritual problems are considered to be caused by alien spirits and/or their "tools," the invading "foreign bodies." These intrusive elements may be what Westerners call *germs*. The alien invaders need to be destroyed or gotten rid of before they kill the person they afflict (de Rosny: 82). Because every illness has these two dimensions, herbs and other local medicines, or even Western drugs can be helpful in dealing with the material dimension of an illness, but all material medicines are considered completely unable to deal with the spiritual dimension of that affliction. The spiritual dimension must be healed by spiritual means. In some cases, materials like Western drugs temporarily alleviate or even entirely eliminate all the visible symptoms of an illness; however they never *heal* the spiritual dimension. The spirit dimension is by far the more important of the two and it is considered the actual cause of the illness. Germs and their ilk are mere instruments by means of which these spirit causes express themselves. This explains why only those people who are under spirit attack actually fall victim to germ infections. If there is no spirit cause, the germs, even if present, remain inactive or non-virulent.

In the same vein human beings have two dimensions. They have a visible physical body and they have an invisible spiritual soul. The spiritual soul is often spoken of as a person's spiritual counterpart because its dimensions and appearance are completely identical to those of the physical one.   This is attested to by those who have "double vision."[2]   Of the two, the soul--the spiritual part--is the ultimate essential for life. When a soul leaves the body, as when it is lost or is captured by a sorcerer, the body slowly deteriorates and dies.

Most illnesses, mental or physical, especially minor ones, are actually caused by friendly ancestral souls-of-the-dead who are merely calling to the attention of the living that some action of bad consequences has been committed in the immediate social context. Very frequently the diseases caused by friendly spirits equate with what Westerners call "natural" diseases, but not always so. Such diseases are readily cured once the offending cause has been discovered and removed.   More serious are the illnesses which involve attacks by malevolent souls-of-the-dead. Such attacks, possessions, or other afflictions are usually the result of the victim or a close kin having violated some major tribal taboo. Or they may be the result of witchcraft/sorcery that grow out of the social tensions within the immediate or the extended family context. A common tribe X proverb says: "Your sorcerer is your sibling or your bodyguard" (de Rosny: 130). However, there can also be unprovoked spirit attacks such as when a sorcerer/witch is trying out his/her powers and strikes a random victim or when somebody decides to get rich at the expense of his/her co-villagers and steals or buys their already stolen souls and enslaves them in order to harness their power for personal gain.

As we have already said, when a soul is stolen during a person's lifetime, the body begins to deteriorate. Tribe X's standard symptoms of a soul's having been stolen or sold are the following: sore throat, fever especially in the late afternoon, great fatigue, trembling, pain that constantly moves, prickly feeling in the eyes, nightmares involving incest, paranoia and depression (de Rosny: 130). Especially dangerous as soul-thieves are white people who move into a native community and who then become rich very quickly. Tribe X believes that people are able to get rich only on the basis of the enslaved souls of others. The self-enrichers have either themselves stolen the souls of tribespeople or they have bought them from some sorcerer/soul-broker who has captured them and who now sells them to the highest bidder. Since the stealing of one's soul is an ever present danger, one should never give one's name or let any part of one's body such as hair combings, nail clippings, etc. fall into someone else's hands, especially not a stranger's hands. Since in tribe X's view, the whole is always present in the part, any unscrupulous stranger or tribal *ekong* sorcerer may use a person's name or parts of his/her body to enslave his/her soul through magic means (de Rosny: 176). This would explain why the African MB Church members accosted the missionaries leaving the Congo (now Zaire) during the 1960's turmoil, angrily demanding that the missionaries turn over the church membership rolls to the locals before leaving.

In fact many Africans today believe that the reason independence from colonialism has not changed their lot is because their souls have been captured and sold to operate the Western industrial/commercial complex. Once a person becomes aware that his soul has been stolen or enslaved, he will waste away and die. Even if he lives for a period, he will never achieve anything because he has been robbed of his vital essence--his soul. Since AIDS, called the "slim" disease, is accompanied by all the symptoms of soul loss or soul-stealing, many Africans are sure that the latter is its cause. In fact tribe X believes firmly that the physical slave traffic of the past has merely been "civilized" and is now operating as *ekong* sorcery (de Rosny: 6).

Even relatively intangible things like actions, spoken words or even unspoken thoughts always have their spirit dimensions. If a word, action or thought becomes a reality, e.g., if a spoken word contains enough spirit power to actually happen, then its spirit dimension has acted. We see this in the case of the young wife of a low-paid government employee in a large African city who was swamped by dozens of her husband's relatives whom she had to house in a tiny apartment and feed without a garden and within a totally inadequate household budget. Utterly frustrated, she sighed to a friend, "I wish I could get out of this impossible situation." When her husband subsequently had a fatal accident in the city street, both she and those who heard her frustrated wish knew that she had become a witch. She uttered a word whose spirit dimension had acted and killed her husband (Loewen, 1976).

For tribe X socioeconomic equality is an inviolable given. Should any person suddenly be observed to be increasing his possessions more than others, the explanation will be completely obvious to his neighbors and relatives: he is getting rich on the labors of the souls he has enslaved. Should someone else in the community at that time be encountering consistent bad luck or misfortune, he will immediately suspect that it is his soul and its power that has been stolen or bought by the prospering fellow villager. Usually one bad luck experience will be accepted as chance, but continued misfortune is definitely caused (de Rosny: 83). In fact, in the language of tribe X, sickness, misfortune and unemployment are all covered by the same word.

In tribe X sin or evil is invariably defined socially rather than morally. There are a few moral absolutes such as incest avoidance, strict observance of certain tribal taboos, etc.; most actions, however, are neither intrinsically right nor wrong. People do many things that could be labeled "sin." Most of these, however turn out to be completely harmless, that is, they produce no visible negative consequences in the social settings. But sometimes even something utterly harmless, will produce enormous negative consequences. (A biblical example of such an action would be Abraham taking the slave girl, Hagar, as his second wife. The action was completely proper from the pastoral society's point of view, but this innocent sex encounter has produced bad results that are still with us today, thousands of years later, in the bitter Arab/Israeli conflict.)

Ordinary persons are completely limited to the here and now. They cannot foresee the results of their actions farther down the road. Hence the people of tribe X depend on the living-dead, the souls-of-the-dead of their deceased ancestors to indicate to them when and which actions will produce bad results. Deceased ancestors have the responsibility of warning their living relatives if and when even a very innocent action will have long-term negative consequences. They must warn the living so that the harm-producing action can be undone or at least that its effect be greatly reduced. Warning messages from the ancestors usually come in the form of benign illness or misfortune, but they could also come in visions or dreams. When such an illness arrives and/or when such a supernatural message is not readily understood, a diviner will be consulted. The latter then consults with the deceased ancestors and determines the precise reason for the warning. Thus for tribe X all illness--mental or physical--is never just happenstance, it is always caused, usually, by a friendly soul of a deceased ancestor who is trying to prevent a major catastrophe from developing.

However, illness caused by a witch or a sorcerer within the fam-

ily or the village. For example, many village quarrels remain harmless. Two people disagree, tempers flare momentarily, others intervene, no major calamity develops, so there are no evil consequences.
But should one of the contending parties have wished an evil and
suddenly--having become an accidental witch--his/her evil desire
become reality, then the opponent or some member of the opponent's
family will fall ill. It could be that the offended individual himself
had witchcraft powers and thus made a spiritual attack on his/her
opponent or his/her kin; that is, s/he sent an evil spirit over which
s/he has control to attack his/her opponent. Others may have to go
to a known witch/sorcerer and pay him/her for a charm, a curse or
even an evil spirit attack.

Thus every illness or calamity is seen as having a spiritual
cause and all evil experienced will be personified as one or more
evil spirits who attack and trouble the patient. One chronically ill
woman, who, after many other healing efforts had failed to effect a
cure, came to an African Independent Church (AIC) where the prophet-
leader diagnosed her case as possession by three evil spirits. Two
of these had been sent by her deceased maternal great-grandmother
and one had been sent by a deceased ancestor from her husband's
family. These spirits had been sent as a punishment for her continual quarreling with her husband. Now at the AIC, after an adequate
number of confession and healing sessions, and a series of consulta-
tions with her husband and other relatives, she was given an emetic
and eventually she herself exorcised (vomited out) all three spirits
whom she personally identified in her vomit. By this means she
received visible evidence that the evil spirits afflicting her had
been successfully exorcized from her. In this case the AIC community
provided the healing social context (Loewen, 1976). More usually
however, it is the immediate family that provides the social context
of healing.

In an ordinary tribe-X-healing, family members of the victim
meet to flush out the witch or the witches who have caused this illness within their own family or circle of relatives. This process
involves accusation of individual members of the family by the
healer. This is a very painful experience for the family, but it is
the only means by which the demons can be exorcised, the victim
healed, and the social context liberated. Such a liberation is especially celebrated if the witches/sorcerers also are "cleansable" (de
Rosny: 56).

The cooperation of family members is considered absolutely
essential for all healing. The family circle provides the accepting
social context in which the possessed/ill person can be healed. One
healer put it this way, "There is no healing or exorcism if there is
no family reconciliation and cooperation. The healer's cannon hangs
fire as long as the family of the possessed withholds the powder"
(De Rosny: 44).

The demonized person may manifest only a benign form of an illness as in the preceding example, or s/he may manifest many of the

more violent symptoms often cited in Western demonization: capacity to speak in unknown foreign languages, foul and blasphemous language (usually directed at members of the family, but in Christian settings sometimes also against God or Christ), intensely violent behavior toward self and others, the manifestation of multiple personalities each with its own voice and persona, severe depression, paranoia, etc. However the exorcism procedure in all cases remains remarkably similar.

At the healer's site of operation other patients, friends and visitors in the healer's compound provide the larger social context, but the inner circle is formed by relatives who have been summoned, often from afar, because they are recognized as part of the social tension network within which this illness and evil possession has developed. And it is this same context which now must cooperate to expel the demons. As already indicated, in the later stages of the exorcism, the healer will "accuse" one or more members of the family of being the sorcerer/sorcerers who have provoked this evil spirit invasion. The healer often makes some very specific accusations. These are based on the information he has gleaned through the patient's confessions, from his interrogations of the patient, from his knowledge of the social situation in general, and ultimately, on the basis of his "second sight" or "double vision" as tribe X calls it. This is the capacity to see the spiritual dimensions surrounding the case which are invisible to ordinary tribespeople.

As an aside, it is interesting to note that in tribe X the Christian helper of the healer, who could perform most of the rituals on behalf of the recognized healer, was deemed incapacitated to obtain "double vision" because of his Christian upbringing (de Rosny: 47).

The above described accusation-and-response pattern usually continues until the social setting which originally sparked the illness/possession, not only the patient, has been "healed." The healing can only come about when all potential or actual "witches/sorcerers" in the situation have spoken the required release formulae for the victim in public. On the strength of the resulting social solidarity, the healer now proceeds to the exorcising phase of the healing. He achieves the exorcism and the banishment of the attacking evil spirits, either by his word of command or by ritual washing or anointing, but more usually, by ritual vomiting done by the patient.

As an aside, it is important to note that in tribe X all social tension and friction invariably involves the spirit world. The bad effects of these tensions lead to evil-spirit-caused illness or catastrophe. Since these evil spirits have been sent, one or more individuals will be singled out as the causers of the resulting illness/possession. But once the healing/exorcism has been successfully concluded, the witches/sorcerers will also have been cleansed and restored to full social acceptance. The next time an illness arises in the family, the social evil causing it will usually be "personified" in a different member of the family. To the outsider this appears like so much scapegoating, but to the society it means that since all people participate in the creation of social problems, all of them must also take turns to be designated as evil witches/sorcerers in causing the troubles in the social setting (de Rosny: 48).

Earlier we mentioned that unprovoked invasion by evil spirits is also possible. It usually happens when sorcerers/witches try out their powers or when someone steals the souls of fellow villagers for his personal enrichment or for resale to others. There could also be unprovoked invasion by alien spirits from neighboring clans or villages when the latter for known or unknown reasons engage in sorcery against their neighbors. Under such unprovoked conditions, the healing/exorcism may have to be one-sided. Even if the agent/agents of such sorcery can be identified on the basis of the healer's double vision, the culprits may not be willing to cooperate in the healing/exorcism. In such cases, once the healer has identified the source of the attack and has exorcised the invading spirit/spirits with the use of power, he at once proceeds to "armor" the patient, indeed the entire family, to be able to deflect any additional evil spirit forces that may be sent against them. The spiritual armor provided by the healer will cause any new malevolent spirits that may be sent at them to "bounce off" the armor and to be "deflected back" toward the senders (de Rosny: 133).

We may be inclined to see soul-stealing as sort of a converse of demon possession, but in actual fact, it has exactly the same negative effects and requires very similar healing procedures of the latter. The legitimate spirit inhabitant of the individual--the soul--has been taken captive and enslaved by more powerful alien spirit forces. The resulting soul loss may involve the same illness symptoms as when a person falls under the control of alien spirits who trouble him/her, ride or possess him/her.

The healer in tribe X is a very important person because he is the group's anti-sorcerer. Since he is endowed with double or second vision and can see those dimensions of the world around them that are beyond the view and knowledge of ordinary mortals, he is able to intervene in most cases of illness, soul loss, or evil spirit invasion. Such "second sight" is probably equivalent to the New Testament gift of discernment of spirits. To me discernment speaks of merely the ability to distinguish evil spirits from the spirit of God or even from a human spirit; however, John Wimber, Dr. John White and others talk about having the capacity to actually and physically see the evil spirits which are afflicting the individual (White: 1987).

Tribe X's healers' greatest enemies are not the invading evil spirits or even the sorcerers who sent them, but the doubts in his powers to heal and exorcise which can occur in the hearts and minds of his family and friends (de Rosny: 37).

Finally, we need to point out that the religion of the African tribe X is basically a therapeutic one. It not only seeks to heal sick individuals, but it also seeks to heal the entire social context which originally gave birth to the disease-causing evil. On the other hand Christianity, by its own doctrine, defines itself as a salvation religion which deals with the forgiveness of biblically defined moral sin in the here and now and with the preparation of people for life in a blessed hereafter (de Rosny: 197-199).

II. Comparison of Worldviews and Cultural Contexts

Based on the preceding description of an African social context of illness/evil spirit attack and healing/exorcism, we now want to develop a way of comparing the worldview and social context of the African situation with the contexts of the New Testament (with an occasional Old Testament reference) and with that of North American society. In the case of the latter we need to make special reference to the evangelical/Christians (including the charismatic movement) because Christians form a definite sub-culture which differs from that of North American society in general. However, it needs to be underscored that most Christians, while professing dissenting views, in actual practice operate more or less fully on the general premises of the scientific/ materialistic worldview of the North American social context at large.

The comparative listing below will show the similarities and differences between the various social contexts and their respective worldviews. This should help us see why certain models of reality develop and how these models then influence the interpretation of events like physical or mental illness, and how they determine the type or methods of treatment that will be considered applicable in cases of evil spirit attack. When we postulate radically different models of reality for different societies, we are not judging the rightness or wrongness of these models. We are merely indicating that it is possible to develop radically different models of reality, because in the current state of our knowledge no models can be comprehensive. All of them must of necessity operate on certain selected premises on the basis of which they choose and interpret only certain features of the reality which surrounds them. The importance of these models does not lie in their rightness or wrongness, but in how closely they correspond to the "reality" the people experience. Faith and confidence in the model and the concomitant practices are extremely important. Mere mental assent or verbal affirmation is not an adequate basis for developing healing/saving faith. Dissonance between the professed model and reality or the actual experience of reality, will always breed doubt in the minds of the participants, and the resulting weakness or lack of faith will seriously hinder the healing/exorcism process.

128   Loewen

African	New Testament	Western Culture Basic Western	Western Christian sub-culture
The whole universe including all matter is alive	The world is peopled with a variety of spirit powers (Col 1:16, Eph 3:10)	The universe is matter. "Spirit" is a matter of super-stition	Profess belief in spirits, at least Spirit of God, but uncomfortable with it, seldom experiencing either God's spirit or evil spirits
Material things can change into spirit and spirits can manifest themselves in material form	Moses and Elijah appeared (Matt 17:37), dead saints appeared (Matt 26:.52-53). An angel appeared and freed Peter from prison (Acts 12.6-11), Aarons rod became a living snake (Exod 7:10)	Impossible!	We believe the NT, but this doesn't happen today
Matter and spirit are the opposite ends of a single continuum e.g. m sp	Matter and spirit a single continuum e.g. Jesus walking through closed doors (John 29.19) Philip disappearing (Acts 8.39)	Matter is real, spirit is super-stition. (Now quarks raise the question of spirit again)	Matter and spirit are separated by an unbridgeable gap; m gap sp
There are good and bad spirits	There are good spirits like the Spirit of God, the angels, etc. There are evil spirits of diverse kinds	No spirits, neither good nor bad	Profess belief at at least in Spirit of God, evil spirits are more problematical
Humans have a body and a soul	Humans have a body and a soul/spirit	Human beings have a body, life and self-consciousness	Believe humans have a body and a soul worth saving, but feel comfortable with life and self
Soul is released on death	Soul released on on death (Matt 27.50, Acts 5.5,10)	Life processes stop	Believe soul survives death
Souls of deceased ancestors become good or bad spirits	Good and bad spirits a part of God's creation(??)	Impossible!	Souls go to heaven or hell

The souls-of-the-dead speak to the living	Resurrected Jesus appeared and talked to the disciples (John 20:.26); dead saints appeared (Matt 26:52-53), Medium/necromancer (Deut 18:11, 1 Sam 28.11)	Dead are dead and gone, communicating with them is so much hocus-pocus	Departed souls do not communicate with the living. Consulting the dead is of the devil
Souls of humans can be stolen, captured, enslaved	Souls of men sold (Rev 18:13), Slaves of devil (Acts 8:23, 2 Tim 2:26)	Impossible!	Souls can become slaves of devil/evil
Humans can be possessed by good spirits	Filled with/indwelt by Spirit of God (1 Cor 3.16, Acts 2:4). Led by the Spirit (Rom 8:14)	Good motivation but no spirit entity	All true believers indwelt by the Spirit of God
Evil spirits can possess, control ride, enter human beings	Evil spirits can enter, possess, control humans (Matt 9:32-33, 15:22, 12:43-45); Judas (John 13:27)	Impossible!	Believe in it, but most have never seen a case of demon possession
Humans can control spirits, good or bad, e.g. a Malawi healer had 17 spirit helpers	Disciples receive power over evil spirits (Mark 6.7)	Primitive superstition!	Theoretically believers have power over evil spirits
Spirits communicate with people	Spirit of God speaks to people (Matt 4:.1, Acts 8:29, 16:7, Rom 8:16); devil to Jesus (Matt 4:1-9), to sons of Sceva (Acts 19:15), to Judas (John 13:2)	So much superstition!	Spirit of God speaks, but devil speaking to people almost unheard of
People communicate with spirits	Jesus to devil (Matt 4 1-10), Jesus to evil spirits (Matt 8:32, Mark 5:8-9)	So much superstition!	Frowned upon, more or less unknown
Evil spirits cause illness--physical	Bent woman (Luke 13:16), blind and dumb (Matt 12:22) dumb (Matt 9:32)	Physical illness caused by invasion of germs or malfunction of the human mechanism, but a growing awareness of psycho-somatics	Try to believe the Bible that evil spirits can cause physical illness, but germ view more convincing

Evil spirits cause illness--psychic	Lunatic (Matt 17:15, Mark 5:1ff)	All psychic illness is the result of nervous malfunction or hormone/chemical imbalance	Try to believe the Bible that evil spirits can possess people and cause emotional disturbance
Illness/affliction the result of wrong-doing/sin	Blind man (John 9.2), weak & sickly (1 Cor 1:29-30), corruption of flesh (Gal 6:7-8). (Also see Lev 26:15-16), Herod (Acts 12:23), afflicted (Ps 107:17)	Guilt may cause emotional problems, might predispose a person to illness, but it never causes it	Find it hard to believe that their own sins cause illness; often see things like AIDS as divine judgment on homosexuality
Illness caused by friendly (ancestral) spirits	Soul's emotional illness cause by a spirit sent by God (1 Sam 16:14), Paul's thorn in flesh condoned by God (2 Cor 12:7-9), God sent diseases (Deut 7:15, 29:22)	So much superstition!	Try to believe Bible account, but find African view preposterous
Ancestral spirits concerned about living relatives	Ancestral heroes of the faith are "cloud of witnesses" that watch (Heb 12:1) Christ our older brother (Heb 2:11, 16-18, Rom 8:29)	Impossible!	Theoretically possible, but practically unbelievable
Human beings can see invisible spirits when their eyes are "opened"	Balaam saw angel (Num 22:31-34) Paul saw Christ (1 Cor 15:8), Jesus saw Satan fall (Luke 10:18), (See also 2 Kgs 6:17, 1 John 4:1-3)	Tell me some more!	Believe the Bible but have never seen any
People can enslave soul-power of others for self-enrichment	Human souls as slaves (Rev 18:13) enslaved to spirits (Gal 4:3)	Unbelievable!	Unbelievable!
People can practice witchcraft/sorcery	Sorcerers (Rev 21:8, 22:15) sorcery (Acts 8:11, Rev 18:23), idolatry, witchcraft (Gal 5:20)	Unbelievable!	Unbelievable!
Close relatives are the most frequent sorcerers	Did he or his parents sin? (John 9:1)	Unbelievable!	Unbelievable!

A name has power	Holy is his name (Luke 1:49), believe in name...to be saved (John 1:12), What power/ what name (Acts 4:7), ask in my name, I give (John 14:13), no other name saves (Acts 4:12), a blasphemous name (Rev 13:1)	A name is a name!	A name is a name, but use doctrinal formula: In the name of the Father, Son and Holy Spirit
Name used for witching/ magic	God's name: hallowed (Matt 6:9), blasphemed (Rom 2:24, Rev 16:9)	Unheard of!	Unheard of!
Whole present in part: magic on body parts like nail clippings, combed out hair, clothes, etc.	Touching Jesus' hem healed (Matt 9:20, 14. 36), Paul's handkerchiefs and aprons healed (Acts 19:12)	Impossible!	Impossible!
Actions can have magic effects	Anointing with oil: consecration (Exod 29: 36, 1 Sam 10:1); healing (Mark 6:13, Luke 10:34, Jas 5:14, 2 John 7); laying on of hands (Matt 19:15, Acts 6:6, 1 Tim 4:14, 2 Tim 1:6); laying hands: healing (Mark 6:5, Luke 4:40, Acts 28:8)	Unknown except champagne for ship launching	Laying on hands/ blessing=mere ritual. Laying on hands: healing, especially by charismatics
Words can have magic effect	Curses (Acts 23:3, Gal 1:9), blessings Rom 16-20, 2 Cor 13:14, Jude 24), praying over	Unknown!	Use religious formulae: May the God...
Thoughts can have magic effect	Evil thoughts lead to murders etc. (Matt 15:9)	Unknown!	Bad thoughts are harmful/ dangerous
Magic amulets and charms	Practiced magic (Acts 8:9-11;19:19), Pharisees wore phylacteries (Matt 23:.5), amulets (Isa 3:20), charms (Neh 3:4) idols of gold, silver (Rev 9:20)	So much nonsense/ superstition!	St. Christopher medals, crucifix worn as protection
Certain people function as mediums to communicate with spirits	Medium at Endor (1 Sam 28:7). There are prohibitions in Bible	In some off-beat cults	Considered forbidden by Scripture

Diviners can divine future or the human unknowable	See (Gen 44:15, 1 Sam 6:2, Jer 27:9, Isa 2:6, Acts 16:16); Use of lots to know God's will (Acts 1:26)	No evidence for it	Some charismatics claim prophetic gifts
Evil spirit helpers can heal or kill	Satanic miracles (2 Thess 2:9, Rev 9:13-21,13:13, 16:14,19-20)	So much hogwash!	Fundamentalists often believe in Satanic miracles
All illness is caused by spirit/ spiritual means	Some illness by spirits	Nothing at all in it!	Evangelicals theoretically believe in it, charismatics probably even more
Sin usually socially defined	Sin morally defined: (Exod 20:1-17), but socially defined (1 John 3:15, Eph 4: 31-32, Acts 5:28, Jas 4:1-5)	Most things relative rather than intrinsic- ally wrong	Sin divinely and morally defined
Illnesses that result from deeds that lead to evil social consequences may strike the sinner himself or sinner's family members	Who sinned he or his parents (John 9:2)? Also see: Job 21:19, Isa 14:21, Lam 5:7; children complete ancestors sins (Matt 23:32-33)	Psychiatry now recognizes that children often act out parents' unresolved problems	Sin usually considered very personal matter, we prefer (Jer 31:30, Ezek 18: 19-20)
Religion is therapeutic	Religion both therapeutic (Luke 4:18, Jer 30:17) and salvationist: (Rom 10:13., John 3:16	Religion largely left over super- stition	Religion is salvation oriented
Spirits serve as messengers/helpers of ancestors or of healers or sorcerers	God sent the Spirit (Gal 4.6), God sent Gabriel (Luke 1.26), Messenger of Satan (2 Cor 12:7)	Superstition!	We believe in angels as messengers, but most have never experienced one
The family is the all-important unit. It is the basis of self-definition and and of ultimate salvation	While the family is the basic unit, the the family-in-Christ, the church, is the real social context (Jas 5.13-16, 1 Cor 12,25-27)	The individual rather than the family is all-important	The person's own self is the all- important unit. One is utterly responsible for one's own salvation or damnation

The living-dead protect the morals and health of the living and the living provide eternal "goodness" for the dead dead	Those who died in faith form a cloud of witnesses who watch the succeeding generations run the race of faith (Heb 12.1)	There is no relationship between the dead and the living	Persons make their own choice to accept Christ and thus be saved. The dead are irrelevant
The expulsion of demons is a family effort	Expulsion of demons is by divine power and authority (Mark 1:27, Luke 4:36,9:17)	Normal psychiatric healing is completely non-coercive, but Peck says exorcism does involve power and a loving, accepting context	Wimber, et al want to expel on the basis of divine power entrusted to them
The ultimate expulsion of evil spirits is accomplished by the victim who vomits them out and identifies them	Jesus expected faith either from the victim (Matt 9:28,14:36) or from the victim's guardian (Mark 9:22-24,5.36, 7:24-30)	Peck admits ultimately it is the patient who must will to be free, the loving context only helps	Wimber often casts out spirits without people knowing what he is doing
Exorcism of evil spirits is a normal, expected happening	Jewish exorcists (Acts 13:10,19:13, Matt 12:27); Jesus (Matt 8:16,9:33, Mark 7:29); and disciples (Matt 10:1), Mark 6:13) exorcised; apostles healed and cast out demons (Acts 3:6,14:10,16:18) non-followers of Jesus cast out demons (Matt 7:22)	Basically psychiatry frowns on exorcism since the discipline does not accept the existence of demons	Some RC and other charismatics are now reviving exorcism, but church at large is skeptical
Exorcism without community support requires armoring victims and family against further attacks	God provides spiritual armor (Eph 6:10-17)	Vaccination, immunization and gamma-globulin shots are material kinds of armoring	Vaccination and immunization, prayer for protection
When God created man with a capacity for choice he had to leave evil as a possibility	No clear statement on origin of evil, but freedom of choice demands that it exist	Believe there is good and there is evil, origin unknown	Ascribe evil to devil

Summary of comparative listing
In order to highlight the similarities and differences between the four worldviews/social contexts listed above we will abstract from them the most salient features, especially as they relate to possession and exorcism.

African Model
1. The spirit dimension pervades all of life; as such it functions as the supernatural dimension of all material phenomena.
2. Sin and evil are defined in social terms, i.e. everything that has negative effects on society is evil and can result in illness.
3. All persistent misfortune, illness or bad luck is caused. Benign afflictions are usually caused by friendly ancestral spirits who are seeking to prevent greater calamity. Serious illness, misfortune, etc. are the result of sorcery usually within the family itself.
4. The immediate family and the local community provide the healing/social context. All actual and potential sorcerers must speak the required release formula before the victim ejects the invading evil spirits. The healer is the catalyst to bring about personal and community healing.
5. Religion is basically therapeutic in the here and now.
6. Life and ritual are pervaded by magic.

The New Testament Model
1. The universe is peopled by hosts of hierarchically organized spirit forces both good and evil. While there is some material/spirit alternation, the pattern is not as all-pervasive as in the African situation.
2. Sin and evil are defined both morally and socially. There exists a strong link between evil and illness. Illness is frequently seen as resulting from specific sins.
3. The church theoretically functions as the accepting healing community. Both the therapeutic and salvationist dimension are present in Scripture; however, the former is often OT, rather than NT based.
4. Healing of illnesses of all kinds and exorcism of evil spirits are both heavily based on the power model. The sufferer has faith in the healer/God and the healer is endowed with divine power and authority to "cast out" the demons.
5. There is a recognizable decrease in the amount of magic involved in religious ritual between the Old and the New Testaments.
6. Over-all the similarities between the NT context and the African one are so extensive that Archbishop Milingo in Zambia found that he could operate on the NT more or less literally (Milingo, 1984).

The North American Scientific Model

1. The universe is a giant material machine and there is absolutely no place for spirits, either good nor bad, (unless quarks, i.e. energy without mass turns out to be spirit).

2. Evil is usually contextually defined, so there are no absolute rights or wrongs; everything is relative. Furthermore evil and good are highly personal matters. Only the individual culprit himself/herself can be punished. Legal technicalities often prevent punishment from being meted out.

3. Individualism is basic: individual self-fulfillment is usually more important than the welfare of the family and society at large. Social responsibility is largely a memory of the past. The result is that individuals often feel utterly alone and abandoned. This loneliness seems to be expressing itself in increasing mental and emotional breakdowns.

4. There is a real yearning for community. This felt need has spawned all kinds of cults, group therapies, etc. By and large no easy answer is in sight for providing a therapeutic community for those who desperately need it.

5. All illness, physical and mental, is seen as materially caused, either by invading organisms or by mechanical or chemical malfunction within the organism itself. Demon possession at best is a metaphor for deep-seated psychic problems. Healing thus involves the destruction or elimination of invading organisms or the correcting of malfunctions and chemical imbalances. However, recently the awareness of psychosomatic interaction has been receiving increasing attention.

6. While the Western scientific context officially has no place for religion, there do appear to be some remnants of magic. It could be said that the scientific context represents the converse of the New Testament: the degree of magic remaining in the West is about equal to the non-supernaturalism that is making its appearance in the NT context.

The North American Christian Model

1. The fundamental characteristic of North American Christianity is acute schizophrenia. Theoretically the church "believes" in the New Testament spiritworld: Spirit of God, angels, evil spirits, demons and Satan. In practice however, it is experiencing no evil spirits and very little of the Spirit of God. In everyday life North American Christians are firmly rooted in and practically operating on the premise of a material universe.

2. North American Christianity is also schizophrenic in its definition of evil. Doctrinally it accepts a moral definition of evil, but practically it invariably finds itself interpreting evil relatively and contextually.

3. I think it is correct to say that North American evangelical Christianity is essentially operating on the "God of the Gap." All unknown good phenomena are interpreted as miracles of God. But each

time science offers a new materialistic/mechanistic answer, "God" retreats and gets smaller. The same is true in the satanic realm. Each new discovery of chemical malfunction in the brain/nervous system, reduces the realm of Satan and of demon possession.

4. Charismatic Christians, deeply aware that "God is growing too small" are actively trying to resurrect the New Testament spirit model. However, unlike in the New Testament where spirits are pervasive, demons at the most, are seen as operating in only 50% of the cases of mental illness. A non-charismatic Christian like Peck reduces that to 5%. The practical result is a constant flip-flop between the material oriented universe and the spiritually oriented one.

5. Theoretically North American Christianity views the church as the accepting, healing context; but in actual fact, very few find community in the church as a whole. Some find it in smaller cell or prayer groups, but even these offer only very limited refuge in times of trouble.

6. On the whole I believe Christians consider that "original sin" by far outweighs "that of God" in each human being. Hence the salvationist emphasis by far outranks the therapeutic one. Thus the church readily defers therapeutic functions to secular specialists or social agencies.

7. The "chosen people complex" and the conviction of the "uniqueness" of their approach to God keeps most evangelical Christians from recognizing people in other faiths who live like Christians even if they don't bear a Christian label. Christians often feel uncomfortable with Luke 4:18-19 and Matt 25:31-46 because these passages emphasize the behavioral and the therapeutic rather than the salvationist approach to Christian living.

III. Summarized Evaluations of Several Current Western Approaches to Exorcism

Because of my own limited experience and also because of the practical limits in the amount of time that was available for the preparation of this paper, I will summarize and critique only two current Western models of exorcism. They are the Wimber-White model, based on White's lectures (White, 1987) and the Peck model, based on Peck's book *The People of the Lie* (Peck, 1983). The critique will be made in terms of the models that grow out of the worldview/social context features presented in the comparative listing in section II.

The Wimber-White model

The Wimber-White approach to exorcism, to my mind, exemplifies fairly accurately the current approach of North American charismatic Christianity. It divides reality into two separate domains: the material-natural world and the spiritual-supernatural world. It essentially represents an attempt to blend the spirit-filled worldview of the New Testament and our current materio-naturalistic worldview of scientifically oriented North American society. Thus this model affirms categorically that there is a difference between mere mental illness and actual demon possession (demonizing in their terminology). They go to great lengths to prove that the Scriptures themselves make a clear distinction between mental illness (insanity) and demonization. In the Old Testament they see the distinction in the case of Saul and David. Saul was obviously demonized (1 Sam 16:23); while David, when he acted out the mad man before Achish, the king of Gath (1 Sam 21:10-15) was merely mimicking ordinary insanity. In the New Testament they document this distinction in the following examples: simple insanity is illustrated in the case of Rhoda, the maid, who tells the praying believers that Peter is at the door and who is then called "mad" by the incredulous believer group (Acts 12:15). In the case of the man living among the tombs at Gerasa (Luke 8:26-36), however, they see a clear-cut case of demonization (White, 1987).

   I personally find the evidence presented somewhat frivolous. First, in the examples of non-demonic insanity we are dealing with (1) a case of feigned madness in the Old Testament, and (2) with a casual incredulous retort in the New Testament. Furthermore, the linguistic evidence cited by White is equally dubious, because the same word used to describe Rhoda's supposed simple insanity is also used of Jesus by Jews who say that Jesus, "is mad and is demonized" (John 10:20). Here "mad" and "demonized" refer to the same phenomenon and function like a typical Hebrew doublet.

   I am in hearty agreement with White when he chides the evangelical mainstream churches for limiting the power of the gospel largely to preaching and to saving souls, i.e. to the salvationist dimension of religion, thereby avoiding its therapeutic dimension. I also concur with him when he rebukes fundamentalist Christians for seeing the current charismatic spiritual manifestations as involving demonic powers. This latter accusation is reminiscent of Jesus' experience, when antagonistic religious people of that day likewise accused him of operating on Satan's power (Matt 12:27, Luke 11:15).

   Finally I am deeply impressed when White (probably in distinction to Wimber who seems to see that up to 50% of mental illness cases involve demonization) goes on to state that many cases which are currently being called demonization by charismatics are not really that. He affirms that human sciences are making important advances in their understanding of the way God has designed human beings. The more we understand this design, he says, the less we have to attribute to demonization.

   As a well-qualified physician and psychiatrist, White then asserts it is safe to say that all psychoses probably have a physical or chemical cause. He cites two very convincing examples.

   (1) A woman, officially diagnosed as having paranoid schizophrenia and with a long history of mental hospital stays, was, on more thorough examination by White and others, discovered to have excess fluid in her pericardial sac. This excess fluid was brought

on by a thyroid imbalance. When the imbalance was corrected, the excess fluid in the pericardium disappeared and her symptoms of mental illness also disappeared.

(2) A deluded boy drove his parents from their home at gun-point and then shot and killed two RCMP officers because he saw the police as aliens from outer space "since they had red-glowing eyes." (The police had responded to the parents' call for help.) In this case White was also able to demonstrate that there were no demons involved. It merely was a case of chemical imbalance in the boy's brain. After a week of proper medication, the boy's delusions disappeared and he was shocked and horrified at the evil he had done.

It may be of interest to append here that White's chemical answers to psychosis, which are so comforting and satisfying to the average North American, would still leave Africans with their most basic questions: Which spirits set these imbalances in motion, and why? Thus we can affirm that North American charismatics still operate on the "God of the gap" principle and that they, in actual fact, do not operate on a truly spirit/spiritual model such as exhibited by the Africans or as seen in the New Testament.

The Peck Model

M. Scott Peck is a well-known practising psychiatrist who grew up in the traditional naturalistic worldview of the North American scene. Then, as a practising psychiatrist, he dabbled in Buddhist and Islamic mysticism, but finally in 1980 he "made a firm Christian commitment" (Peck, 1983: 11). He admits however, that defining a "true Christian" is a very difficult business. Much of verbalized and practiced Christianity, he correctly says, has little or nothing to do with Christ.

Peck begins by saying that the general North American view of reality has no room for the supernatural. He asserts that 99% of all psychiatrists and the majority of ministers do not believe there is a personal devil, but all firmly believe that there is an evil principle in this world (1983: 182). Contrary to most psychiatrists, Peck defines psychotherapy as a form of exorcism, but says he, there is a basic difference: exorcism proper involves the use of power which regular psychotherapy avoids (1978: 185). In fact he feels that no one individual alone has either enough love or enough power "to exorcise demons." That is why he feels five or more people are necessary for effective exorcising. He describes two cases of exorcism in which seven and nine people, respectively, cooperated. These people worked for several days from twelve to sixteen hours a day to achieve the exorcism (1983: 189). However, Peck points out that the use of power need not violate the self of the victim. Power may be employed only with the expressed permission of the patient (1983: 187). Since demons represent "the spirit of lies and deceit," Peck says the exorcists must be careful to address either the healthy part of the patient's self or the sick sub-conscious (the demons). They should never permit flip-flops, for these are a standard device of the demonic confusion process (1983: 195,209).

According to Peck, the function of the exorcists is to provide the accepting, loving, self-expending social context necessary for exorcism and healing to take place (1978: 186,199,208). This warm but power-charged social context is an absolute necessity for successful exorcism, because the principal reason people sell out to Satan or to evil, or let the latter overwhelm them, is because of absolute loneliness (1983: 199) and the ontological fear that no one loves them. Thus the healing context must have enough love, acceptance and strength to permit the demonized person to risk letting go of his crutch of evil (1983: 199). The community of love and acceptance must be truly Christian in function, though not necessarily so in name. Thus at the two exorcisms described, the participants included self-professed agnostics, nominal Christians and some practicing Christians, but all were people who could truly love, accept and give themselves on behalf of the suffering victim (1983: 199). Peck adds that fundamentalist or moralistic Christians often are too judgmental to be able to form a strong, genuinely loving and accepting community.

However, it is most interesting to note that Peck says it is not the love and power of the exorcist(s) that will ultimately exorcise the demon(s) but rather the patient's own choice to be free. In the final stages of both of the successful exorcisms described, the patients grabbed a crucifix and fervently prayed to be free. No sooner had they expressed their choice to be free and had taken the step of faith, believing that this would happen, did the release come (1983: 197).

In evaluating these experiences, Peck says that 95% of what happened in these demon possessions and exorcisms can be explained in terms of known psychiatric dynamics. However, says he, there remains 5% which cannot be explained at this time. Following Martin (1976) Peck calls this left over 5% *the evil supernatural* or "The Presence" (1983: 195-196). However, Peck quickly adds that this "Presence" no more has horns, hooves and a forked tail than God has a long white beard (Peck, 1983: 206).

Peck does admit that he finds himself in a real quandary about this 5%. While he calls it "The Presence" and hence classifies it as supernatural, he also says that it may only be the patient's own diseased subconscious. He says that currently it is "impossible to discern exactly where the human Shadow leaves off and where the Prince of Darkness begins" (1983: 209-210).

He continues on this evil presence which he also calls "the spirit of lies and unreality" and says that "it finds truth and reality absolutely incomprehensible." Since science is dedicated to increasing our knowledge of reality, he sees a scientific approach to exorcism equal in validity to the supernatural approach (1983: 208).

IV. Toward a Definition of Demon Possession and Exorcism Within the Categories of the Western Scientific Worldview

I personally found Peck "a man after my own heart." To my mind he goes a long way toward providing us with the basis for developing models--for both spirit possession/exorcism and for spiritual growth--which are solidly anchored in the Western scientific worldview. In other words he potentially provides Western Christians with models that eliminate the current Christian schizophrenia which I have decried. Let me therefore summarize some of the ideas which Peck provides.

I wholeheartedly agree with Peck (1978: 194ff) that the universe we inhabit is real and that it follows laws and patterns that are predictable. I also agree with him when he says that human beings generally are poor observers of nature and of natural processes. They easily succumb to magic, superstition and prejudices; and as a result, they often see what they want to see, instead of what really is there (1978: 195). I further agree that human beings, both religious or scientific, easily succumb to tunnel vision (1978: 222ff) and to dogmatism which, be it religious or scientific, is an ultimate evil (1978: 222-223).

I am greatly encouraged when Peck says that we are beginning to see the possibility of the "unification of science and religion" (1978: 228). In fact in his two books (1978 & 1983) Peck proceeds along the road of the scientific model for 95% of the way (1983: 195-196), but then he suddenly changes the paradigm and begins to speak about the inexplicable 5% residue as the supernatural. Here I want to invoke Peck's own plea for humility (1978: 193-197). Let's admit that we do not currently know how to explain every-thing in terms of the scientific-psychiatric model. (In fact, I would even be willing to make the area of our ignorance much bigger than Peck's 5%.) I am afraid that when he switches models, Peck is falling prey to the traditional fallacy of using the supernatural (God for good, Satan for evil) to explain the areas of our ignorance. J.B. Phillips has aptly described this phenomenon in his book *Your God is too Small* (Phillips, 1971). I personally sense that this use of the supernatural to "explain away" the areas of our ignorance is not only illogical, but in actual fact, intellectually dishonest.

Let's acknowledge that we still have many "steps of obedience" to master in the process of bringing the divine image in us (Gen 1:27; 2:15,19) to full fruition.

If we follow Peck's wise suggestion and begin to look at ordinary day-to-day events but with a "scientific" orientation (1978: 231) we can learn bit by bit what lies beyond the boundary of our current knowledge. Let's heed his warning that it is very easy to fall into the trap of attributing two events happening in a sequence to cause and effect. Because of this fallacy we often see miracles where none exist, e.g. when we pray and then notice that the swelling in a joint went down (1978: 231). However, we also need to be

aware of the fact that when we say "the patient died of a
meningococcal infection," we are clearly operating only at a very
superficial level. On a deeper level we need to recognize that the
patient succumbed to the meningococcal infection only after his
usually reliable natural defense system failed (1978: 238-239).

When Peck speaks about the unconscious as our friend, I find
myself in wholehearted agreement, because I too have experienced it
as a helper who urges me to overcome my resistance to doing the
good/right, often warning me or instructing me by what seem like
idle or stray thoughts (1978: 245) or by Freudian slips (1978:248).

The Proposed Model

In the spirit of unifying science and religion I now propose an
alternative model of evil spirit possession and exorcism based on
the Western scientific worldview. This model posits God, that is,
Spirit (John 4:24) as the First Cause which created and organized the
world we know and the human beings that inhabit it. Next, invoking
the theological concept of progressive revelation, I want to propose
a model of evil, illness and demon-possession that is based on
mechanico-material premises of the scientific worldview.

I therefore define demon possession as follows:

(1) Human beings were created with a capacity for choosing good
or evil. Thus there exists in every human being, not only a divine
image, but also an id, that is, a capacity for self-will and for disobedience to God's design.

(2) When such self-willed human beings "do their own thing" in
defiance to the Creator's design, they misuse divine energy and thus
produce evil.

(3) Furthermore, human beings find it very hard to "own" their
evil deeds, so they habitually try to project them outside of themselves, as when they say, "the devil made me do it."

(4) Sooner or later, however, they find that the evil they tried
to externalize is really still inside of themselves and so they
experience it as an alien presence--an "evil spirit." If the presence
of the evil becomes intolerable, they may split it off their ego and
treat it as a separate personality.

(5) In a similar vein when a very young child is sexually abused
by an adult who had been trusted implicitly, the child may be unable
to cope with the evil experience and so splits off a part of its
fragile ego, thereby creating a personality other than itself which
supposedly experienced the evil.

(6) The intense awareness of the evil within makes the persons
(both the evil-doer and the evil experiencer) feel utterly evil and
totally unlovable. This may result in a retreat from reality into the
realm of "mental illness."

(7) Persons suffering very extreme cases of alienation and ego
fragmentation experience what Christians call "the demon possession."

I now define exorcism in terms of the same model:

1. Because "demon-possessed" persons feel utterly alone and

unlovable, the "ice-cold core" of evil within them needs to be "melted down" by selfless acceptance and unlimited love exercised by concerned fellow human beings. But, as Peck says, few people have developed such a capacity to love the unlovely, hence it may be necessary that a group of concerned people "pool" their love in order to provide "enough warmth for enough time" so that the "bound" person can risk letting go of his "evil spirits."

2. If the love and acceptance of such a healing community of human beings reaches adequate proportions, then the bound persons may finally be able to risk wanting to be freed; and once they own their evil, and let go of it, to experience the love and the acceptance of God.

The Unexplained 5%

As we have said, Peck states there remains a residue in demon possession and exorcism which human beings still are unable to explain in terms of science. I want to call this residue: the area of our current ignorance--the area in which we still have not learned to follow the design of the Creator to discover the laws by which he set things in operation.

Dr. E.A. Nida, one of my leading spiritual and intellectual mentors, used to say that the triennial workshops, which the Bible Societies conducted for their technical staff, were absolutely necessary because staff members needed to collectively project/probe what lay just beyond the boundary of their current knowledge. He used to use the following model:

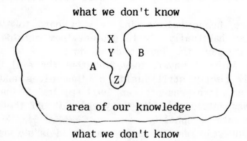

He said: If A "feels" that X lies just beyond the boundary of his knowledge; and B, working from a different vantage point, suspects that Y is just beyond the boundary of his knowledge,then maybe the group as a whole could theorize what Z might be. If we then went back to our individual places of work and continued our research, sooner or later one or another would be able to prove experimentally that X, Y and Z did exist, thus enlarging the area of our knowledge.

In this spirit I want to say humbly (because I am neither a medical specialist nor an expert in physics) that I suspect that just beyond the boundary of our knowledge in the area of our current ignorance the following "knowledge-gap-pluggers" are emerging as possible answers to Peck's still inexplicable 5%:

(1) An increasing number of serious medical thinkers, Peck included, are considering the possibility that all diseases involve both the *psyche* and the *soma*, that is, that the human psyche (spirit) is somehow involved in causing our normal forces of resistance to disease to fail (Peck, 1978: 239). This "psychic" dimension provides a non-material cause (the African's spirit cause) on the basis of which material agents like microbes and chemical imbalances produce physi-cal and mental illness.

(2) A recent study of some carefully selected volunteers, who lived in close uncomfortable quarters in Antarctica to study the effects of stress on human beings, revealed that the individual who "went berserk" and who had to be removed before the midpoint of the experiment was reached, had developed almost no "strange" antibodies, while the other individuals, who successfully completed the experiment, had developed an abundance of hitherto unknown antibodies. Since there were no known germs in the environment, the researchers suggested that maybe these individuals had developed antibodies which had helped them overcome stress, irritation, frustration, anger, etc. This raises the question: Can the human body produce antibodies against evil? (PBC Series on Antartic Cold Adaptation Expedition.)

(3) Medical science has become aware that certain cancers (and AIDS) are caused not by complete microorganisms such as germs, but by virus materials, basically DNA material containing genetic information. Like evil spirits or Satan who cannot operate except they take control of a body (Peck, 1983: 206) this destructive DNA information cannot function unless it is able to take control of a human cell. Only if it is able to take over a human cell, can it reproduce and perform its destructive function. The aim of this "body-less invading power" is to put the human body's immune system to "sleep" (or in the case of AIDS to completely destroy it) so that the evil "alien force" can reproduce and finally enlist the body's own immune system to destroy healthy body cells. This raises the question: Is this viral DNA material equivalent to what the Bible calls evil spirits, i.e. "intelligent negative power that has no body"?

(4) The discovery of quarks in the course of smashing the atom and studying its smaller component parts (MacCormac, 1983: 47-70) have a two-fold interest for us here.

First of all, they go beyond Einstein's law of relativity ($E=MC^2$) in that quarks are manifestations of energy which apparently has no mass. This raises the question: Is science in the process of discovering spirit, i.e., "power without a body"?

Second, we are here dealing with a very fundamental power in atomic structure. In the Scriptures the "Spirit of God" is often used as a synonym for the "power of God." Compare the Hebraistic doublet "the Holy Spirit will come upon you, the power of the Almighty will overshadow you" Luke 1:35, (for additional discussion see Loewen, 1983: 217-218). Since quarks form one of the most elementary energy

sources in atomic structure: Are we on the threshold of discovering
the power which brought the universe into existence and which keeps
it functioning even today?

Concluding Plea

I am deeply aware that I am here "playing with fire" as far as
many Christians are concerned. But leaning on Peck's admonition:
"The path to holiness lies through questioning *everything*" (1978:
193), I am attempting something that I have felt should be tried for
many years already. My effort here may be premature or it may even
be dead wrong, but it represents a genuine attempt to make a statement of faith while keeping "both feet" in the psycho-mechanical
model of Western science which taught me the value of honesty at all
costs.

Furthermore, I want to avoid the danger of trying to operate in
our day and in our setting on the New Testament worldview of 2,000
years ago, and thus becoming what James calls "double-minded people
who are unstable in all their ways" because they are "tossed too and
fro by the waves" of supernaturalism from one side and of naturalism
from the other side to the point where unqualified faith becomes a
practical impossibility.

Notes

1. Tribe X represents an effort to give a fleshed-out picture
of a West African culture. Many of the specifics are drawn from de
Rosny (1985) with author and page numbers in parentheses, unless
otherwise indicated. This will allow the serious reader to study the
cultural context in more detail.
2. Double vision is the capacity to see the spiritual dimension
of the universe and of human beings. It is a capacity that only few
people have. Healers have it. It is dangerous to ordinary mortals
because the spirit dimension does not appreciate being watched.

BOOKS CITED IN THIS PAPER

Loewen, Jacob A., "Mission Churches, Independent Churches, felt need in Africa," *Missiology* 4 (1986) 405-425.

-----. "Clean Air or Bad Breath?" *The Bible Translator* 34 (1983) 213-219.

MacCormac, Earl R., "Religious Metaphors: Linguistic Expressions of Cognitive Processes," J.P. van Noppen, ed., *Metaphor and Religion*, (Brussels: Wettelijk Depot 1085, 1983) 47-70.

Martin, Malachi, *Hostage to the Devil.* New York: Reader's Digest Press, 1976.

Milingo, E., *The World In Between.* Maryknoll, New York: Orbis Books, 1984.

Peck, M. Scott, *The Road Less Travelled.* New York: Simon & Schuster, 1978.

-----. *People of the Lie.* New York: Simon & Schuster, Inc., 1983.

Phillips, J.B., *Your God is Too Small.* London: Epworth Press, 1952.

Rosny, Eric de, *Healers in the Night.* Maryknoll, New York: Orbis Books, 1985.

Songer, H., "Demonic Possession and Mental Illness," *Religion in Life* 36 (1967) 119-127.

White, John. Tapes of lectures. Christ & the Ruler of Darkness (#2), Mental Illness and Demons (#3), Visualization, Guided Imagery & the Ghost of Carl Jung (#4), delivered at the seminar: "Spiritual Oppression, Mental Illness and the Christian Response," in the Brighouse United Church, Richmond, B.C. Jan 30-31st, 1987.

Response to Jacob A. Loewen

Robert L. Ramseyer

In response Loewen's thought-provoking paper I would like to offer a very brief synopsis of what I understand Loewen to be saying and then focuse on what seem to be the basic issues which the Loewen paper raises, issues with which I feel this consultation needs to wrestle. I do this realizing that this is quite arbitrary and that the issues which I see may not be those which Loewen intended or which others in the consultation see as critical. I am especially conscious of this because Loewen and I are by training anthropologists and may have an agenda which is not shared by those whose training is in very different disciplines.

Synopsis

Loewen's perspective is stated very clearly in his first sentence. Exorcism and spirit possession can only be studied in specific contexts. I understand this to mean that these are not universalizable phenomena, things which can be found in most any socioculture setting, things which exist objectively "out there" apart from cultural interpretations. This in itself is probably a proposition which will be questioned in this consultation.

Loewen proceeds to give us a careful picture of a model of reality which he attributes to "tribe X" somewhere in Africa. This is a model of reality which is full of spirits--spirits which act much like human beings and which interact with humans in socially defined ways. In contrast to that, he describes a North American model which is all material and has no room· for spirits or spirit forces at all.

In the African model all illness and misfortune is caused by other human beings using spiritual forces. Such action may be either deliberate or inadvertent. Someone within the family of the victim is most often involved. Only after this relationship with other humans has been dealt with and words of release have been spoken by the perpetrator, can the exorcism take place. Exorcism then, of necessity, usually takes place within the family circle.

With the "spiritual" African model of reality at one end of the continuum and the North American materialistic model at the other end, Loewen places the New Testament model and the model used by North American Christians today somewhere between these poles. Loewen is quite critical of the North American Christian model which is essentially unintegrated and which he calls schizoid. North American Christians profess to believe in spirits because they are found in the Bible, but their basic model is the materialist one which has no room for spirits. The result is a model which attributes to the spiritual what cannot be explained by the material model, an area of experience which is progressively shrinking. The dissonance between the spiritual and material models leaves many Christians without a dependable model for understanding reality and leads to an essentially unstable faith.

Loewen also contrasts African religion, which he calls "therapeutic religion" because it heals both the victim and the social context which gave birth to the illness or misfortune, with Christianity, which he calls a salvation religion because it is concerned with the forgiveness of moral sin and the preparation of people for life in the blessed hereafter.

Loewen's basic position is that all models of reality are partial and incomplete, reflecting the experience of a people with a particular social heritage at a particular time and place. However, Loewen also believes that God has given human beings the ability to eventually understand the design that God has built into the universe. Advancement in the natural and social sciences is the result of that ability.

Critique/Issues

1. Loewen contrasts a spirit-filled African model with a North American model which has no room for the non-material. It seems to me that the contrast could be more helpfully stated as that between a essentially social African model and a mechanistic North American model. Both models are an attempt to make the experienced world predictable to those who must live in it. In the African setting it is society, the ways that human beings interact with each other, that is dependable and predictable. In North America it is the machine, a universe of impersonal laws of cause and effect, that is dependable.

What is disturbing in North America then, is not the possibility of non-material somethings existing around us. Loewen raises the issue of quarks. Quarks are not really a threat to the North American world view. What is a threat is the possibility of some-things around us that have something like free will, that have some-thing like personality, that operate on the basis of social relation-ships rather than impersonal universalistic laws of cause and effect. It seems to me that magic in the North American setting it seems to me is precisely an attempt to get such unpredictable beings back into a setting where they can be dealt with in an impersonal pre-dictable way.

2. What is the relationship between a people's model of reality and real "reality"? Loewen talks of our models as being only par-tial and incomplete, but his insistence on dealing with spirit pos-session and exorcism only in specific settings seems to imply that there is a mutual relationship between reality and a people's model of reality, that a model of reality affects what reality actually is.

As an example, it seems clear that in many African Christian churches God speaks to the leaders of those churches quite clearly through dreams and visions. I venture to say that God does not regularly communicate with most of us here in that same way. I believe that God communicates with African Christians in that way because that is what they expect, and that God does not communicate with me in that way because that is not what I expect. In other words, human beliefs affect what really is.

Similarly, since Loewen mentioned quarks, I would also mention that in quantum physics the presence or absence of an observer apparently affects what actually happens, how particles act depends on whether or not they are being observed.[1]

The issue I am raising is simply this: Is the African world in fact full of spirit beings who operate socially much as human beings do, and is this in fact because the African model of reality has a place for such beings? Similarly, are there far less spirit beings in North America because the North American model of reality has little or no place for them?

Put baldly, is "reality" out there somewhere existing on its own or does it depend on our expectations of it?

3.   What relationship do we today have to the model of reality which lies behind the New Testament materials?   Loewen seems to place the New Testament rather near the African model, less dependent on the action of spirit beings to explain everything, but much more dependent on the action of spirit beings than is the contemporary North American model.   Is what Loewen calls the New Testament model to be normative for people today who like to think of themselves as New Testament Christians?

As noted above, Loewen feels that most evangelical Christians today have been unable to integrate the New Testament and North American models.   The model on which most North American Christian exorcists operate distinguishes clearly between problems which can be explained mechanistically, by cause and effect, and those which are the result of the activities of spirit beings.   This seems to me to fit well into the North American model of reality.   It is analogous to our attributing some of our problems to mechanical failure, and some to human error or evil.

However, as Loewen also says so clearly, it is not enough to explain everything that we can explain mechanistically and then assign whatever is left to either God or the devil.   Such are areas of human experience which are steadily shrinking as our areas of scientific explanation grow.

4.   This leads to what I see as our fundamental agenda from the Loewen paper.   What is an integrated holistic model of reality for North American Christians today, and specifically what is the place of spirit beings/ forces in that model?

Loewen helps us to see more clearly what it is not.   It is not the incorporation of a few spirits into an essentially mechanistic model.   It is not explaining all that we can mechanistically and then assigning the left-overs to spirit beings.   It is not dividing reality into the natural and the supernatural when that is essentially merely another way of talking about what we can explain and what we cannot explain.

Although Loewen himself says that as Christians we should not be afraid of an all-material model of mental illness, demonization, and exorcism, I personally believe that the logic of his argument throughout this paper calls us rather to a model of reality which is able to see all events as having material, spiritual, and social dimensions; a model of reality which sees that all events need to be understood mechanistically, spiritually, and socially; a model of reality which sees that in everything mechanistic, social, and spiritual forces are at work. I believe personally that developing such a model of reality is the agenda which Loewen's paper ultimately lays before us.

Note

1. "The electrons not only know whether or not both holes are open, they know whether or not we are watching them, and they adjust their behavior accordingly. There is no clearer example of the interaction of the observer with the experiment. When we try to look at the spread-out electron wave, it collapses into a definite particle, but when we are not looking it keeps its options open." John Gribben *In Search of Schrodinger's Cat.* (Bantam Books, 1984), 171.

REPRESENTATIONS OF GOD AND THE DEVIL
A PSYCHIATRIC PERSPECTIVE
FROM OBJECT RELATIONS THEORY.

Gerald Kauffman

Introduction.

Psychoanalytic thinking has historically attempted to make God a projected image of our earthly father. The super ego model, under which God is experienced as the critical parent, thereby causing neurotic dysfunction, is based on nineteenth century medical research by Freud and others who emphasized experimental and scientific methodology. This paper thus gives considerable attention to Freud to test aspects of his contribution in relation to ongoing usefulness to psychiatry and especially in relation to God- and devil-concepts, focused by the agenda of this consultation. While the skills of observation and description (egopsychology) and theoretical frames of reference (object relations theory, see Appendix I for definitions) remain valuable, the usefulness of classic psychoanalytic theory for interpreting various issues, and particularly religious ones, is now being rightfully challenged.

This paper thus attempts to draw together some of the current thinking on how we experience God and the devil. Freud's psychohistory, which led to his misinterpretation of data, will be used as a case example in Part I (see also Appendix II). The humbling reality is that each of us, like Freud, is entangled in a psychohistory which affects our view of religious issues. Part II will then introduce W. R. D. Fairbairn's view of "object relations," in which human experience of reality is conceived in a significantly broader dimension than that provided by Freud. Within this context then, a theoretical view of exorcism will be given in Part III as a response to Fairbairn's paper.

If psychiatry has anything to say about religious experience, it is that egopsychology and object relations theory allow us to understand, or at least to talk creatively about, how persons experience transcendent objects. Psychiatric theory "[b]y its very existence,...creates new phenomenon for the observing eye. It should be remembered, however, that theory exists to assist in the understanding of complex reality; it is not reality itself. [What it does is provide] a way of talking about observable phenomena in order to understand them" (Rizzuto: 11).

I. Our Object Representations of Religious Images

Ana-Maria Rizzuto, in *The Birth of the Living God*, posits that although Freud does not express it in those terms, his thinking provides the foundation for object relations theory. She points out that Freud argues that gods and demons are "creations of the human mind" (1913) which are based on "revivals and restorations of the young child's ideas" of father and mother (Freud, 1910: 123).

"Psycho-analytic theory would later call [these] object representations, an essential concept in the theory of object relations" (Rizzuto: 15). Freud, Rizzuto notes, places the Oedipus complex at the pivot of human's creation of God, both at the anthropological and individual levels. Psycho- analysis, says Freud, shows that "God is, psychologically, nothing other than the exalted father....Thus we recognize that the roots of the need for religion are in the parental complex" (Freud, 1910: 123). As Rizzuto notes, however, Freud excludes potential object relationships, such as son-mother, daughter-father, and daughter-mother, in favor of placing the inner image of God solely in the context of a father-son relationship. It is this "paternal element as the source of the concept of God" (Rizzuto: 16) which was, in Freud's view, psychoanalysis' contribution to an understanding of religion.

Thus Freud's theorizing about God and devils illustrates both his convictions about object relation of people significant in childhood, and emphasizes the power he attributes to the way these representations shape individual and social life. What Freud can not and does not do, is explain "the belief in a Divine Being" (Rizzuto: 36).

From her own clinical work, Rizzuto concludes that images of God are created in working through ongoing developmental issues, and from sources other than actual parents. "This is because object representations are not entities in the mind; they originate in creative processes involving memory and the entirety of psychic life" (Rizzuto: 44). The formation of an image of God is thus a process "marked by the emotional configuration of the individual prevailing at the moment he forms the representation--at any developmental stage" (44). Though Rizzuto concurs with Freud in his emphasis on the Oedipal period, since resolution of the Oedipus complex brings to a close one significant period of development, and since repression takes place, she does not accept Freud's conclusion that this period of development is the definitive one in the formation of a God representation. She argues that to explain things as Freud does reduces one's image of God to a "representational fossil" (46).

Rizzuto believes that just as it is possible to have mature relationships with one's parents, so it is also possible to have a mature relationship with one's God representation. Yet it is not simply a matter of relating maturely to a representation formed in childhood. "Those who are capable of mature religious belief renew their God representation to make it compatible with their emotional, conscious, and unconscious situation, as well as their cognitive and object-related development" (46). I would caution, though, that we must be careful not to equate maturity and belief. Maturation has nothing to do with the presence or absence of the human need to experience the representation of objects of Good and Evil. Regression in psychological terms to less "mature" states of ego function is necessary, essential, and healthy for a meaningful religious experience.

Rizzuto draws on Pruyser to suggest that one way of describing this "regression" psychologically is to speak in terms of primary and secondary process thinking. Primary process thinking is that "in which wishes derived from drives find pleasurable fulfillment in images which are at odds with the fabric of reality or fill up gaps in it" (Pruyser: 60). This kind of thinking includes the "products of dreams, poetic imagination, artistic playfulness, fabrication, and delusion" (60) as well as many religious ideas. Secondary process thinking, on the other hand, is the thinking in which "respect for the undeniable features of reality prevails over the strength of wishes" (60).

Pruyser finds that since both wishes and reality testing mechanisms are always a part of human experience, the conflict between primary and secondary process thinking rarely leads to a decisive victory of one over the other. "More often, we find perpetual compromises between the two, with ever-shifting outcomes and greater or lesser degrees of success" (60). Therefore the belief that all primary process thinking is psychotic regression (since by definition psychosis must include primary process thinking), and that all secondary process thinking is the only healthy way to live, is false. Healthy emotional maturation is not a linear experience, and neither is spiritual growth. An integral part of being truly human is our

capacity to create non-visible but meaningful realities capable of containing our potential for imaginative expansion beyond the boundaries of the senses. Without these fictive realities, human life becomes dull animal existence (Rizzuto: 47).

Rizzuto concludes that "God, psychologically speaking, is an illusory transitional object" (177). She cites Winnicot, who posits that God comes into existence in the transitional space which is the "realm of illusion in which experience is initiated" (Winnicott: 14).

This early stage in development is made possible by the mother's special capacity for making adaptation to the needs of her infant, thus allowing the infant the illusion that what the infant creates really exists. This intermediate area of experience, unchallenged in respect of its belonging to inner or external (shared) reality, constitutes the greater part of the infant's experience, and throughout life is retained in the intense experiencing that belongs to the arts and to religion and to imaginative living, and to creative and scientific work (Winnicot: 14).

Rizzuto thus sees a positive value of illusion. The theses of her book are as follows:
1. God is a special type of object representation created by the child in that psychic space where transitional objects--whether toys, blankets, or mental representations-- are provided with their powerfully real illusory lives.

Figure 1: Formation of the God representation in the transitional space (178).

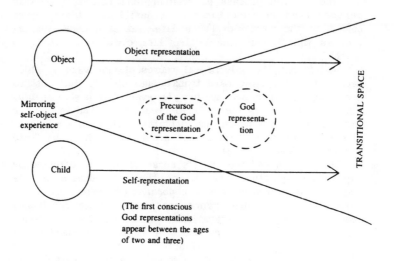

2. God, like all transitional objects (Winnicot, 1953), is located simultaneously "outside, inside, and at the border" (2). God is "not a hallucination" and "in health...does not 'go inside' nor does the feeling about it necessarily undergo repression. It is not forgotten and it is not mourned" (5).

3. God is a special transitional object because unlike teddy bears, dolls, or blankets made out of plushy fabrics, he is created from representational materials whose sources are the representations of primary objects.

4. God is also a special transitional object because he does not follow the usual course of other transitional objects. Generally, the transitional object is "gradually allowed to be decathected, so that in the course of years it becomes not so much forgotten as relegated to limbo.... It loses meaning...because the transitional phenomena have become diffused...over the whole cultural field" (5).... [Yet] instead of losing meaning, God's meaning becomes heightened by the oedipal experience and all other pregenital events that have contributed to the reelaboration of his represen-tational characteristics....[T]hroughout life God remains a transitional object at the service of gaining leverage with oneself, with others, and with life itself. This is so, not because God is God, but because, like the teddy bear, he has obtained a good half of his stuffing from the primary objects the child has "found" in his life. The other half of

God's stuffing comes from the child's capacity to "create" a God according to his needs.

5. The psychic process of creating and finding God—this personalized representational transitional object—never ceases in the course of human life. It is a developmental process that covers the entire life cycle from birth to death.

6. God is not the only mental representation used by children and adults alike as a transitional object. Many others are available. In our culture, however, God has a special place, because he is the cultural creation offered to men for their private and public (in official religions) reelaboration of those primary ties that accompany each of us "unto the grave" (Mahler: 1972).

7. The child's and the adult's sense of self is affected by the representational traits of the individual's private God.... [O]nce created, our God, dormant or active, remains a potentially available representation for the continuous process of psychic integration. As a transitional object representation, God can be used for religion because he is beyond magic.... (Rizzuto: 177-80).*

Rizzuto thus argues that it is impossible for a normal child in the Western world to complete the Oedipal cycle without having formed at least a rudimentary representation of God. During the rest of that child's development, he or she may then choose either to revise or not to revise that representation. But if "the God representation is not revised to keep pace with changes in self-representation, it soon becomes asynchronous and is experienced as ridiculous or irrelevant or, on the contrary, threatening or dangerous" (200).

Although Rizzuto focuses primarily on the image of God, I might add that a similar diagram also holds true for a conceptualization of the representation of an evil object. Hence in Figure 1 one may put *Devil* in the image-making functional role where *God* occurs. The formation of the Devil representation also occurs in the transitional space between the child and object-representation.

Satan is also a special type of object representation created by the person in that psychic space where transitional objects are provided with their powerfully real illusory lives—as well as an object who is created from representational materials whose sources are representations of primary objects.

*Ana-Maria Rizzuto, *The Birth of the Living God.* ©The University of Chicago Press, 1979. Used by permission.

Therefore in understanding a person's representation of God and Satan it is necessary not only to explore the mythical images but also understand significant relationships that influence that particular experience. Some persons relate in an intentionally harmful and maliciously exploitive way toward others. If that person is a parent or person whom the child (or older person) trusts, he or she then seeks to please that person even though they are completing an evil transaction. This affective attachment is described further in Fairbairn's paper.

II. How Negative Object Relationships Affect our Experience of God.

In the opening comments of his article "The Repression and the Return of Bad Objects," W. R. D. Fairbairn gives object relations the place he feels they deserve: "...[L]ibidinal attitudes are relatively unimportant in comparison with object relationships, and. . .the object, and not gratification, is the ultimate aim of libidinal striving" (103). This clearly lays aside the myth that psychoanalytic psychiatry is concerned only with impulse gratification, which it never was. Furthermore, Fairbairn challenges the assumption that the superego is the prime mover in requiring the ego to repress material. He believes that "what are primarily repressed are neither intolerably guilty impulses nor intolerably unpleasant memories, but intolerably bad internalized objects" (105).

On the basis of clinical evidence about sexually abused and delinquent children, Fairbairn then goes on to conclude that although internalized bad objects are present in the deeper levels of every individual's mind, whether that individual becomes delinquent, psychoneurotic, psychotic or "normal" depends on three factors:

(1) the extent to which bad objects have been installed in the unconscious and the degree of badness by which they are characterized, (2) the extent to which the ego is identified with internalized bad objects, and (3) the nature and strength of the defenses which protect the ego from these objects (108).

Fairbairn thus lays the foundations of psychopathology "in the realm of internalized bad objects, and not in the realm of internalized good objects, (i.e. the realm of the superego" (113). He illustrates his point with a case history from Freud of a young artist named Christoph Haitzmann who made a pact with the devil. In reflecting on the case, Freud concluded that there was a close association between the devil with whom the pact was signed and Christoph's father. Christoph was not completely healed until he took vows with a religious brotherhood, thus replacing his pact with the devil with a pact with God.

Fairbairn argues that Freud misses the point, however, when he incorrectly attributes Cristoph's illness to the libido theory instead of realizing that the whole point of a pact with the devil is

that it constitutes a relationship with a bad object.
[A]lthough the heuristic, no less than the historical, importance of the libido theory would be difficult to exaggerate,
a point has now been reached at which the theory has out-
worn its usefulness and, so far from providing impetus for
further study within the field of psychoanalytical thought is
actually operating as a brake upon the wheels (115).

According to Fairbairn, the ultimate aim of the libido is the
object. Thus what appear to be inhibitions against libidinal expression are in fact inhibitions against object seeking. In these circumstances, the libido is "operating in the same direction as repression. It is captivated by the repressed object, [and]...is driven into
a state of repression by the very momentum of its own object-
seeking" (116). Freud himself posited that "repressed" material
offers no resistance to treatment, but this view fails to account
for negative therapeutic reaction. Fairbairn thus sees that:

  ...[T]he actual overcoming of repression would, accordingly,
  appear to constitute a less formidable part of the analyst's
  difficult task than the overcoming of the patient's devotion
  to his repressed objects--a devotion which is all the more
  difficult to overcome because these objects are bad and he
  is afraid of their release from the unconscious" (117).

Fairbairn concludes that "it is only through the appeal of a good
object that the libido can be induced to surrender its bad objects....
[I]t may well be that a conviction of the analyst's 'love' (in the
sense of Agape and not Eros) on the part of the patient is no
unimportant factor in promoting a successful therapeutic result"
(117).

  Fairbairn suggests that the ultimate purposes of the analytic
treatment should be, first, to help the patient release repressed bad
objects from the unconscious, and second, to help dissolve the
patient's attachment to these bad objects. For both of these purposes to be fulfilled, there needs to be successful transference and
an analyst who can be the patient's good object. Yet transference
alone is not enough, and several principles of technique must also
be borne in mind:

  (1)...all situations should be interpreted, not in terms of
  gratification, but in terms of object-relationships (including, of course, relationships with internalized bad objects);
  (2)...the strivings of the libido should be represented to the
  patient as ultimately dictated by object-love and as, therefore, basically "good"; (3)...the libido should be represented
  to the patient as only becoming "bad" when it is directed
  towards bad objects ("sin" always being regarded, according
  to the Hebraic conception, as seeking after strange gods
  and, according to the Christian conception, as yielding to
  the devil); (4)...all "guilt" situations should be converted
  by interpretation into "bad object" situations; (5)...inter-
  pretations in terms of aggression should be sedulously

avoided except perhaps in the case of melancholics, who present a very special problem for analytical technique (118).

The fourth principle is, to me, one of the key ingredients in the reasoning behind, and the effectiveness of, the religious ritual of exorcism. Fairbairn has spent a lot of time earlier in the paper on "guilt as a defense against the release of bad objects" (112). The concept of guilt as a defense correlates well with my perception of one of the unique dynamics of the ritual of exorcism. After the "possessed" individual is carefully led through the universal struggle of allegiance, the plan of redemption is discussed, and the known sin confessed, then he is assessed for allegiances he has made by design or default to something or someone other than Christ as Lord. If he is not experiencing freedom in the identification with Christ as Lord, then the exorcist instructs the "possessed" person that he will deal with him not as a person (the observing ego) but with the evil spirits (the internalized bad objects that have exerted influence in his life). The evil spirits represent the allegiance which consciously or unconsciously is keeping him from cognitively and affectively experiencing personal and spiritual peace.

Thus the exorcist does not condemn the fragile ego by becoming the critical super ego and increasing the "possessed" person's repression through increasing guilt. Instead he helps his "patient" identify with a Christ that he can incorporate as a part of his ego ideal. This decreases the resistance to exposing the bad objects, and the person's ego is assured of a stronger good object to replace the bad objects. Just as positive transference, the use of special interpretation, and the therapist functioning as the good object are critical to the recovery and therapy, so the techniques that increase guilt, which can be used as a defense, are also to be avoided in exorcism.

III. Discussion of the Ritual of Exorcism in Response to Fairbairn.

Fairbairn is rather dogmatic in his belief in the importance of the internalized bad objects. To them, he traces the "origin of all psychopathological developments.... It becomes evident, accordingly, that the psychotherapist is the true successor to the exorcist. His business is not to pronounce the forgiveness of sins, but to cast out devils" (113).

I agree that internalized bad objects are one way people experience what can be conceptualized psychiatrically as a representation of devils. But I would take issue with his phrase that "the psychotherapist is the true successor to the exorcist." It is not the therapist's business to "pronounce the forgiveness of sins" (even though some patients experience therapy as if that is happening) because the therapist is not addressing directly the nature of one's allegiance to God. The crucial factor in Jesus' clinical work was his ability to differentiate between those who needed healing of diseases and those who needed demons cast out. It is not as clear to me how he healed physical diseases as how he cast out demons. When he met a person whose allegiance was to Satan, either by admission or by inability to experience Jesus, the incarnate God, as Lord, and that person desired a "change of heart," he showed his authority over the powers of "other gods" or the "presence of darkness" and cast them out by his own command.

To me, it is the lack of cognitive and affective allegiance to Jesus Christ as Lord that is sin. Moral misconduct, on the other hand, is a transgression. It was Adam and Eve's switch of allegiance that was called sin. I don't want to get into a feud over semantics of sin and transgression, but I believe good psychotherapy can help people not "transgress" against God or others better than coercive or moralizing preaching or psychotherapy, but it can *never* address the issue of *sin* in terms of allegiance to God or to the devil because it does not have that world view.

Exorcism as a religious ritual can not be categorically ruled out because psychotherapists feel they can "cast out demons" or bad objects. This is where the capacity of psychiatry ends. If a person's allegiance is to Jesus as Lord and he can experience the presence of the Holy Spirit in himself and through others, then I believe the psychotherapist is able to help remove "bad objects" and the therapist's relationship as Fairbairn describes it may be the treatment of choice. But (speaking from my faith frame of reference), if the person wills to experience Jesus as Lord and cannot because of the influences of the power of the ruler of this world (through cognitive and affective deceptions), then I as a therapist have been unsuccessful in assisting with complete emotional health until the person can be freed from other allegiances by the usual ways of repentance and conversion, or, if that is unsuccessful, by the ritual of exorcism. Otherwise, as Scott Peck describes in *The People of the Lie*, the transference is so distorted that therapy is very difficult at best, or unproductive at worst. Psychotherapy can speak to how exorcism is experienced phenomenologically by the exorcist as well as the person experiencing it, but only in the religious belief system can one explain why it is effective.

Much has been written about the trance states and various belief rituals. The importance of the ritual of exorcism is not in the presence or absence of a trance but in the capacity of the person to be able to shift allegiance to Christ as Lord and not cognitively or affectivley be bound to other allegiances. Psychiatry can remain descriptive of the process, but its theories do not allow it to be prescriptive. Each person needs to be evaluated on an individual basis as to whether the issue is one of allegiance, guilt-transgression from a spiritual standpoint, or a problem with healthy allegiance but a rupture of ego strength in which the pattern of disturbed object relations or disturbed biochemistry calls for

psychiatric help.   The most difficult situation is where pastoral
care for emotional and spiritual growth doesn't appear adequate and
psychiatric help is also needed, or where psychiatric intervention
has helped but not promoted total healing.

Appendix I

A Comment on Ego Psychology

Ego psychology, which includes object relationships, furnishes us
with a framework in which to understand different types and styles
of religious experience.   The *ego*, described functionally, is made up
of twelve different factors: reality testing, judgment, sense of
reality, regulation and control of drives, object relations, thought
processes, ARISE, defensive functions, stimulus barrier, autonomous
functioning, synthetic functions, mastery-competency.   These functions, partly because of their biological and maturational corol-
laries, have generally been understood as existing on a continuum of
immature to mature, or, in psychopathology, of psychotic to normal.
One ego function that helps us understand the dynamics of religious
experience is ARISE, Adaptive Regression in Service of the Ego.
Thus I would encourage us to lay aside the value judgment that
"maturity" with its corollary defenses is better in all situations
and simply use the continuum of ego strength as a descriptive grid.

This allows a functional dynamic clarity to the frequent
metaphors and analogies of children that Christ, St. Paul, and others
used in describing our entrance into the Kingdom, our relationship
to Christ and the Holy Spirit, and our development in Christian
maturity.

Appendix II

Reflections on Freud

Freud's superstition and how his own personal conflicts affected
his life and view of religion are addressed nicely by Meissner:
For the hardheaded agnostic and objective scientist that
Freud proposed to be, he was an uncommonly superstitious
man. The fact has not escaped observation. Jones (1955)
comments on Freud's tendency to 'unrestrained imagination,'
and Jung (1963) mentions the mystical side of himself that
Freud seemed to have to deny--an aspect that Jung himself
would hardly have overlooked. As Wittels puts it, 'In
Freud's mentality the mystical gift of the seer is con-
tinually at war with the need for mechanical description....He is afraid of his own supreme talent, and throughout
all of his life as an investigator he has been imposing a
curb on himself' (Wittels, 1931: 79-80; Meissner: 26).
In the conclusion of his chapter, "Freud's Religion" Meissner writes:
There is little doubt that Freud's religious views, which
maintained an admirable consistency from his earliest writings on the subject through the final pages of *Moses and
Monotheism*, reflected at every step deep psychological
forces and unresolved conflicts within his psychic economy.
Freud's rationalism and his agnostic disbelief were not free
from conflict and clearly rested on powerful underlying
motivations. His somewhat superstitious nature and his
mystical leanings were matters of significant difficulty for
him which he sought to deny and to overcome but clearly was
never able adequately to analyze or to resolve.

His *Todesangst* was perhaps the clearest example of this
superstitious trend, but it carried with it a strong mystical
bent and a leaning toward superstition that attracted him
first to Fliess and later to Jung and at the same time laid
the ground work in both these relationships for playing out
the deep-seated ambivalence and for the eventual development
of conflict. In both cases, it seems clear that Freud's
unresolved mystical trends were being projected and dealt
with in part in an externalized form (Meissner: 54-55).
Meissner then notes how Freud's conflict arising from his superstitious trend and mystical bent, on the one hand, and his denial of
transcendent religious reality on the other, played itself out in
relationship to his Jewishness. Unable to either embrace or reject
the religion of his fathers, he identified with Hannibal in his never
fulfilled quest to conquer Rome. Hannibal's quest provided the model
for his own unsuccessful but ever-striving endeavor to conquer
Catholicism and Christianity. Significantly, his ambivalence, inter-
acting with his Jewish identity, drew him irresistably to Moses, who
both revolted against "the religion of his fathers and created a new
religion" (55).

Indeed, Freud's struggle with these powerful conflicting themes arises "from unresolved infantile conflicts, particularly his ambivalence to his father." In addition to bearing the "guilt of his murderous Oedipal wishes...toward his father," he bore also the mark of Cain, carrying "the guilt of the survivor for his infantile murderous wishes toward the baby Julius" (55-56). Moreover, Meissner says, he carried in his mind the fusion of two other powerful figures, his mother and his old Catholic nanny, his original seductress. From these he had learned the basic Catholic beliefs and "the overpowering mysteries of heaven and hell" (56).

Hence, as Meissner claims, "Freud was never able to free himself from these deep seated entanglements and their associated conflicts and ultimately what he taught us about religion, religious experience, and faith must be taken in the context of these unconscious conflicts and the role his thinking played in his attempt to deal with them." These forces arising from Freud's inner conflicts and shaping his religious views must be taken into account when assessing Freud's "psychoanalytic approach to religion " (56).

Freud did name a "God" for himself. In his desire to have a system of belief that could correct itself--which he did not see religion being capable of--he gave himself to what he saw as the essence behind the scientific method. In his writings to Wilhelm Fliess we read:

"Education freed from the burden of religious doctrines will not, it may be, effect much change in man's psychological nature. Our God *logos* is perhaps not a very almighty one, and he may only be able to fulfill a small part of what his predecessors have promised. If we have to acknowledge this we shall accept it with resignation. We shall not on that account lose our interest in the world and in life, for we have one support which you lack. We believe that it is possible for the scientific work to gain some knowledge about the reality of the world, by means of which we can increase our power and in accordance with which we can arrange our life. If this belief is an illusion, then we are in the same position as you. But science has given us evidence by its numerous and important successes that it is not an illusion (Freud, 1927: 53-55; Meissner: 54).

He later commented, in his writings to Oskar Pfister, that:

[c]omplete objectivity requires a person who takes less pleasure in life than you do; you insist on finding something edifying in it. True, it is only in old age that one is converted to the grim heavenly pair *logos kai ananke* (reason and necessity)" (Meng and Freud, 1963: 86; Meissner: 80)....

Pfister summarizes the Freudian viewpoint in one trenchant sentence: "The God, Logos, hurls the God of religion from the throne and reigns in the realm of necessity, about whose meaning we, in the meantime, do not know the least" (Pfister, 1928: 172; Meissner: 96).

Pfister wrote prolifically on the pitfalls and the flaws of the
Freudian belief system. Meissner summarizes:
  ...Pfister totally rejects Freud's attempt to substitute natural science for religious belief. To do so, he argues, would
  be to destroy much of what is finest and noblest in human
  nature and achievement. Moreover, it would undercut and
  destroy any realistic basis for ethics and morality
  (Meissner: 98).

Thus, the man who gave us a way of thinking about representation
of God and the devil--which may be at points useful--was unsuccessful in his attempt to do away with God and religion. It is clear
that he substituted the "God" of *Logos* and *Ananke*, maintained by the
defenses of intellectualization and rationalization, for his parents'
and his nanny's belief in transcendent object and reality.

Works cited

Freud, S.   *Leonardo Da Vinci and a Memory of His Childhood.*   In
    Standard Edition 11.   Ed. James Strachey.   New York: W. W.
    Norton.
--------.   *Totem and Taboo.*   in *Standard Edition* 13.   Ed. James
    Strachey.   New York: W. W. Norton.
W. R. D. Fairbairn.   "The Repression and the Return of Bad Objects
    (with Special Reference to the 'War Neuroses')."   *Essential
    Papers on Object Relations.*   Ed. Peter Buckley, M.D.   New York:
    New York University Press, 1986.   102-126.
Mahler, M.   "On the First Three Subphases of the Separation-
    Individuation Process."   *International Journal of Psycho-Analysis*
    53: 133.
Meissner, W. W., S. J., M.D.   *Psychoanalysis and Religious Experience.*
    New Haven: Yale University Press, 1984.
Pruyser, P.   *A Dynamic Psychology of Religion.*   New York: Harper
    and Row, 1968.
Rizzuto, Ana-Maria, M.D.   *The Birth of the Living God.*   Chicago:
    University of Chicago Press, 1979.
Winnicott, D. W.   "Transitional Objects and Transitional Phenomena."
    International Journal of Psycho-Analysis 26: 137-43.

Selected Bibliography

Bellak, Leopold, M.D., Marvin Hurvich, and Helen K. Gediman.   *Ego
    Functions in Schizophrenics, Neurotics, and Normals.*   New York:
    John Wiley and Sons, 1973.
Horner, Althea J.   *Object Relations and the Developing Ego in
    Therapy.*   New York: Jason Aronson, Inc., 1984.
Kernberg, Otto, M.D.   *Object Relations Theory and Clinical
    Psychoanalysis.*   New York: Jason Aronson, Inc., 1984.
Mackey, Richard A.   *Ego Psychology and Clinical Practice.*   New York:
    Gardner Press, Inc., 1985.

PSYCHIATRY/PSYCHOLOGY: A RESPONSE

Ruth Detweiler Lesher

The biases I brought to my preparation for this consultation on bondage and exorcism are at least two: 1) from a clinical perspective, the tendency to fit mental health problems into the existing categories acknowledged by the DSM III-R (1987) manual and accepted by a majority of clinicians, and 2) not having taken very seriously angels or demons as part of my spiritual life, theology, or cosmology.

It seems to me that a psychological/psychiatric study of exorcism might include at least these components: 1) a review of how paradigm shifts and worldview affect explanations of events, 2) an examination of the nature and cause of suffering and evil, and 3) an overview of the development of psychopathology, its diagnosis and treatment. I will try to include both clinical and faith implications because my desire to be faithful affects both my clinical work and how I make sense of the world.

I. Paradigm Shift

The most radical shift in my belief since preparing for this consultation has been the emerging acknowledgement of the existence of angels and demons as spirits. This happened by finding myself singing songs about protecting angels to my six month old son, Benjamin, almost unawares. It also, of course, came from the discovery that angels and demons are treated as existing phenomenon in Scripture and in other cultures. I tried to include in my readings some study of angels as well as demons and found that at some points in history there was little distinction between the two. Perhaps angelology should be given as much or more attention than demonology in our consultation.

But, before taking the topic of demon possession seriously, I need to contemplate the nature of the reality of angels and demons. That has literal cosmic implications for me. I am a Westerner and had relegated angels and demons to medieval mythical constructs like gnomes and fairies which are no longer used to explain events. My view of reality was two tiered. As Paul Hiebert said:

As a scientist I have been trained to deal with the empirical world in naturalistic terms. As a theologian, I was taught to answer ultimate questions in theistic terms...I had excluded the middle level of supernatural but this-worldly beings and forces from my own world view" (Hiebert, 1982:43).

People tend to use the ordinary immediate experiences and observations of their lives to explain both the natural world of objects and the social biological world of living things. This would be considered the imminent and natural level.

At another level ("the middle") are beings (animate) and forces
(inanimate) that cannot be directly perceived but are thought to
exist on this earth, e.g. gods, ghosts, angels, demons. This category
also includes astrological forces, magical rites, evil eye and
witchcraft. The phenomena of both this "middle level" and the third
tier are supernatural (i.e., beyond immediate sense experience).
Because they are beyond natural explanation, the events are based on
inference from what can be perceived or from supernatural experience.
    The *third tier* is the transcendent world or worlds (heaven and
hell) beyond this one. It may also include transcendent time
(eternity). For example, the Jewish concept of Jehovah was one of
transcendence and thus contrasted to the gods of the Canaanites who
were deities of this world, of the middle zone. Jehovah entered the
affairs of this earth but abode above it (Hiebert, 1982).

Historical Perspective

    Before psychiatry and psychology existed as disciplines cultures
seemed to acknowledge that certain illnesses were the result of natural occurrences and others the result of supernatural causes. The
Hebrews made a distinction between the diseases and misfortunes
caused by possession by evil, and those caused by sin or the natural
environment. According to Isaacs (1987) and the Swartley/Finger
study (1987), the Hebrews did conceive of spirit possession, or of an
illness that had a spiritual origin" (1 Sam 16:16). "The later
Hebrews also could conceive of the spiritual being, Satan, as bringing about misfortune and illness. But illness, misfortune, and—
especially important here—mental illness could also have a mundane
origin" (Isaacs, 1987:265). For example, they recognized "madnessess
due to drunkenness (Jer 25:16) as well as [those] due to unforgiveness and hatred (Hos 9:7). Despair and misfortune also cause
insanity (Deut 8:34)" (Isaacs, 1987).
    Both the Egyptians and the Greeks conceived of certain illnesses
as the result of natural occurrences and others as a form of possession. In these ancient cultures and in many other cultures currently, people distinguish between possession by gods or spirits and
other forms of illness. If the modern contention that demon possession was attributed to all mental illness because of no other
explanation was ever true, it must have been later, perhaps in the
14th-16th centuries.
    Much like Peter Berger's discussion of the rediscovery of the
"supernatural" so are we rediscovering the messengers of this God
"signalling his transcendence as well as his presence in the world
of humanity...angels signal God's concern for this world both in
judgment and in redemption," (Berger, 1979). Angels, then, might be
thought of as God's signals in reality. Billy Graham's book, *Angels*,
is full of accounts of these signals of the transcendent God making
himself known in our earthly midst but in an unseen way by others
(nonempirical).

The rationalism, materialism, and empiricism of the sciences has been challenged over the last few decades by Michael Polanyi, Thomas Kuhn and many others. Joseph Chilton Pearce wrote about *The Crack in the Cosmic Egg*. So often, if we turn to the field of physics, we find more insights than we expected ahead of our current world view, discoveries more compatible with phenomenon like demons, angels, or spirits. Even Gregory Bateson has now written a book with his daughter called *Angels Fear*, which is essentially about the middle zone. The secular world and the scientific world (or parts of it) are more open to the "supernatural" or nonmaterialism than some Christians at a philosophical level. In the social sciences there are many references to the spiritual, the meta, the trans, and the pretrans.

So from a philosophy of science or world view perspective, addressing the topic of demon possession may primarily be an issue of one's cosmology which may not quickly or consistently change. That is, some people may be working with demons but not have considered very carefully how they deal with angels in their lives. Or, they may consider all the evil in their lives to be an external spirit-like force rather than just some aspects of evil (i.e. they see the devil in every reference to spirit or force and begin to fear or feel helpless in relation to evil).

The change in my cosmology is to be open not to the "possibility of transcendence" but to the reality of transcendence breaking into my everyday reality without seeing it--the middle zone, the angels and demons and the unseen war of the spiritual world.

II. Theology of Evil

In addition to examining one's cosmology or world view, the questions of bondage and exorcism need to be seen in the context of the larger issue of the Christian response to suffering. A theology of suffering is a subset of a theology of evil. Acknowledgement of the existence of angels and demons may shed an interesting light on the theology of suffering or evil, particularly with the questions, 'Why did God allow this to happen to me?" (God's omnipotence) or "How do we pray for protection and understand it if we are not protected?"

I believe that a theology of evil deserves consideration along with a theology of suffering in order to address adequately the topic of bondage and exorcism. Exorcism and bondage seem to be pieces of the larger questions of why and how evil came to exist in the world, why there is suffering in general, and how Christians should respond to evil and suffering on both the individual and corporate level. Again, angels need to be as much a part of a theology of evil and suffering as demons. In fact, the consideration of angels and demons may have some interesting implications for our pacifist positions and theological responses to the demonic in social evil. As Mennonites we seem to have worked more at responses to sociopolitical evil than to personal evil. In these discussions, however, our cosmology didn't seem to be as threatened as it is in this discussion on exorcism and deliverance.

Further clarification of the differences between evil and the demonic is needed. Is the demonic supernatural power, a force, the absence of good, something more or different than sin? Does it have form to it, even though unseen? Is it a being that may not always be perceivable? How does one distinguish between the evils of materialism, war, and political oppression and the demonic? Wouldn't the same cosmology allow for belief in demonic possession and protective angels? If this holds on an individual level, can one grow in the confrontation of the demonic corporately or socially and increase prophetic/intercessory praying for peace? Increased confidence in relying on God for protection might follow from belief in the possibility of angels, be that for personal safety, or from the snares of wealth, fame, or war.

Are there some significant ways in which our theological response to corporate evil can be applied also to individual demonic evil? Should there be some consistency in one's theology of suffering and evil on a corporate and individual level? Mennonites have been known for refusing to use violence to alleviate oppression. I believe that prophetic ministry to sociopolitical structures is as much as or more important as deliverance is to individuals. The larger question to me is: as we now stand between the breaking in of God's presence in the resurrection and the fullness of God's kingdom here on earth, how should we as Christians confront evil or respond to suffering, be that individual or corporate? Are we to be doing more than waiting together through the long afternoon in solidarity? And I don't mean to minimize that. Or do we shoot Hitler to bring an end to destruction? Could it be that our role in releasing individuals and groups from oppression needs to be equally nonviolent and without force? In prayer and solidarity? The power is of the Holy Spirit and in Jesus name.

III. An Overview of the Development of Psychopathology, Its Diagnosis, and Treatment

Gerald Kauffman has given the bulk of his attention to a theory of the development of psychopathology that I believe he feels could help to explain the development of someone who is demon possessed. I will come back to that a little later. First, I'd like to deal with the easiest matter to discuss, the diagnostic issue. One of the main questions to me as a clinician coming to the study of bondage and exorcism has to do with whether one can identify a distinct symptom cluster to distinguish demon possession from other forms of mental illness. This is not an easy task and many papers have attempted to do this at various levels of success (Bach, 1979; Sall, 1976 and 1979; Virkler, 1977).

The following problems with attempting to do this should be noted:

1. There are no consistent symptoms or behaviors in a demon possessed person in Scripture. Demons were cast out of persons with what we would currently consider physical symptomatology as well as from persons whose symptoms would correspond with psychiatric diagnoses.

2. The behavior of the demon needs to be distinguished from the possessed person in the Gospel accounts.

3. There is significant overlap among existing psychiatric diagnoses.

4. For many of the symptoms associated with demon possession, there is another psychiatric diagnosis or two with the same symptoms.

5. Some people claim all illness is demonic; others claim all *mental* illness is demonic. Some claim that the Bible distinguishes between natural and supernatural causes of disease.

6. There is a need to distinguish voluntary possession from involuntary possession.

7. Psychiatric problems coexistence with demon possession.

To my pleasant surprise, a week before this consultation, the librarian at Philhaven sent me an article in which T. Craig Isaacs (1987) summarized some research done as part of his doctoral dissertation which looked at the question of whether possession is a phenomenon independent of the current commonly accepted psychodiagnostic categories. The research done by Isaacs (1987) indicates that it is.

Let me briefly describe the parameters of his study. The criteria for possession were: persons believed by experienced and competent exorcists to be possessed and whose symptoms were alleviated by an exorcism. Exorcists were chosen who gave equal validity to physical and psychological disorders as to possession. Exorcists who viewed all nonphysical disorders as works of demons or the devil were screened out. (Two Episcopal priests and two Episcopal lay persons provided the fourteen cases for this study.) Psychodiagnosticians (four psychologists, one psychiatrist) were asked to assess the applicability of the current DSM III categories and then later to assess the applicability of a newly created diagnostic description.

I think the question Isaacs addresses in his research is *the question* from a clinical perspective, that is: *Are there symptoms demonstrated in demonic possession that are independent of any current forms of psychopathology?* My first thoughts on how to clinically approach the questions of this consultation were to consider the diagnoses of patients that came closest to descriptions of demon possession and then study them more closely for symptom differences. I knew immediately which categories of the DSM III-R came closest to my understanding of demon possession. They are Borderline and Multiple Personality Disorders. One reason for this comes from my own experience in working with someone who I considered and treated as having a Borderline Personality Disorder, but who also was exorcised twice of forty some demons.

Let me briefly review the clinical descriptions and symptoms which are considered in diagnosing Borderline and Multiple Personality Disorders and related diagnoses. Although some authors have written about the similarities and differences between diagnoses such as schizophrenia, manic depression, and demon possession, I find these diagnoses to be easier to distinguish from demon possession because of less overlapping symptoms as well as less intuitive or countertransference questions, and because of their response to medications.

CLINICAL DESCRIPTIONS (DSM-III-Revised, 1987)

Borderline Personality Disorder (at least five of the following)
1.   a pattern of unstable and intense interpersonal relationships characterized by alternating between extremes of overidealization and devaluation.
2.   impulsiveness in at least two areas that are potentially self-damaging, e.g. spending, sex, substance use, shoplifting, reckless driving, binge eating (do not include suicidal or self-mutilating behavior covered in (5)).
3.   affective instability: marked shifts from baseline mood to depression, irritability, or anxiety, usually lasting a few hours and only rarely more than a few days.
4.   inappropriate, intense anger or lack of control of anger, e.g. frequent displays of temper, constant anger, recurrent physical fights.
5.   recurrent suicidal threats, gestures or behavior, or self-mutilating behavior.
6.   marked and persistent identity disturbance manifested by uncertainty about at least two of the following: self-image, sexual orientation, long term goals or career choice, type of friends desired, preferred values.
7.   chronic feelings of emptiness or boredom.
8.   frantic efforts to avoid real or imagined abandonment (do not include suicidal or self-mutilating behavior covered in (5))

Dissociative Disorders
The essential feature of all these disorders is disturbance in integrative (ego) functions of identity, memory, and consciousness. The disturbance may be sudden, gradual, transient or chronic. If it occurs primarily in identity, the person's customary identity is temporarily forgotten, and a new identity may be assumed or imposed (as in multiple personality disorder), or the customary feeling of one's own reality is lost and is replaced by a feeling of unreality (as in depersonality disorder). If the disturbance occurs primarily in memory, important personal events cannot be recalled (as in psychogenic amnesia and psychogenic fuge).

Multiple Personality Disorder
a.   The existence within the person of two or more distinct personalities or personality states (each with its own pattern of per-
ceiving, relating to, and thinking about the environment and self).
b.   At least two of these personalities are personality states which
recurrently take full control of the person's behavior.

Kenny (1981) analyzed the similarities of possession and multiple
personalities and according to Isaacs (1987) came to the conclusion
that the essential difference between the two was a culture specific
bias. That is, those cultures that believe in a spirit world will
understand the phenomenon as due to possession while those cultures
that do not observe such a belief may turn to the more rational
explanation encompassed by the theory of multiple personality. This,
then is further evidence to me that the issue of world view is crucial to the question at hand.

Let's return now to Isaacs' (1987) research. Isaacs found seven
features held in common by all fourteen of the cases he studied:
1.   The experience of being controlled by someone, or something,
other than one's self, with a subsequent loss of self control in one
of four areas: thinking, anger or profanity, impulsivity, or physical
functioning. (These may seem to take the form of delusions which
characterize psychotic states, yet the thinking is not truly
delusional since the person does not accept these as his or her own
beliefs, but experiences these thoughts as those of the controlling
identity.)
2.   A sense of self which fluctuates between periods of emptiness and periods of inflation, though one period may predominate.
This fluctuation is not due to external circumstances but corresponds to whether the person is feeling in control of him or herself or is feeling out of control.
3.   The person experiences visions of dark figures or appari-
tions and or the person hears coherent voices which have a real, and
not a dreamlike quality. (These differ from the hallucinations of
the schizophrenic in that these voices and visions are experienced
as completely alien and separate from him or herself, without a
dreamlike quality. The person can maintain contact with reality.)
4.   Trances, or the presence of more than one personality. If
more than one personality, these are only observed during a trance
or if present in normal consciousness, the person is able to maintain
an independent sense of reality respective to the other personality.
Also there may be variations in voice or in the ability to speak or
understand a previously unknown language. (According to Isaacs,
this differs from multiple personality disorder in that either the
other personality is only present when the person is in a trance
state or the person does not lose his or her own sense of reality
and have it replaced by the other personality's sense of reality. In
a multiple disorder only one sense of reality is present in any

moment of time, while in the possessive state many senses of reality may be present.)

    5. Revulsive religious reactions, such as extreme negative reactions to prayer, or to religious objects. The inability to articulate the name of Jesus, or the destruction of religious objects (even when the person desires to have someone pray for him or her).

    6. Some form of paranormal phenomena such as Poltergeist-type phenomena, telepathy, levitation or strength out of proportion to age or situation.

    7. There is an impact on others: paranormal phenomena, stench, coldness from the feeling of an alien presence or a feeling that the patient has lost a human quality, is experienced by someone other than the patient.

    Isaacs concludes that the diagnostic criteria for the "Possessive States Disorder" must include symptoms 1, 2 and at least one of 3, 4, 5, 6 and 7. The criteria that are seemingly unique to the possessive state are features 5, 6 and 7. The symptoms of 1-4 may be found in many other disorders, but the pattern in which these features occur is what Isaacs feels makes possession unique.

    If one were to seek an explanation for the development of the phenomenon of demon possession without appealing to evil spirits--in other words, a more acceptable one in our Western psychological and psychiatric community--I would utilize the one that Dr. Kauffman has shared with us. It is a model of ego or personality development that I appreciate and use frequently. It is the most helpful theory I know of for understanding the development of borderline and multiple personality disorders which I see as closely related to each other. If I were not allowed to use or did not know of the demonic possession option I would use these diagnostic categories: Multiple Personality Disorder or Borderline Personality Disorder. In fact, I would use this conceptual model and related treatment approach with some persons who may also be possessed.

    Freud developed his theories about mental illness with the intent of making the treatment of emotional problems a much more scientific, almost biological, enterprise. Object relations theory continued with theory development and "scientific explanations" but no longer felt the need to make the treatment of mental disorders a biological (instinctual) endeavor. Object relations theory is a series of inferences about how an infant's experience in the world, particularly of his or her caretakers (objects), interacts with his or her own development to form his or her personality.

    What Dr. Kauffman has described is how trauma, withdrawal or smothering of a child at different stages in life can dramatically influence the child's view of him or herself and the world. More specifically, but very briefly, the origins of borderline and multiple disorders is purported to lie approximately in the 15 to 22 months stage of development when the child is moving toward separating from mother or father and toward autonomy and independence. Death, withdrawal, or clinging by the caretakers at this point may result in the child's internalizing a split experience of withdrawal from the parents for individuating and also feeling reward from the clinging parents for not separating. The withdrawal experience of the parent is internalized affectively as abandonment and depression; the clinging experience is internalized as a wish for reunion or fusion with the parent. In addition, the rewarding experience of the parent is considered the good parent-part and gets connected with a good self-part and good feelings. And the same process develops from the withdrawal: a bad-parent part representation connects with a bad self-part representation a chronic angry feelings. The person later acts this out by withdrawing from others when it is feared that he or she may be abandoned by them. To get rewarded for not becoming a person and smothered for remaining a non-individuated person is terrible and confusing.

The interpsychic development of the infant is thwarted and results in problems with ego development. The psyche itself develops a particular way of protecting and defending itself. The interpersonal style of borderline's and multiple personality disorders is recognized by clinging dependence alternating with distancing as they view others and their therapists as either all good or all bad. Masterson (1976) describes six basic strategies to be characteristic of borderline's attempts to defend against abandonment depression: homicidal rage, suicidal depression, panic, hopelessness and helplessness, emptiness and void, and guilt. All these traits are also typical aspects of multiple personality symptomatology.

One final clinical postscript is not directly related to much else that has been said. I have always found it most ironic that those patients, often middle aged, who carry the most concern about having grieved the Holy Spirit or about some failure in their spiritual life, report excessive guilt feelings, frequently confessing sin, and are suicidal or even homicidal, but hesitate to acknowledge it because of their religious convictions and tremendous sense of condemnation--these are the very patients that are most likely and very frequently responsive to shock treatments (ECT). This most inorganic/mechanistic, yet not understood, treatment radically alters these person's views about themselves, and their faith, and relationship with God. One thing this illustrates is that what the patient says, or what may appear on the surface as the expression of the persons problems, may be far from the etiology of that problem.

In conclusion then: (1) As a clinician, I am faced with a dilemma of discovering that my theology of evil and my world view, and the way I function as a psychologist would tend to try to fit demon possession into a multiple or borderline personality disorder diagnostic label. However, as I reflect further, my spiritual practices (i.e. prayer and the belief system associated with spiritual disciplines, etc.) leave more room for a middle zone in my cosmology. The intuitive feelings I have as a clinician when around a person who I believe may have been demon possessed along with a Borderline Personality Disorder (as described in Isaacs' study), nudge me in the

172 Lesher

direction of choosing to expand my beliefs and give more intellectual credence to the middle zone (i.e. the world of spirits that do
enter our reality). I believe that this change in my world view will
have a greater impact on my theology than my clinical practice. The
number of demon-possessed patients I encounter is very small, but
may increase as more attention is given to this middle zone in our
culture.

I would like then, to call ourselves and the church, to give
greater attention to spiritual development and a theology more consistent with the spiritual reality of angels and demons, both good
and bad spirits, that enter invisibly into our material or empirical
world. Not only do I think this needs to be incorporated into our
theology of evil and suffering but also into our worship as has been
called for in some of the other excellent papers (i.e., in our bap-
tisms, in the eucharist). With regard to who should exorcise demons,
I think both prophets and exorcists need to be deeply rooted in a
spiritual community. And I think psychologists or psychiatrists
should participate in the discernment of demon possession because I
think it is rare (but increasing) and most likely when it does exist,
there are other coexisting psychiatric problems that also need to be
addressed. I also think the follow-up community is as important as
the deliverance rite itself and should be a prerequisite for exorcism. I have a lot of thoughts about how a demon possessed person
should be treated from a therapeutic perspective, but that will have
to be for another time.

References

Bach, P. J. Demon possession and psychopathology: A theological
relationship. *Journal of Psychology and Theology*, 7 (1979), 22-
26.
Bateson, G., and M. C. Bateson. *Angels fear: Towards an epistemology
of the sacred.* New York: MacMillan, 1987.
Benner, D. G. and B. Joscelyne. "Multiple personality as a borderline
disorder." *The Journal of Nervous and Mental Disease*, 172
(1984), 98-104.
Berger, P. *A Rumor of Angels.* Garden City, NJ: Anchor Books, 1969.
*Diagnostic and Statistical Manual of Mental Disorders - Third Edi-
tion, Revised* Washington, D.C.: American Psychiatric Associa-
tion, 1987.
Graham, B. *Angels.* Garden City, NY: Doubleday, 1975.
Hiebert, P. G. The Flaw of the Excluded Middle." *Missiology*, 10
(1982), 35-47.
Isaacs, T. C. "The Possessive States Disorder: The Diagnosis of
Demonic Possession." *Pastoral Psychology*, 35 (1987), 263-273.
Kenny, M. G. "Multiple Personality and Spirit Possession,"
Psychiatry, 44 (1981), 227-358.
Meigs, J. T. "Pastoral Care Methods and Demonology in Selected Writ-
ings." *Journal of Psychology and Theology*, 5 (1977), 234-246.

Pearce, J. C.   *The Crack in the Cosmic Egg: Challenging Constructs of Mind and Reality.* New York: Pocket Books.

Sall, M. J.   "Demon Possession or Psychopathology?: A Clinical Differentiation." *Journal of Psychology and Theology,* 4 (1976), 286-290.

Sall, M. J.   "A Response to 'Demon Possession and Psychopathology: A Theological Relationship." *Journal of Psychology and Theology,* 7 (1979), 27-30.

Virkler, H. A. and M. B. Virkler.   "Demonic Involvement in Human Life and Illness." *Journal of Psychology and Theology,* 5 (1977), 95-102.

Masterson, J. F.   *Psychotherapy of the Borderline Adult: A Developmental Approach.* New York: Brunner/Mazel, 1976.

JANE MILLER'S STORY AND TESTIMONY
(as told at the Conference)

Today I would like to just tell you a thumbnail sketch of how I came to the way of life that I now have. I was raised a Baptist and I guess I took my religion nominally like most Sunday Christians do. I then had a catastrophe in my life; I had six children and I lost touch with reality completely. There is a long story leading up to that point, but for now I'll just say that the diagnosis when I was taken to the psychiatrist was postpartum neurosis.

The following week the psychiatrist changed the diagnosis to total schizophrenia, and then I was hospitalized. I had shock treatments. I had psychotherapy every day and after a period of three months of treatment in the hospital I was released for a short period of time. But my touch with reality didn't last; I lost touch once again.

This time, because our financial resources were used up, I was taken to Tulane University School of Psychiatry and was taken on as a teaching case. I spent another year and a half there. I experienced drug therapy but no more shock treatments because I had all that one could have. I had therapy every day in the beginning. When I began to get a little better I had therapy about only three times a week. By sheer desire to be free I would crawl up to the edge and be led me up to a realm of almost light; then I would slide right back down to the pit again, and this happened over and over again. The psychiatrist would change the medication and then I would be better for a few days or a few weeks, but then again I would lose touch completely.

I was very very highly motivated because I had six children and a husband that I loved very much. I wanted so desperately to be free. One day the psychiatrist said to my husband, "Mr. Miller your wife is going to be committed to an institution for permanent care because there is not anything that we can do. My suggestion to you is that you put your children in foster homes or remarry or whatever you can do, but don't look back, because Jane will never be normal." At that juncture my husband was not able to turn me loose. He could not face the fact of living without me forever. As crazy as I was he said, "I'm going to hang on as long as I can watch her."

At that time I weighed 88 pounds, I hadn't eaten a meal in three months, not anything solid because my throat would not swallow it. I didn't sleep at all; I ran, I ran and ran and ran. He had me on a kind of track where I would run and I'd fall on the ground and as soon as I'd get my breath I'd run again for miles and miles; I was on 150 milligrams of Thorazine four times a day and Stelazine on top of that, Phenobarbital on top of that and I still could not lie down.

Here I must interject this. The same day that the psychiatrist told my husband that, and I was not appraised of that at all, that same day I had an experience with God—and I want to point out that regardless of how crazy I was externally, there were/are three parts

174

to me: I'm spirit, I'm soul and I'm body. Before I was born again
my spirit was dead.   But when Jesus Christ came and I was born
again, he made my spirit alive. He quickened it, made it alive and
the relationship that I had within was in the spirit and I communed
with Jesus Christ as Lord in the Spirit. But my soul was possessed
of devils and my body responded likewise.   I just say that for
clarification, because at the moment that I knelt at the foot of my
bed and prayed, capitulating all and everything to God, my Father,
relinquishing every right and hope, indeed relinquishing everything
to him in total abandonment, *in 48 hours I was healed.*

It happened like this. A woman who had been in the neighborhood
and heard about my illness had asked her pastor, Sam Fife, to begin
to pray for me. They had been praying for a couple of weeks and
they had been seeking the Lord as for what kind of relationship they
might have with me, if there was anything God would lead them to do
to help. Fife was a former Baptist minister who had received the
baptism of the Holy Spirit and had begun to see in scripture healing
and deliverance truths. On this particular Wednesday, the day after
I had prayed like that, the woman came and knocked on my door and
said, "I want to tell you that Jesus loves you and he doesn't want
you to be sick like this." Then she said, "Let me introduce you to my
pastor."

The pastor came and spoke with my husband and he said to him,
"Let me read to you Mark, the fifth chapter, since you are a Baptist
deacon I know that you must believe that the Bible is the word of
God." Dick said, "Yes, I do." He read to him Mark 5 and when he
finished my husband said, "My God, that's my Jane." I wept this
morning at the story we heard[1] because it has a lot of meaning for
me because I experienced many of the same things. I don't think the
story came from a thin imagination.   That writer must have known
something of what it was like. At any rate, he said, "Mr. Miller, I'm
a believer" and he turned to Mark 16:17 and said, "as such I have the
power in Jesus to cast these spirits out of your wife, these devils
out of your wife, and she will be whole. Do you want me to do it?"
And Dick said, "Absolutely." Then he said, "I don't choose to do this
alone; I like to have my church group with me; it will take them a
little while to get here; and I'll go aside and pray and contact
them."

So late in the night they came back and as they came into my
bedroom I remembered the single cry in my spirit saying "Oh God,
help me; let this be real," and yet my mouth shouted out, "Get out of
my house, I don't want you in here, you have no place here," and many
other things to dissuade them. I was amazed as I watched them; they
didn't respond at all to anything that I said. It was almost as if
they could hear my spirit. They just filed right on in, came and
knelt around my bed and lifted their hands. They spoke in a language that I had never heard. I didn't know there were such things
as speaking in tongues. I didn't know what they were saying, but I
was so impressed that they were holy. Everything in me said these

people are holy and I remember crying out inside. I said, "God, don't let me be a party to a farce, but let it be real. God, let this be real." He began by putting his hand on my head; it began to burn like crazy. Yet there was that difference in myself, because the voice was screaming, "It's burning, burning," but the spirit within me didn't sense a burning.

It was almost like it was theatrics. I felt like theatrics was taking place because within me I felt just this cry to God. This continued for some four and a half hours with him commanding spirits to name themselves and to come out (there is a tape of that and I won't go into a lot of detail about it); the spirits spoke to him, he spoke to them back. Then at a certain time he seemed to know when he was finished, though he had never spoken to me during the entire session. He spoke to demons and spirits. His challenge was only to them. When he cast one out there would be a retching like and it seemed like something was departing, but I didn't view it that way. I was still crying out, "God, let this be real."

When he was finished he said, "Jane." He called me, and it was like I'd come from a long way. I just came up to meet him, sat up and when I looked around I realized that all the hell of all these years was gone. The burning brick in my middle was gone. The anguish that I'd experienced and the ripping and tearing that I didn't tell you about, was gone and I was absolutely at peace. It was as if my prayer had been completely answered. Now instead of having a soul and a body that was out of control, it seemed as if the spirit, my very real being, was in complete control and I was one person again. I looked up at my husband and smiled. He cried, because the film that had been over my eyes for two years was gone, and he could see Jane for the first time in years. I sat up and looked around. Everyone was rejoicing, worshiping and praising. Brother Sam said to me, "You need to get some sleep." I lay down while all the people had coffee and talked about what happened after a deliverance. They were all in the kitchen while I was in my bedroom sleeping the sleep of an undisturbed child.

When I awakened in the morning I got up and fixed myself a big breakfast. I ate it all and swallowed it with no difficulty. And I want to tell you something. Nobody had to tell me how to pray. My hands could go up and I could shout, "hallelujah, praise God Almighty," with all the fervor that the people the night before had used. It seemed so natural to me because I was so free and so thankful. I went outside and the light of the sun was so bright; I could feel the breeze on my face and I could see the blue sky and the green leaves of the trees. I hadn't realized how dull and drab everything had been until it was all clear and I was seeing and feeling reality again. I loved my children and drew them to me.

It wasn't very long until Brother Sam came in and he said to me, "These spirits are going to try to come back. It's very urgent that you understand how to be filled with truth, because when the house is swept and garnished he takes seven other spirits more able then himself and he returns to the place from which he has come. So its urgent that you be filled with truth." He began to teach me from the Scriptures. He said, "Jane, you roll out of bed in the morning praising God with all your being. Do not allow any thoughts in your mind. Do not allow any feelings to come. But just give thanks unto God and praise unto God. Get on your knees and pray. If you don't know what to say, then say *Jesus.* If you say it a thousand times, that's not too much. Pray and read your Bible and let God minister to you from the Scripture." I did all these things with all my heart, but I was not able to keep them out indefinitely; but I did last five days. That was pretty good.

On Thanksgiving day Sam had to come back. It just took about an hour and a half that time to cast the spirits out. He had to do this three more times, five times all together, over a period of a month. Immediately after the deliverance during this month that I was being dealt with, my son was in the hospital with a fractured skull. This made it a very difficult time. It was almost as if Satan was determined that I was not going to be able to hold on to my deliverance. But at the end of that month I received the baptism of the Holy Spirit and was strengthened with might and power through that experience. From that time forward I was empowered and able to ward the spirits off myself.

The next few years I spent just learning and knowing how to anticipate various different types of things. I think this is very important for us to understand that Satan attacks in various ways. When I stood strong in my mind--and it took a little while until the insanity that was there was really put under foot, he began to attack my body and I had various physical ailments. I vomited up huge blood clots at one time. At another juncture I was paralyzed from my waist down. I had numerous different physical manifestations, and in my spirit I knew those things were demons spirits. I knew also that I could overcome them with the same fervor that I had overcome the insanity. I think that part is important to say because sometimes there is a question about how much power Satan has over the physical. I tell you he can make any kind of manifestation; but the power of Jesus Christ can heal that very manifestation.

Since that time I have given my life to walk before the Lord with all my heart. I never desired to have a ministry, but in seeking to walk before the Lord with all my heart there has been a ministry that has come forth to share and to pray for others and to minister deliverance to others, and to just minister the word of God. I've never been to school; I have no formal education. But I've been schooled in God's word as the Holy Spirit has drawn me to see and to understand his truth. Hallelujah! I'm very thankful for the privilege of ministering to others, because as their need draws God's movement from me it strengthens me.

It will be 27 years this November since my deliverance. When I went in for the evaluation after my deliverance, Dr. Epstein who was the head of the board of psychiatry at Tulane University, said to me,

"Jane, I do not believe in the Jesus that you talk about, but I cannot deny what I see with my eyes. You do not need us now. But when you do we will be here." I said, "Dr. Epstein, how long would I have to stay within normal limits for you to believe that I had a true miracle that's lasting." He said, "Schizophrenics do some really strange things. I would say from three to five years would convince me that your experience was what you say it is." It was eight years later, I think, that I was in New Orleans and went and shook his hand and said, "Do you remember me?" and he said "Oh, yes, I remember you." I'm not sure exactly what he meant, but he didn't forget me!

I had a good time with those psychiatrists, I'll tell you. Some of the things that those spirits pulled were just terrible. I had 22 doctors that I was a teaching case for; they were in their resident year. Every one of them had different personalities. They all looked different and so I responded differently to everyone of them. They would get together and check their notes, but nothing fit because the response in me made a difference whether they were tall, dark and handsome or whether they were short and bald. Now realizing some of the ways that the spirits worked, I see it wasn't fair to them. Spirits don't do anything according to the book; they just play the game. Some of the things that I now hear people have done and said, I remember and recognize in my own experience. You can't put too much stock in what you are getting out of a demon possessed person.

I want to say to you how much I appreciate the privilege of being here and sharing with you and being able to cross the line. To be here with you is such a privilege. I want you to know how much I appreciate it and I hope my story and my life experience will be some help as you seek to understand these things which we all seek to understand better.

Note

1. The story read by James Waltner for the morning devotional was "The Gadarene Set Free," pp. 87-89 in *To Walk in the Way* by Urie A. Bender (Herald Press, 1979).

THE CASE OF JANE:
PSYCHOTHERAPY AND DELIVERANCE

Mervin R. Smucker and John A. Hostetler

In the early 1960s, Jane, a woman plagued by a long history of severe emotional disturbance, was suddenly and dramatically cured of her mental illness through the technique of demon deliverance. Today, over 25 years later, Jane is a living testimony to the effectiveness of her cure. She is a devoted lay minister in the Christian group which was founded around the time of her deliverance. (Although this group has no official name or title, it is commonly referred to by members themselves as the "Body" or the "Body of Christ.") Jane continues to share her story and experiences, using them to teach and witness. Several of the actual deliverance sessions are available on tape cassette, and can be purchased from her Christian group by anyone who wishes to use it as a tool for spiritual growth. Thus Jane's experience is unusually well-documented, and has reached many people who were not present at the time. Jane's experience occurred following a period of hospitalization at Tulane University where she was being seen by a psychologist/clergyman.

The information presented in this paper was gleaned from a number of different sources, including interviews with both Jane and her former therapist, Dr. David Reed. The Reverend Sam Fife, who conducted the deliverance sessions, is no longer living. (He died in a plane crash in South America during one of his ministry travels in 1979.) However, as previously mentioned, several of the sessions are on tape, and Fife's teachings and sermons are available on tape or in transcriptions from the Body of Christ group, of which he was the founder. These personal contacts, as well as the availability of information about both the therapy and the deliverance sessions, have provided us with a unique opportunity to explore the effects of therapy and demon exorcism on the same individual.

In this paper we propose to give a brief summary of Jane's life history, including personal information relevant to her various psychiatric diagnoses and treatments. Then we will examine in greater detail the deliverance sessions and Jane's response to them. The scope of our paper does not allow for a full-scale analysis of the case. Rather, our primary purpose is to describe the healing process in both religious and psychological language, in order to inform and stimulate further discussion.

Life Story Summary

Born in 1931, Jane grew up in Texas. Married at the age of 16, she gave birth to six children by age 27, and was hospitalized at age 27 (shortly after the birth of her sixth child) for what appeared to be a severe schizophrenic breakdown. She then underwent treatment at a private hospital at Houston, Texas, for nearly a year. The following year she was brought to Tulane University, and after nearly a year of custodial care and treatment was discharged without recovery. Reverend Sam Fife, a Baptist minister and faith healer found her in a highly disturbed psychological state.

He conducted a total of five intense demon deliverance sessions with Jane over a period of one month before she was "healed." Today, over 25 years later, Jane is completely cured of her mental illness and is an active member of a community-oriented Christian movement.

Childhood

Jane was the second child of her mother (age 35) and the first child of her father (age 40). At age 15 months Jane experienced "malnutrition from nursing" and fell into a coma. She was subsequently weaned and given to her 15-year-old half-sister for rearing, as Jane's mother left home to work. At age 2 Jane was toilet trained by her sister. Jane's dependency on her sister continued to increase until age 5 when her sister married and moved out of the house. The loss of her mother surrogate was psychologically traumatic for Jane as she began to manifest symptoms of depression, fear, and hysteria, while regressing to a state of incontinence. Jane's grandmother then became her primary caretaker, which intensified the conflictual relationship that already existed between Jane's mother and grandmother. Jane subsequently developed storm phobias and a pervasive fear of destruction by God for being "bad."

A year later Jane caught scarlet fever, fell into a coma, and was given an emergency hospitalization. Following this experience, Jane recalled having a profound fear of death as well as of her grandmother. At age 7 she came down with pneumonia, went into a coma with delirium, and was accused (presumably by her grandmother) of melodramatics. (Jane's "illnesses" were later interpreted by her psychologist at Tulane University Psychiatric Clinic as expressions of her rage towards her passive father and "uncaring" mother for abandoning her.)

At age 8 Jane again fell comatose (for unknown causes) and was subsequently "saved" by her grandmother. By this time, Jane had developed a marked emergency adaptation and was no doubt experiencing considerable secondary gain from such dramatic behaviors. (In light of the profound emotional deprivation which Jane had experienced from early infancy on, her hysterical behaviors and comatose states no doubt served to get her the kind of care and attention from parental figures which she otherwise was unable to obtain.)

Jane began menstruation at age 12, a development for which she was ill prepared. The following year her grandmother died, after which she moved with her parents to a home in Dallas where her dramatic and regressive behaviors intensified. Most notably, she began to exhibit nightly hysterics until her mother would come and sleep with her.

Several years later at age 16 Jane developed a steady relationship with an Air Force recruit named Richard, and married him. Jane describes her early marriage as an attempt to escape from her home environment.

Marriage and Motherhood

After Jane and Richard's wedding, which took place at an army camp, Jane developed a number of phobias, began having nightmares and "hysterics," and gave birth to her first child (a male). She reacted with panic, loss of libido, and guilt. Yet, she was determined to make her marriage succeed.

After two subsequent miscarriages, Jane had her second child (a female) at age 20, an event which triggered hypomanic spells, intense mood swings, obsessions, and violent nightmares with night screamings. Her husband reacted to her hysterics with ridicule and scorn and became increasingly cold towards her. Jane had her third child (a male) at age 21 and reacted with intense feelings, frustration and anger towards her maternal role. She also developed a car phobia, began having death dreams and visual hallucinations and manifested periods of extreme confusion and lability.

At age 24 Jane began experiencing frequent states of derealization, developed a house phobia. The birth of her fourth child (a male) during this same year was followed with more hysterics, depression and pneumonia. She was subsequently hospitalized for a brief period and was found to have abnormal electroencephalogram (EEG) rhythms. She continued to experience nightmares, stress with her husband, and a house phobia accompanied with a strong desire to retreat from her home role.

Jane gave birth to her fifth child (a male) at age 26. Her depression worsened as she became increasingly dependent on her children for "reassurance of being needed." The following year, at age 27, she again became pregnant and remained in a fugue state during the last two months of her pregnancy.

Psychiatric Hospitalizations

Following the birth of her sixth child (a male), Jane was given a complete hysterectomy, became severely depressed and anxious, experienced a temporary loss of speech, and was hospitalized. The following is Jane's own account of what she experienced on the day of hospitalization:

One bright, beautiful day, when the baby was just a few weeks old, I was trying desperately to do the necessary morning chores when I became aware of an overwhelming desire to lie down. My body felt heavy and it seemed as if my feet were made of cast iron. Somehow I felt if I gave in to this desire I would be trapped in my bed, unable to get up. It was this fear that drove me out into the yard, into the sunlight to escape the tentacles of the bed in my room. My fear was so intense, I could only walk back and forth in

the yard. Inwardly, I was screaming: "Help me! Help me!"
Yet, I was unable to speak a word, unable to cry for help to
a living soul.

My husband came in from a dental appointment and
wondered why I was pacing in the yard. It was some time
before he could realize and accept the fact that I could not
communicate with him. I heard the words he spoke, but it
was as if I were hearing an echo. I could not speak.

He called my sister and together they arranged for a sit-
ter for our five boys and one girl. They took me to a
psychiatrist who had been highly recommended.

After a three-month stay in the Houston hospital's psychiatric
ward, where she received electro-shock treatment and daily therapy,
Jane spent an additional three months at her sister's home rehabili-
tating. She continued to experience intense feelings of guilt as
well as increased feelings of ambivalence and uncertainty about her
marriage. Around this time her husband lost his business, and the
family moved to New Orleans where he found new employment. At one
point shortly after her breakdown Jane's husband left her, con-
templating suicide, but returned after three weeks.

Several months later, at age 28, Jane had another major relapse
and underwent inpatient treatment at the Tulane University
Psychiatric Clinic in New Orleans. According to the psychiatric
report, she was diagnosed as having a *Chronic Schizophrenic Reaction, Undifferentiated Type* and an *Episodic Behavior Disorder,
Secondary to Complex Psychomotor Epilepsy*, although her case appears
far more complex than her diagnoses suggest. Her symptoms included
periods of dissociation and hysteria, multiple levels of awareness,
abrupt changes in awareness levels, visual hallucinations, suicidal
feelings, murderous impulses towards her children, numerous phobic
reactions, chronic depression, severe anxiety and nervousness, nightmares, anorexia nervosa, extreme guilt and fear of punishment from
God, and periods of compulsive religious ritualisms. Physiologi-
cally, she suffered from periods of temporary loss of sight and
speech, irregular EEG rhythms, a mild temporal lobe disturbance,
psychomotor epilepsy, dizziness, and borderline hypoglycemia.

Therapy

Jane's psychologist and therapist at Tulane, Dr. David Reed, who
was also a clergyman, initially saw Jane three times a week, then
twice a week, and then once a week over a period of nearly a year.
The clinical appearance of Jane, as described by Dr. Reed, "was that
of a thin, dark-haired, attractive young housewife who spoke with
good intelligence and great flare for drama." From the beginning of
therapy, Jane expressed considerable concern about her periods of
"loss of control." She saw herself as being in reality two Janes,
with the good Jane being modest, pious, and devoted to her family
responsibilities, and the bad Jane being rebellious, angry, and wanting to abandon all family demands placed upon her. She frequently

expressed a desire to overcome this perceived split in her personality and would often say at the beginning of treatment, "I want to learn to be the same people."

In the therapy sessions themselves, Jane exhibited dramatic symptoms that looked quite different from week to week. She would frequently have hallucinations in the office which she experienced in vivid technicolor. According to her therapist's report, "She would have visions when closing her eyes. They were like movies, like traffic going in front of her." On certain days Jane would wear something black and somber to the office and refuse to talk. Then slowly she would reveal that she could not talk because she saw the letters S E X written on the wall behind her therapist. (Dr. Reed noted that in addition to a long history of emotional deprivation which culminated in an impulsive marriage, Jane had a strict, fundamentalist religious background which emphasized *aggression* and *sex* as being especially sinful.)

Throughout the course of therapy crises continued to occur in Jane's family. Her husband was always upset about what was happening to Jane and nearly left her on numerous occasions because he was so fed up with her illnesses. Her husband was out of the home nearly all of the time, which both angered Jane and wore her out. At times, she would have "attacks of rage," and behaviors which were extremely upsetting to her husband. Then Jane would become extremely sorry and feel guilty about what she had done. In general, she would handle personal crises with a strong reference as to whether or not God was acting in her life.

Because of her strong religious orientation, she began at one point in therapy to go to Sunday school at a local church in her neighborhood as part of her "recuperation." The minister of the church came to see her therapist in an attempt to keep Jane from showing up at his church because of her "bizarreness."

The weekend following her deliverance, one of her sons suffered a fractured skull and nearly died. Remarkably, Jane responded to this crisis by snapping out of her illness and "nursed him back to health in a significant fashion." According to her therapist, "she hadn't been that organized in years."

For Jane, the therapy had its ups and downs. Admittedly, Dr. Reed and the psychiatric staff at Tulane University were "shooting in the dark" with Jane and were quite perplexed as to what the nature of her treatment should be. A variety of drugs and placebos were used, but none had a lasting effect on her. A "supportive model" of talking therapy was used with her throughout. While Jane did establish a good working relationship with her therapist, she revealed that "again and again he led me gently upward to reality, only to have some unseen thing drive me down again."

Deliverance

Finally, as Jane later recalled, "after the last of a long series of drugs and therapy proved ineffective, the inevitable had to be faced." The day before her husband was going to have her committed to the state hospital, Jane accepted an invitation to attend a Bible study in the home of a neighbor which was being conducted by Reverend Sam Fife. (Reverend Fife had been told about Jane and her problems before the meeting that evening.) Afterwards, Fife offered to take Jane home so he could speak to her husband. Citing the biblical accounts given in the book of Mark, chapters 5 and 16, on demon possession and the casting out of demons, Fife was able to convince Jane's husband that she was indeed demon possessed and obtained permission from him to perform an exorcism on her.

Fife then proceeded to employ the age-old technique of demon exorcism with Jane in a manner reminiscent of what we find reported in ancient literature, where the priest would address himself directly to the spirits within the individual, labeling and identifying them by name in order to provoke their response. In the taped sessions we can hear Rev. Fife and Jane conversing in a dramatic fashion, with Jane speaking for the spirits within her and speaking of herself in the third person. Initially, Fife's focus is primarily on convincing Jane that she is demon possessed, that he has the power to cast the demons out, and that she must therefore turn to him and away from psychotherapy. During the healing session, Fife's speech occasionally lapses into *glossolalia* (the ancient practice of speaking in tongues), a sign to the healer and the believer that the priest is invested with the power of God.

What Jane herself experienced during the "healing" session is perhaps best portrayed in her own account, beginning with the initial conversation about demon possession which Sam Fife had with her husband, Richard:

He turned to Mark 5:1 and read through verse twenty. I do not have the words to express the complex emotions I experienced that evening. There were two distinct personalities active within my being, though I had no idea what was actually transpiring, or the reason for it. As he continued teaching from the Scriptures I sat for a few moments with a growing apprehension over his words. Now my vision began to blur and the room seemed to darken. Suddenly I ran through the haze into my bedroom. Terrified, I locked the door. A fear of this man seized me, and at the same time, the personality within that was my true self, was begging desperately, "Oh God! Help me! God! Help me!... Richard continued to listen and to question Reverend Fife, and soon it became evident that there was a great similarity between the man possessed of unclean spirits in Mark 5 and my condition!...

Reverend Fife called some of the believers from his congregation and asked them to come to my house to pray for me. Finally, Richard convinced me to open my door. Since he realized that my fear had been aroused by this man, he made no further mention of him or his plans to cast the

unclean spirits out of me. The time was shortly before mid-
night. Knowing it would take over an hour for his people to
arrive, Reverend Fife spent the time alone, in prayer.

When the people began to arrive, an indescribable
hysteria seemed to engulf me. I was literally thrown into a
frenzy, screaming and shouting and ordering eveyone out of
my house. They took no offense, nor did they seem to be
aware of my ill-temper, but knelt around the room, completely unmoved by my threats and violence. They began to
praise God in a very unusual manner, with hands held high in
the air, saying, "Hallelujah! Praise the Lord!" All the time,
the real me was silently crying, "God, help me! God, help me!"
After a period of praising God, Reverend Fife began to speak
the command: "You unclean spirit, in the name of Jesus, come
out of her." When he spoke to this spirit, it spoke back to
him. I knew that I was not doing the talking, though it
appeared to be me.

This went on for nearly three hours. There were nineteen
unclean spirits that were cast out. They named themselves;
each had a distinct personality. As each came out, they
made me retch, though I was not physically ill.

When the last unclean spirit was gone, I sat up and
looked around. I was absolutely amazed that I was no longer
afraid! I was overjoyed to realize the turmoil, fear, confusion and guilt I had lived with for years was gone! It
simply wasn't there! The most remarkable physical change
was my eyes. My husband said he looked into my eyes, and
for the first time in two and a half years, he could see
'Jane' there. The cloudy far-away look was gone. As he
tells this, even today, tears of joy and gratitude appear on
his face.

The time was 3:30 a.m. The minister and congregation
went home, praising God for victory. I fell into a deep
restful sleep, the first sleep without sedation I had experienced for months!

After the first deliverance session was completed, Reverend Fife
warned Jane that the demons would return and try to repossess her.
He thus instructed her to roll out of bed in the morning on her
knees, to go about her daily work all day long singing "Oh the Blood
of Jesus," to read from the Bible whenever she had a spare moment,
and to keep her mind "so filled with Jesus and truth that there will
be no opening for these spirits to get back in."

Apparently, Jane was able to successfully carry out these
instructions for several days. However, five days later, Jane's husband called Reverend Fife to report that Jane was again acting
strange and requested that he come and see her. Suspecting that
some of the demons had returned, Fife took one of the church deacons
and his wife along with him as well as a tape recorder. Fife was
particularly interested in making a recording of the event "so that

there would be evidence with which to teach the people of God's church of the reality of this enemy that we're fighting." When Fife and friends went to Jane's house that morning, they were greeted at the door by her husband. The following is Fife's own summary of what ensued:

When I entered Jane's home, she ran for the bedroom in fear as soon as she saw me. Her husband then led her back, made her lie down on the couch, and I began to command the spirits to come out of her. At first they tried to deceive me by causing Jane to say, "I'm just sick and I don't feel like having anybody pray for me." But as I continued to exert faith, they grew angry and began manifesting themselves by causing Jane's tongue to run in and out very fast, like a snake's when he is angry. Then they began to talk through her declaring that they would only come back again if I cast them out. I forced them to talk for more than an hour knowing that Jane with her conscious mind could hear herself saying those things and knowing it was some force other than herself making her say them. Her faith was thereby strengthened, and her own power to resist them was increased.

Fife then proceeded to cast out, one at a time, each of the demons, who identified themselves by name as Thaddeus, Danis, and Lucius. Each time a demon was cast out, the following sequence would take place: Fife would order the demon to come; he would "speak in tongues" loudly and rapidly; then Fife and the group would repeat together in raised voices "In the Name of Jesus come out of her. In the Name of Jesus, In the Name of Jesus...", followed with repetitions of "Hallelujah, thank you Lord." As each demon was declared to be coming out, Jane would cough loudly and "uncontrollably" for a minute or two, after which she would become silent for a period. When the last demon was cast out, Jane suddenly appeared very normal—almost as if nothing had happened—and, in a friendly and lighthearted manner, invited the group to stay for dinner, offering to make them a pumpkin pie.

Following this second demon deliverance event, Jane appeared to be quite normal for the next three days, until, as Fife relates, "the demons pulled an insidious trick on her in order to get back in." According to Fife, the demons tricked a neighbor boy into throwing a clod of dirt with a piece of broken brick in it at her seven-year-old son, which hit him in the head. Jane rushed her son to the hospital where she learned from the X-rays that his skull was not only fractured, but that the fractured piece was pressing inward on the brain and needed to be surgically removed. Fife reported that this event "was such a shock to Jane's mind that it opened her mind up and these demon spirits rushed back in." When Fife arrived at the hospital, he found her sitting there "jerking from head to toe." Fife then drove Jane to his church, called some of his people to the scene, and again cast the spirits out.

Following the third exorcism, Jane reportedly was normal for nearly a week. But then, as Fife relates, the demons crept back in "through an insidious manner," and he was again called upon to cast them out. Some time later, the demons returned and "possessed" Jane for the final time. Fife gives the following account of that event:

The last time the spirits got into Jane, she had come to church on Sunday night. As I was standing behind the pulpit preparing to start the church service, I noticed that she was acting rather fidgety, and suddenly I saw her jump up and run out of the church toward her car. I knew what had happened, and I ran out the side door and caught her at her car, brought her back in, and we bound the spirits so they remained quiet until the church service was over. We then took her down to my home, and for the fifth and last time we cast the spirits out. As God had told us, we sent them by faith into a far country [into the land of Palestine]. The leading spirits which had been tormenting Jane were never heard from again. Of course, there were other demons around who sought to get back into her, but Jane herself had reached the point that she was strong enough in knowledge and faith and truth, and she was able to resist them and was completely healed.

Jane continued her therapy sessions at Tulane University while the exorcisms were being performed. She apparently did not mention anything to him about them until sometime after the fifth and final deliverance session had been completed. Dr. Reed noted a significant improvement in Jane's behavior at the time but did not press her for further information. When she shared the deliverance experience with him, Dr. Reed requested a conference with Reverend Fife in order to learn more about how Jane had been healed. Following his individual meeting with Fife, Dr. Reed invited him to share the Jane story with some of his professional colleagues at Tulane University. The following is Fife's own account of that event:

This scientist was so impressed that he asked me to appear the next Saturday before the Board of Psychiatry of Tulane University which I did. The following Saturday I appeared before twenty psychiatrists from Tulane. The leader said, 'We've been tremendously impressed with this woman's healing. We're interested in your methods and techniques by which it has been accomplished." They gave their whole seminar to make my presentation. I took the Bible, showed them what it had to say about demon spirits, about the power that is in the Name of Jesus to cast them out, and then played this tape recording for them. When I finished, a great number of them asked me to make them a separate copy for the university, and I was asked to write a paper, a thesis, on the subject for the university which I did.

In the paper which Fife wrote on Jane's healing, he put together a list of "clinical symptoms" which to him indicated demon possession, which were remarkably similar to Dr. Reed's own clinical observations. Fife's list of her symptoms in his own words are as follows:

1. Nervousness to the point of abnormal activity, such as not being able to sit still, crossing her legs and shaking the foot that is off the floor, making silly motions with the hands.

2. Seizures whereby she lost control of her body and shook uncontrollably.

3. Desire to hurt self during the seizures.

4. Her desire to hurt her children.

5. Tormenting thoughts with tremendous fears of horrible punishments from God.

6. Horrible nightmares.

7. Her description of technicolor visions she had periodically.

8. Periods of dizziness.

9. Halting speech which demonstrated her inability to think or follow a line of thought clearly because of confusion of the mind injected by spirit forces.

10. Periods in which the eyes would become glassy and then sometimes cloudy.

11. Increased blinking of eyes, a twitching of the body, and then complete loss of sight and confusion of speech. This specific episode happened during a period when I was explaining the reality of the demoniac spirits, their work on the human personality, and my commission and authority as a minister of Jesus Christ to cast them out. This was obviously the spirit personalities venting their fear of me and their anger at me on the patient because I understood them and their work and was going to drive them from their home.

12. The extreme fear of me and my prayer that Jane demonstrated as I told her I could cast the demonic spirits out confirmed beyond all shadow of doubt that Jane's case was demon possession and the spirits were trying desperately to keep her away from me and my prayers.

Deliverance vs. Psychotherapy

During a recent talk which Jane gave about her deliverance experience to a group of college students, she was asked to comment on the psychologist's role and the way in which he helped her versus the function of the evangelist, and whether there was a place for both. Her response was as follows:

Definitely, I believe definitely so. I don't believe the two years that I was under psychiatric care was a waste. Now this is mystical; this is hard to talk about in a group like this. Because it is mystical, we are talking about two levels of creation, the spirit creation and natural man. But

I believe that I could not have experienced the deliverance that I experienced until the spiritual relationship with God was right. As mentioned before I had a spiritual experience with God. It triggered a supernatural moving in my life where a man [Sam Fife] came right out of nowhere. Prior to that time, I was exposed to psychoanalysis and psychotherapy and all this, and their attempt was to erase the misconceptions and the error that was in my mind and in my subconscience and fill it with reality of truth. I understand this is the purpose of psychology and psychiatry, to take away those things that are terrorizing from past experiences and to put truth and reality in its place. And so, Dr. David Reed commented to Sam Fife, "You did in a few moments what it would take us with our methods 15 years to do, but it was the same thing." Sam's revelation was that all the error and untruth and misery that was there was contained in personalities. He would cast them out and then fill me with truth very quickly and very simply, whereas the psychiatrists were dealing with one fallacy and then another. I spent hours upon hours in those years just talking, talking, and talking. They would help me to see how this or that was not a good concept. They would help me search out a better one and I searched until I found it. I think it was extremely beneficial. But I couldn't have lived long enough to have gotten it all done, piece by piece, like that. Together we needed to pull out the source of the lies and cast them aside, and then leave me free to walk in the source of truth.

As a scientist and student of mental health, Dr. Reed was open to learning from the experience of Jane's healing through deliverance. In a brief paper entitled, "History of a Healing: A Case of Demon Exorcism," he explores the use of demon exorcism and the psychological processes upon which this technique relied. He begins his paper with the following notation:

...It should be noted that the story is an unusual one. It has a vivid and dramatic quality which is difficult at first to accept. It seems anachronistic, as if we should be sitting in some temple of Aesclepius learning how to cast out the demons from the sufferers who come to us feeling plagued by the gods. But it offers us an opportunity to explore that process which is the *raison d'etre* of our professions, be we associated with medical, para-medical, or religious disciplines, that of healing itself.

In his paper, Dr. Reed identifies a number of predisposing factors and influences that he believes enabled her to respond so well to Fife's techniques.

1. Both Dr. Reed and Jane agreed that "without the preparation and the groundwork of the therapy, the healing would not have had the affect that it did." The good therapeutic alliance he developed

with Jane enabled her for the first time to "finally rely on a non-demanding adult."

2.   Dr. Reed believes that the most crucial factor in Jane's healing was the dramatic change that took place in her husband's attitude. He went from initially being an unsupportive, manipulative and absentee husband/father to becoming a kind, supportive, and active husband and family man. Dr. Reed feels that Richard made this change "when he saw a make-or-break situation for Jane to get better, or never to get better."

3.   Another important variable in Jane's healing had to do with her own belief system which was heavily rooted in dualism (good vs. evil) and which needed strong doses of existential experience. As Dr. Reed noted:

...she's got to have a visceral sense that God occurs, or over time it doesn't hold true for her. That is the way she was brought up. Her grandmother ...[for example, one evening] she announced to the family that this is the night that Jesus was going to take her. She went upstairs for the night and died. She was 95. Her family had a very strong belief in the presence of God in everyday life. What happened with Jane was that she had wandered so far from the beaten path that according to the hymn she needed God's help to get back to it. According to the illness, she had unfortunately matured at a time when the integrated mechanisms in the midbrain had broken down. She needed help to get it back together.

4.   In Jane's original cognitive formulation of her illness, she had described herself as "two people," a factor which lent itself readily to demon-God dualism (spirit-body).

5.   Jane's own susceptibility to the power of suggestion (along with her dualistic bent) enabled her to accept Fife's dichotomous categories (e.g. that she was demon-possessed; that the forces of Good and Evil were waging a war within her) and to ultimately feel expiated from guilt. Fife was able to convince Jane that it was not she who was "bad," but the demonic forces (i.e. an external force over which control is difficult and for which responsibility should not be taken) penetrating her essence. Thus she was not personally responsible for wrong-doing; she needed only to become stronger to ward off the demons when they would return and again try to penetrate her. In this way, Fife was able to increase her self-esteem and sense of self-worth and absolve her of guilt and shame.

6.   The group support and personal attention which Jane received during the healing sessions, and which was maintained through the supportive church community to which she belonged after that, offered a kind of personal validation and ongoing support that was previously unknown to her.

Sam Fife, who had initially portrayed the psychiatric profession as "giving up on Jane" later apologized to Dr. Reed for "painting psychiatry at Tulane as being hopelessly outclassed." But, according to Dr. Reed, Fife explained, "It's part of the method. You can't go halfway on these things. You either believe or you don't." As Dr. Reed concluded, "If Fife had any doubts, he couldn't speak in tongues again. He couldn't heal. The Spirit wouldn't move him ."

Jane Today

Following Jane's healing, she and her family became active members of Reverend Fife's church congregation. As part of a closely-knit, supportive community, Jane was able to maintain a well-adjusted and fulfilled life. Several years later, Jane and her family joined the "Body of Christ," a community-oriented Christian movement which Fife founded and in which Jane has become a very active participant. Jane's continued well-adjusted state was also confirmed by Dr. Reed, who reported being in contact with her by phone at five and ten years after the healing. Today Jane continues to be active in the "Body of Christ" and to enjoy good health.

PASTORAL CARE OF THE DEMONIZED PERSON

Mark H. Winslow

I have been asked to address the subject of pastoral care for the person facing spiritual bondage associated with demon powers. I am not an expert on pastoral care in this area, nor am I a professional scholar. I am a pastor who has been called upon to exorcise demons from eight Christians and non-Christians over the past four years.

Before going any further, let me say that I prefer to use the terms "demonized," "infested," or "invaded" rather than the term "possessed." Possession is usually a misnomer, since the invading spirits rarely *totally* possess a person any more than pesky cockroaches, no matter how numerous, possess our homes. Secondly, I prefer to use the term "deliverance" to describe exorcism. This is because many faulty, illegitimate and even dangerous methods of exorcising evil spirits are found throughout history and in many cultures. I do not wish to confuse deliverance from demons by the Spirit of Jesus with these other practices.

I got experientially involved in deliverance ministry for the first time in 1983 when I was finishing up my Clinical Pastoral Education as a hospital chaplain in the Chicago area. My first case was with a hospital employee--a woman in her late twenties who was an elect high priestess of a satanic coven. She wanted out of the coven and wanted the demons out of her. At that point I knew a bit about the supernatural and demon "possession" and that deliverance was possible. But I had no experiential contact with either the phenomena or the procedures of remedy until then. I am indebted for my initial practical experience in deliverance ministry and many subsequent insights to Dean Hochstetler of Nappanee, Indiana, who consented to work with me and a group from our Chicago congregation on that first case. Dean knows more about this ministry by experience than any other Anabaptist Christian I have yet encountered.

In my current pastorate in Allentown, Pennsylvania, I find myself helping two to three demonized persons a year with varying degrees of success. Deliverance is not something I do nearly as often as preaching, visiting, counseling and administrating, but it *is* something I do as it is called for. In 1983 I urged Marlin Miller and Dave Augsburger to consider how Associated Mennonite Biblical Seminaries could take the need for deliverance work more seriously and actually prepare students to do this work in the same fashion that we intentionally train people to counsel, preach, evangelize, and so on. I want to thank the seminary for listening to people like myself and for taking the initiative to arrange this consultation.

I believe that Jesus' mission directive in its most basic form calls us to do three things that Jesus gave priority to--preaching and teaching, healing, and casting our demons.

Almost all congregational leaders in North America know how to preach and teach. Some know how to bring healing. But very few know how to diagnose and cast out demons. This is a sad state of affairs. As segments of our culture move away from historical Christianity toward materialism, new age spirituality, witchcraft, shamanism and other myriad forms of occult beliefs and practices, I expect demonization of individuals to continue to be a problem and to probably increase in frequency and scope. Add to that the demonic infestation that sometimes begins in tandem with the emotional, physical and sexual abuse of children in our society, and you have a recipe for demonic bondage in our time.

I believe that everyone going into practical ministry with people whether it be as pastor, mission worker, counselor, chaplain or whatever, ought at minimum, to know the telltale signs of demonization or demonic influences as differentiated from other spiritual, emotional or physiological disturbances. And many more of us need to know how to do the actual work of deliverance.

I used to think that demon invasion was rare. I now know that it is more common than I had previously thought. Most of us, Christian professionals included, can't recognize demonization for what it is even if we see it. I used to think that a few people spread around the country who were exorcists would be adequate for the needs. I now know that Christians who can do the work of deliverance are too few and too far between for the many people who need the help they can offer. Last year a man visited me for deliverance work for three weeks. He came from Toronto--over 500 miles away. It is hard for me to believe that some Christian in Toronto couldn't help him. Yet in all his searching he was unable to find someone near him to help. I am coming to see that we face a two-fold problem. Competent deliverance workers are too few and too far between, and we don't have an effective cross-denominational network or association for referral to a worker close to a person's geographical area.

So I am convinced that the attitude I once had that a few exorcists around the country are enough to meet the demand and that we ourselves don't really need to know more about this topic is not a healthy response. We pastors cannot afford to leave deliverance to the few deliverance workers any more than we can afford to leave all the counseling to the Christian psychotherapists.

Having given some perspective on who I am and what I believe, I would like to delineate what I see to be the essential elements in the pastor or any other Christian helper, professional or otherwise, that enable capable pastoral care for those who are experiencing demonic bondage or invasion. Keep in mind that I do not seek to be exhaustive about such traits in this brief paper.

Qualities of a Christian Deliverance Worker

1. *It is essential that the Christian helper have full intellectual belief and faith in the supernatural worldview of the Bible.*
Recently I was at one of the largest and most prestigious mainline
Protestant churches in a neighboring city. I took home a printed
copy of the sermon of the week because the pastor there is well
known for his pulpit work. One of the texts for the day was Mark
6:7-10. Verse 7 says, "Calling the twelve to him, he sent them out
two by two and gave them authority over unclean spirits." The
pastor explained the verse in these words: "He gave them power over
unclean spirits. In 1987 we would say, he gave them power to heal
mental disorders and illnesses."

Here was a Doctor of Theology rejecting in a single sentence the
existence of evil spirits without so much as giving a reason why.
Jesus clearly believed in the reality of demons and spent much of
his ministry expelling them from people. Demon invasion and
deliverance are a fact of life in the New Testament, in early
Christian literature, and in literature that spans the centuries
since then. This pastor, like many other persons in our time, is
blinded by an overly rationalistic worldview which has no room for
the unseen spirit realm spoken of time and again by the Holy Scriptures. It is a grave error when Christians try to reduce the supernatural worldview of the Bible to the rationalistic, materialistic
worldview of many in the 20th century. The worldview of Jesus and
the New Testament is the standard by which we are to judge the
ideologies and philosophies (including therapeutic belief systems) of
our contemporary culture and not the other way around.

The Scriptures teach, and the experience of many of the Church
past and present confirms that God is a personal God and that God's
archenemy, Satan, is also a personal being. Jesus certainly believed
the physical world was host to an unseen realm where elect spirits
(angels) and fallen spirits (demons) worked to influence, protect,
guide or destroy humans. One of Satan's prime objectives toward the
Church is to convince us that he and his demons are not real or that
they are currently no threat to us or our world.

The coven priestess told me that the demons in her were not
afraid of some of the chaplains I worked with but that they were
terrified of me. I asked her what it was about me that terrified
them. It wasn't my formal education or my helping skills. It was,
she said, "what you believe." It was my belief in the reality of the
unseen world of the spirits and Jesus' authority over it that fright-
ened them because my faith made me a formidable adversary.

I believe in the supernatural realm. I believe that people experience things that cannot be explained apart from reference to the
supernatural activity of God, Satan, elect angels and demons.
Because of this conviction of mine, some call me a mystic. I do not
particularly care for that term because my own understanding of
Christian mysticism connotes believing in things for which there is

no scriptural warrant. I believe that my position is intellectually defensible and confirmed by the experience of many believers past and present. The Lord Jesus Christ has power over all things, seen and unseen, and desires to use his people to challenge the destructiveness of the demons against individuals or institutions.

If a so-called Christian rejects the supernaturalism of the Scriptures and argues against the existence of demons and their power to cause destruction in people's lives today (including Christians) it is they who have departed from historical, orthodox Christianity, and the burden for defending their heretical position falls necessarily upon them. But such people will have limited impact for God anyway. They are like a traveler setting out to travel the U.S. with a map of only the state of Indiana that they sincerely believe is the map of the entire U.S. They are going to get frustrated, and lost, and will miss a lot of significant sites along the way. No effective traveler knowingly sets out with an inadequate map. But that is what Christians who say that demons don't really exist or that they can't harm us or that deliverance ministry is unnecessary today are doing. No Christian can cast out demons if he or she believes that they are nonexistent, that they don't invade people and take up residence there, and that Christians can't or shouldn't take authority over them through the power and delegated authority of Jesus Christ.

2. *The Christian helper must believe that the extraordinary as well as the ordinary gifts of the Holy Spirit are still operative today.* Some believers, notably from Reformed and fundamentalist perspectives, have been taught that all the extraordinary gifts of the Holy Spirit like healing, tongues, discernment and prophecy passed out of existence in the first century church after the early church was established. I believe this interpretation is faulty.

1 Corinthians 13:8-12 is appealed to often to make the case that the extraordinary gifts of the Holy Spirit are no longer operating in our time. The usual argument says this passage teaches that these gifts passed away when the early church was established and the New Covenant put in written form as the New Testament. It is claimed that this is what is referred to in verse 10 as when "the perfect comes." Thus, it is claimed, these extraordinary gifts of the Holy Spirit were no longer necessary after the establishment of the Church and the written record of God's revelation in Jesus, so they died out in the first century.

Other Christians, including myself, maintain that these extraordinary gifts *are* present in today's Church and have been since the beginning. They never passed away. The "perfect" of verse 10 refers, according to this second interpretation, to the return of Jesus Christ and the final consummation of the Kingdom of God in the future--and not to the establishment of the Church or the canon of Scripture in early Church history.

It is not essential that Christians who are effective in dealing with demonized persons embrace this second interpretation. But it is my observation that believers who are effective in this ministry either already believe that all the gifts of the Holy Spirit are still operative today or are rapidly moving in that direction.

3. *The Christian who is capable of helping those with demon problems must have a theoretical knowledge of the capabilities of demons, the characteristic signs of demonization, and the theological rationale and methods for their expulsion.* The ministering person needs to know something about *the capabilities of demons to inflict physical, emotional, and spiritual pain and injury upon people as well as their capacity to heal and deceive.* The demons in one man I worked with would give him a severe case of diarrhea and other body pains, and would create an unbearably unpleasant smell around him that would effectively keep him from attending worship faithfully as he desired. Another demonized man had controlled sleep patterns that kept him up all night and in a deep, trance-like sleep all day so that his employment opportunities were severally hindered. I saw the suicide demon in one young woman (which subsequently identified itself and was expelled) compel her to run and attempt to throw herself under the wheels of an oncoming car, as friends and I managed to reach her in time to restrain her.

Demons have tremendous power to inflict injury and death, to communicate instantaneously across great distances, to heal while bringing the victims of their healing into greater spiritual and emotional bondage, and to do other things that we can hardly fathom. These capabilities are described in some of the credible literature on this subject and have been observed in our experience also.

The Christian who would be an effective spiritual warrior for the Lord needs also to know what the symptoms of the demonized person can be. The marks of infestation are often different, but a single characteristic or especially a constellation of them may move the helping believer to consider (not conclude, initially) that demon infestation may play a role in the person's problems.

The *identifying characteristics of demonization* should be learned by the helping Christian through books, journal articles, and ministering persons familiar with the phenomena. There are many marks of invasion, and many symptoms can be explained in physiological or psychological terms only, rather than in terms of spirit influence. When, on the basis of seeing several marks of possible demonic influence in a person, or when I have a strong intuitional sense that demons may play a role in the person's problems, I will sensitively approach them for permission to do further diagnostic work. I might say something like this: "Ronald, sometimes with people who are experiencing the things you've told me about, it has been my experience that demons can be one of the underlying factors involved. I'm not saying that is the case with you, but it might be. If you would be willing, I can test further to see whether demons might be part of your problem. Does that make sense to you?"

So far, everyone to whom I have asked that question has been willing to allow me to test for the presence of demons in their

lives. Some have been relieved, along with me, to find that demons
play no invasive role in their lives. Others have been relieved,
when demons were present, to know that indeed they were not crazy,
that there was hope and that there was someone who understood and
could help them.

The last theoretical aspect that can and should be learned by
the Christian before any direct contact with a demonized person is
*the authority we possess as ambassadors and servants of the Lord
Jesus Christ.* We also need to know how to use that spiritual
authority along with our human sensitivity and skills to determine
whether demons are present in an individual and to expel them. In
seminary through my reading I was able to come to some understanding of what demons can do and what demonization may look like to
the observant Christian. And I had learned that demons could be
decisively dealt with by Jesus Christ. But it was not until I met my
first case that I realized I didn't know *how* to use my authority
because I had never read anything or heard or seen a fellow
Christian tell me or show me how to do it. While a lot can be
learned from reading and speaking with others who have ministered
before in this area, it is perhaps unrealistic to expect Christians
to learn how to do the work of deliverance without a mentor or
teacher who will work with the person at least once. Jesus had his
disciples watch him preach and heal and deliver before he sent them
out to do likewise. Dean Hochstetler has been that person for me in
respect to deliverance work. I have since learned from other ministers in person, print or on tape. Like preaching, counseling or
evangelism, we rarely learn to do it except with a model who we can
watch, learn from, and from whom we gather a holy confidence in God
as we get started. As a pastor, it is the *deliverance workers* who
have really taught me the most important things I know in this field
and who have taught me some methods of working.

4. *A fourth essential element for the Christian helping those
with demon problems is that the helper be emotionally and
spiritually healthy.* The mistakes one can make in trying to help a
demonized person are many and the demons will exploit our own emotional and spiritual weaknesses in order to thwart our attempts to
be used by Jesus Christ to cast them out. We need not be perfect,
but we do need some measure of emotional health and spiritual fit-
ness to effectively do this work. My own experience shows that
deliverance work calls for the use of the full range of our emotional makeup--aggressive, persistent authority on one hand, and
empathetic, transparent caring on the other. The old adage, "Know
Thyself"--know your own strengths and weaknesses--is perhaps as
important as knowing Christ in this work. We have probably all read
in the newspapers about mentally unbalanced persons who murdered
family members to get rid of the supposed demons in them. A reading
of the European and Colonial witch persecutions of past centuries
reveals much about the emotional sickness and spiritual error of the

Christians involved in these persecutions and executions. These extremes illustrate how the helping person can be blind to his or her own sinfulness and emotional ill-health or theological error-- with disastrous consequences. The Christian who can be used effectively by God against demons must have a humble assessment of their strengths and weaknesses and their own potential to be influenced by evil lest they be drawn into the vortex of evil themselves.

5. *Christians who would be able to help persons infested with demons must have experiential contact with such persons.* Reading, reflection and prayer can help prepare us to help such persons, but nothing is quite as useful as finally witnessing this phenomena first hand in the presence of another competent deliverance worker or a team of such persons gathered to dispatch them. This should come as no great surprise. An action-reflection cycle is the hallmark of our best educational efforts in society and in the Church. Our seminary students get field education in such disciplines as counseling, chaplaincy, urban ministry, congregational leadership and so on. Those who will work with people in the Church also need a field education in deliverance ministry. To learn deliverance work we need examples of that work who we can watch in action, learn from and take the reins from in our own fledgling first attempts.

6. *The Christian deliverance worker must have the ability to integrate insights from other helping disciplines and their practitioners.* When people come to us with a problem, that problem may be physical, emotional or spiritual since we are composed of body, intellect, emotions and spirit. The "presenting problem" may originate in any one area or be located in several areas of a person's life. Pastors can mistake a physiological or emotional illness for a spiritual one. And physicians or psychiatric workers can mistake a spiritual problem for a physiological or emotional one. Whatever our discipline, there is a tendency to diagnose the problem as located in our particular area of expertise and remedy. As the old saying goes, "To the person whose only tool is a hammer, everything appears to be a nail."

One of the most harmful things that I have seen done, chiefly among charismatic and pentecostal believers is the casting out of demons from a person where there was no visible, discernible, communicating presence of invading spirits. I saw this happen several times years ago before I knew what I know today.

The only demons Jesus has ever used me to cast out were discernibly visible to me. I didn't just imagine them to be there, or "see them with the eyes of faith." I had first determined them to be present by the way they responded to my addressing them with Christ's authority. They either spoke directly out of the victim's mouth, or the afflicted person reported their responses and communicated to me.

When Christians "cast out demons" that were never there in the first place, it is emotionally and spiritually (and likely physically)

harmful to the person, to the Christians who (often with good intentions) victimized the person, and to the more widespread acceptance
of an intelligent and balanced understanding of this subject.
Ideally, the deliverance worker needs a Christian physician and
Christian psychologist or psychiatrist who is competent to diagnose
and differentiate with him or her, the difference between emotional,
physical and spiritual problems. But it is not just the deliverance
worker who needs to be able to integrate and respect the expertise
of the other helping professions. These other helpers must be able
to approach their own disciplines from the standpoint of a biblical
worldview. If they are only nominal Christians with no tolerance for
the realities that the deliverance worker and the demonized person
knows firsthand, they will neither deserve or receive the cross-
disciplinary cooperation that is called for in many cases.

Part of the great value of a consultation like this one is that
we can learn from one another and learn to trust and work a a team
with the hurting and demonized persons with whom we come into contact. One thing we can keep learning is when to be humble and defer
and refer to the expertise of our colleagues and when to challenge
each other's reductionism of the person's problem to the area that
just happens to be our field of specialization.

The insights of the biblical worldview and the Christian religion and the insights of other disciplines can be integrated to help
all manner of people, the demon-infested included. That does not
mean that there will not be some loose ends that we will simply have
to leave hanging because we are not omniscient as God is. I think
Satan will do his utmost, though, to resist and frustrate the
integration of these helping disciplines in a Christian manner. We
cannot afford to be one dimensional thinkers and practitioners in a
world that is clearly not one dimensional.

Requirements for Deliverance

Before I list some of the most helpful resources I have found
for the Christian in deliverance ministry, I want to mention several
things that I require of persons who want me to help them if they
suspect or if it is confirmed that part of their problem is demonic
oppression or invasion.

One requirement is that the person must be willing to entrust
their life to Jesus Christ as Lord and Savior if they have not done
so already. To cast demons out of someone who has no intention of
becoming or remaining a Christian is a vain pursuit, because the
person will not become personally empowered through Christ to resist
future demonic attacks and intrusions.

A second requirement is that the person understand before we
begin working that embarking upon this course will entail close
follow-up pastoral care with their pastor or myself or another
pastor who understands what they have experienced and can be a
resource for them to remain free of spiritual bondage in the future.

One dilemma I face, which illustrates the importance of what I am saying in this paper, is that there really are few pastors who have even a book knowledge of this subject, let alone a working knowledge of the supernatural phenomena and the spiritual dynamics for recovery and defensive spiritual warfare. It's akin to a surgeon having to refer a patient who has undergone successful surgery to a general practitioner who has never done surgery and knows very little about that patient's affliction. The pastoral care I am speaking of for follow-up might mean a meeting between pastor and person every 2 weeks, every week or every other day for as long as needed to aid that person's spiritual recovery.

Third, I do not let persons I am working with stay in our home. Some deliverance workers do this, and I believe the hospitality and modeling of Christian relationships in the home can be of immense value to the person seeking deliverance. Having demonized individuals in our home does not frighten us, but at this point, it is too disruptive of our family life and my other pastoral duties. However, if others are able to host the person seeking help in their home for a period of time as counseling, prayer and deliverance sessions are in process, this is a real advantage and the person could recover faster. But care must be exercised not to foster an overdependence on the part of the person seeking our help.

I like to have several other committed Christian folks with me as we go into a deliverance session. This makes the often exhausting work easier and we take turns addressing and commanding the demons, counseling the person, praying in earthly or tongues languages, reading Scripture, and singing hymns. This also gives firsthand ministry experience to new people. I would never invite a non-Christian and would shy away from inviting nominal Christians from participating in these sessions for their own safety and well-being and so as not to hinder God's work in us.

I find that occult activities in the family lineage (even when the demonized person themselves has not been the active participant) and harbored bitterness, anger and resentment go hand-in-hand with demonization. Some Christian psychiatrists have recently noted that demonization is often present with the disassociation that results from such traumatic events. Demonization is also sometimes misdiagnosed as multi-personality disorders.

It is very important to use counseling, listening, prayer and confession, and absolution before and during the deliverance sessions with a person. It gets at the roots of the problems and makes the confrontive work against the demons easier for us.

Method of Deliverance Ministry

Normally I have initial contact with the person by way of their letter or phone call or personal visit to me. It is during this initial contact that I listen and ask questions to determine whether there is sufficient reason to suggest demon activity. If I believe there is, I tell them that demon activity is possibly part of their problem and give them assurance that Jesus Christ can help them through me. I then schedule a time to interview them in person. Sometimes I ask them to read and complete the response pages of a little pamphlet entitled, "Clearing the Land; Preparing for Deliverance." I ask them to bring this read and completed pamphlet to our next face-to-face interview.

The next face-to-face interview lasts 1-2 hours and is a more indepth attempt to see the nature of the person's problem as physiological, emotional, spiritual or a combination of several. After 1-2 hours of gathering information, I know whether or not I want to check for demon activity.

At this point if I suspect demons are involved, I will ask the person for permission to test for demonic presence in the way noted before. I will also assure them of the greater power of Christ and of our safety through him.

Having obtained permission to test, I will first offer prayer that we and our families will be protected and unharmed, that any demons present may not call for reinforcements or split off into other parts of the body or to other locations or people, and that Jesus Christ will grant us wisdom, power and discernment. In my prayer I forbid violence on the part of any demons present.

After praying I will say to the counselee, "Ron, I am no longer addressing you, but I will instead be commanding the spirit world." I will then begin to issue commands such as, "I am a servant of the only true God and his son the Lord Jesus Christ. I command any evil spirits present to pay attention and identify themselves now. Who are you? What is your name?" I remind them of the blood of Calvary and the open tomb that has shattered their power. I remind them of holy truths from God's Word to bring pressure to bear upon them. Reading Scripture and singing hymns and simple choruses can be employed here as elsewhere to pressure the demons to respond.

Demons will eventually, if present, either speak directly out of the victim's mouth (not necessarily but possibly in a different tone or voice) or will flash thoughts, phrases and sentences into their victim's mind which (s)he in turn, must be counseled to repeat ver-batim to the deliverance worker.

Demons are liars and deceivers by nature. They will lie, tell half-truths, use illogic, and stall to win their victory and stay in the victim's life. They may threaten to kill or to enter the Christian helpers present. They must then be told that they have no power or right to do so. They will leave no tactic unused if it will help them avoid being cast out. They may attempt to bargain with us, and will attempt to convince us that they have gone, when in fact they have not.

The deliverance minister wants to find out (1) the names of the demons, (2) how many there are, (3) which demon is the head in authority over the group, (4) what their purpose or task is in the life of their victim, and (5) what grounds or legal claim, if any they have for being in the victim's life.

When gathering information from demons it is important that the Christian worker not ask for any information that would not be relevant to the deliverance and continuing freedom of the person. It is possible to cross over the line from seeking relevant information to trafficking with demons, which is expressly forbidden by Holy Scripture. It is wise for the deliverance worker to keep notes of relevant communication the demons give that is *verified.*

Demons are liars by nature. But one question that they will not lie to is this: "Omni, you have just told me that your purpose in Ron's life is to keep him away from Christian fellowship. *Will you tell the Lord Jesus Christ on the day he judges you* that it is your task to keep him away from Christian fellowship?"

"No."

"Then what is your purpose in his life?   Tell me by the authority given me by the Lord Jesus Christ!"

"My purpose is to deceive him into thinking that he is crazy and no one can help him."

"*Are you willing to tell the Lord Jesus Christ on judgment day that that is your purpose in Ron's life today?*"

"Yes."

The second response by the demon is the true one. The deliverance worker should never accept the response of any demon as true and valid unless it has been verified in the preceding manner.

If it is determined in the interview with the afflicted person or a demon reveals that there is some special ground or legal claim that a demon has upon the person (because of a curse, ancestral bondage, fetish, blood pact, continuing sinful practice, etc.) then attention must be given to specifically breaking this legal ground through various resources given to us.

When we have found out their names, number, who is in authority, what their purpose is and if they have any legal claim to inhabit the person, then we are ready to expel them.

"Where is the Lord Jesus Christ sending you?"   I will ask. Invariably the answer given is, "to the pit," "to the fiery abyss" or some similar response. "Then go where Jesus Christ sends you now!" I command. I command them time and time again in many different ways until it is either evident that they have all gone or until some have gone and my energy and persistence for the day are exhausted.

I have never seen a person completely set free in one deliverance session. But I have seen people completely free after two or more such sessions. Care must be taken to instruct the person in practical means of spiritual warfare and continuing spiritual growth to insure their continuing freedom. I usually write up an account of my work with a person and send a copy of it to their pastor, as well as giving a copy to them.

Even then, it is common for a formerly demonized person to become re-infested for any number of reasons. Another session or more will be needed unless the person is able to deliver him or herself with Christ's power.

This description of my method is only a bare outline. Case studies, relevant literature, journal articles, tapes, actual experience and the Holy Spirit will teach us further.

As any good deliverance worker will admit, there are no experts in deliverance--only continual learners. May my brothers and sisters in the Body of Christ forgive any errors or omissions in this paper and may God grant us together a growing ability in the Church to know how to be used of the Lord Jesus to set demonized persons free.

THE RENUNCIATION AND AFFIRMATION

As God is my witness and judge I affirm that I am a child of God purchased with the blood of the Lord Jesus Christ (Rom 6:3-11). I acclaim him as my only Lord and Savior and specifically renounce Satan as my lord and God. As one completely accepting the finished work of Christ on Calvary for my redemption, my only hope of eternal life, I now renounce and repudiate all the sins of my ancestors in their working or effect upon me. Since I have through the Lord Jesus Christ's own blood been delivered from the power of dark-ness and translated into the kingdom of God's dear Son (Col 1:13), I now cancel and nullify all demonic working or effect that has been passed on to me from my ancestors.

Because the Lord Jesus Christ has become a curse for me by hanging upon the tree (Gal 3:13), I cancel every spell or curse that may have been put upon me with or without my knowledge. As a child of God covered by the blood of the Lord Jesus Christ and trusting utterly in the atoning power of the blood of my savior Jesus (Eph 1:7), I cancel, renounce, and nullify every agreement or pact I have made with Satan including blood pacts. I renounce any and every way that the devil has gotten hold of me and nullify and renounce every ground that I have ever given to Satan that gave him power or claim over me. I cancel and nullify any powers, gifts, or workings in me which are not of Abba, Father, or pleasing to him.

I belong entirely and solely to the Lord Jesus Christ. As one who has been crucified (Gal 2:20) and raised with Christ and now sits with Him in the heavenly places (Eph 2:5-6), I sign myself eternally and completely over to the Lord Jesus Christ. It is my intention to pray daily that our Lord Jesus Christ will have full control of my total life. All of these things I do in the name of the Lord Jesus Christ and by his absolute authority over all things, rulers, authorities, and powers (Eph 1:18-23). Amen.

date:_____name_____

witnesses to the signing of this renunciation and affirmation:

_____

_____

Practical Resources for Pastoral Care

1. Koch, Kurt, *The Devil's Alphabet*, Kregel Publications, Grand Rapids, Mich, 1971. 156 pp. (A description of satan's traps including astrology, blood subscriptions, firewalking, fortunetelling, magical healing methods, palmistry, rod and pendulum, spiritism, tongues, witchcraft, and many more).

2. Koch, Kurt, *Between Christ and Satan*, Kregel Publications, Grand Rapids, Mich, 1971. 192 pp. (More indepth on fortunetelling, spiritism, magic, healing and occult literature, cases of deliverance).

For understanding the Christian's spiritual authority over the demons:

3. MacMillan, J. A., *The Authority of the Believer,* Christian Publications Inc. 23 pp. (Principles in the letter to the Ephesians.) Available from Faith and Life Publications, 632 N. Prosperity Lane, Andover, KS 67002.

4. Ensign, Grayson H. and Howe, Edward, *Bothered? Bewildered? Bewitched?: Your Guide to Practical Supernatural Healing*, 1984, Recovery Publications, Cincinnati, Ohio. 310 pp. (Perhaps the single most helpful practical volume on the hows of Christian healing and deliverance in print today.) Available from Grayson Ensign, Recovery Publications, P. O. Box 7531, Amarillo, TX 79114.

5. Rockstad, Ernest, *Enlightening Studies in Spiritual Warfare*, Faith and Life Publications, Andover, KS, 1985, 94 pp. (By a knowledgeable practitioner of and teacher of deliverance. Many helpful tracts, booklets and tapes also available from Kansas address listed under #3 above. Write for pricelist.)

6. Koch, Kurt, *Occult Bondage and Deliverance*, Kregel, 1971, 198 pp. (How to begin to distinguish between demonic bondage and psychiatric illness illustrated with many good examples from his ministry.)

7. Koch, Kurt, *Christian Counseling and Occultism*, Kregel, 1972, 338 pp. (Koch's magnum opus on the subject, full of case studies.

For cross-disciplinary dialogue:

8. Montgomery, John W. ed., *Demon Possession*, Bethany Fellowship, 1976, 371 pp. (Papers presented at a Notre Dame symposium sponsored by the Christian Medical Association in 1975. The phenomena are viewed biblically from the perspectives of history, law, literature, anthropology, missions, psychiatry, pastoral care and theology.)

Journal articles:
   9. McAll, Dr. R. Kenneth, "The Ministry of Deliverance," *The Expository Times*, July, 1975, 296-298.

All below are from *Journal of Psychology and Theology*, an evangelical forum for the integration of the two disciplines, Rosemead School of psychology, La Mirada, CA.
   10. Virkler, M. B. and H. A., "Demonic Involvement in Human Life and Illness," JPT 5 (1979), 95.
   11. Sall, M. J., "Demon Possession or Psychopathology?: A Clinical Differentiation," JPT 4 (1976), 286.
   12. Bach, P. J., "Demon Possession and Psychopathology: A Theological Relationship," JPT 7 (1977), 22.
   13. Sall, M. J., "A Response to (P. J. Bach's) 'Demon Possession and Psychopathology: A Theological Relationship,'" JPT 7 (1977), 27.
   14. T. Craig Isaacs, "The Possessive States Disorder: The Diagnosis of Demonic Possession," *Pastoral Psychology*, Summer 1987, 263-273.

Response to Mark Winslow

Marcus G. Smucker

The Winslow paper emphasizes the importance of (a) taking seriously the reality of demon possession, (b) including deliverance as a regular dimension of pastoral ministry, (c) embracing a belief system that enables and enhances a deliverance ministry, and (d) attending to the emotional/spiritual health of the pastor engaged in deliverance ministries. This paper also calls for a "biblical world view" which accepts the extraordinary gifts of the Spirit, a knowledge of the capability of demons, the ability to identify characteristics of demonic activity, the authority of the servants of Christ to deal with the demons, and the ability to integrate insight from other helping professions in the practice of exorcism. In his emphasis Mark seems primarily concerned with the actual experience of deliverance rather than also focusing upon pastoral care of persons leading up to and following such an experience.

In my response I will reflect upon concerns raised by the paper as well as include some broader considerations of the need for pastoral care of person traumatized by evil.

Pastoral care must be concerned about how belief informs practice in ministry. As pastors we must give attention to how we apply theology and doctrine in specific situations and circumstances. Certainly this is true in our encounters with evil.

Throughout the years of my experience in ministry I have been confronted with difficult questions about the nature of evil and concern for persons traumatized by evil. Questions about appropriate responses in ministry have been matters of continuing and at times urgent concern for me. This concern was highlighted because one of the members in the congregation I served was an exorcist, although most of his ministry was outside the congregation. Because of encounters I had with a variety of expressions of evil I have read some of the literature related to this, e.g., Don Jacobs, Don Basham, Derick Prince, Paul Miller, Matthew and Dennis Linn, Francis McNutt and others. In a practical sense I found the Catholic literature most helpful.

The phenomena of evil is difficult to understand and hard to define. That is apparent again in this conference. Different world views, diverse opinions about what is real and a confusing array of terms and concepts make it difficult to develop a theological frame of reference from which to practice care for persons traumatized by evil. It is often the task of pastoral ministry to act with certainty in the midst of ambiguity. Many of us have found ourselves in that dilemma. It is the nature of pastoral ministry to have to respond to difficult situations, ready or not, and to learn from what we do, as well as to be guided by what we already know. However, in the midst of all this ambiguity and uncertainty the pastor does need to be grounded in a belief system and theological frame of reference that will facilitate his or her work.

In this sense Mark appropriately addresses the belief system as essential to pastoral care of traumatized persons. Ministers must be practical theologians. Anyone involved in a ministry to persons traumatized by evil must have a theology of evil, both structural and personal. Pastors are exposed to a vast range of persons who come for help and will often encounter seemingly bizarre and evil phenomena without advanced warning. In the midst of such pressure and ambiguity pastoral ministry requires an operational sense of what to do and why.

In his paper Winslow laments the lack of persons in the church available to deal with evil. I question this assessment. I believe there are many more pastors who encounter and respond helpfully to evil than one would imagine; most times these experiences do not get telecast. Winslow further comments about the lack of attention to methodology in deliverance.

Questions of methodology are important not only to teach practical ways for responding to evil but methodology and procedures in themselves tend to help shape our thoughts about God, our understandings about the nature of evil and our view of human nature. We need to study methodology both to learn how to do what we are to do as well as to look again to what we really believe about God, evil and human nature.

Certainly one key issue in methodology is *discernment*. Winslow's paper points to the significance of discernment, stating that pastors should know the "identifying characteristics" of demons. Pastors need clear guidelines for determining how they diagnois a situation as well as what procedures they follow in making interventions in a person's life. However the Winslow paper does not indicate what he believes the "identifying characteristics" to be. Nor have there been any guidelines emerging from this conference to aid pastors in such discernment. Rather there seems to be significant confusion in our discussions as to what we are addressing. Some speak of "the demonic," others of "demons"; some use the term "possession," others "infestation"; some speak of deliverance, others of exorcism; and some speak of levels of severity of demonization. Do these all refer to the same phenomena? How does one discern what it is that we are discussing? How does one discern severity of evil in a persons life? It seems apparent in practice that sometimes there is exorcism for demons that are not present. What are the assumptions that lead persons to determine whether or not to do exorcism?

Another issue of methodology is the *context* for deliverance ministry. I believe a pastor involved in such ministry should seriously consider how this relates to his overall ministry in a congregation. If deliverance occurs in the context of a congregation there should be appropriate teaching to enable members to understand the nature of this ministry. The congregation should be protected from undue preoccupation with phenomena of evil and in severe situations only spiritually mature persons should be involved as participants or witnesses. The people of God must not become overly engrossed with concern for evil, but concentrate on the saving grace of God.

A third issue related to methodology concerns *consultation* and teamwork. Mark has not indicated in his paper how he received consultation in relationship to other professionals or members of the church community. Personally I believe that there should be a diverse team involved in the process of discernment of the nature of the problem. Also it seems to be an axiom that the greater the severity of the problem the broader the need for consultation and team involvement (Lewis Smedes, ed. *Ministry and the Miraculous: A Case Study at Fuller Theological Seminary* [Pasedena: Fuller Theological Seminary, 1987], p. 74).

A fourth issue in methodology concerns *accountability*. I believe persons involved in deliverance ministry do well to regularly give account of their work to someone who can review with them what is occurring in their ministry. Particular attention must also be given to the effects of such a ministry upon the congregation as a whole, and on the family of the person or persons involved, as well as to the spirit of those who are involved in this ministry. Exorcism is not a work for individualists.

At this point I would like to make a few comments concerning the broader dimensions of pastoral care of traumatized persons. Mark calls for a "close follow up pastoral care...to aid the person's spiritual recovery." Without question this is a very important consideration. I believe that the pastoral care which precedes and follows more extreme interventions must be viewed as part of the entire experience of healing. I submit to you 14 considerations that I believe are important for the minister or team involved in healing persons who are traumatized.

Persons ministering to those who are traumatized need:

1. To have formulated their understandings about God, human nature and spiritual reality to serve as a frame of reference for guiding and evaluating their ministry.

2. To be an "incarnate" presence with the traumatized person; to express God's compassion and care.

3. To become aware of the health of the systems in which the person lives, i.e., family, church, work, etc., and facilitate healthy, responsible relationships within those systems.

4. To observe and deal with any destructive patterns that may have emerged because of the trauma, e.g., tendencies toward becoming dependent, experience of alienation or other patterns ingrained in the person's life.

5. To encourage the person to affirm the basics of Christian experience, e.g., repentance, confession, regeneration, worship, moral development.

6. To initially pursue healing within the normal channels of ministry and experience in the congregation. Care must be given to avoid overstating the problem, unwittingly reward erratic behavior, or unnecessarily stir up fantasies that intensify the problem. Care

must also be given to avoid intensifying destructive patterns by having the person become negatively stereotyped within the community.

7. To be aware of and use resources outside the congregation or the pastor's own giftedness to foster personal, emotional and spiritual growth; be willing to refer to others or get assistance as needed.

8. To be willing to walk with the person throughout the journey to wholeness and help him or her to maintain victory by being anchored in God's love.

9. To enable the person to experience the acceptance/love of others and as rapidly as possible to facilitate a normalization of life.

10. To encourage the person to assume responsibility for him/herself as soon as possible as much as possible. Included in this is the encouragement of regular spiritual disciplines involving prayer, reading of Scripture, worship, etc. Love for God and love for others should be a clear goal for spiritual growth.

11. To involve the person in some ministry to others as soon as possible.

12. To attend also to the church community in which this ministry occurs in order to provide (a) adequate community teaching and awareness of the problem, (b) understanding in how to respond to such traumatized persons, and (c) awareness and experience of God's grace, love, and power.

13. To develop a broad emphasis upon healing within the congregation and view "deliverance ministry" within that context (James 5:13).

14. To maintain order in the congregation, i.e., to not allow evil manifestations and/or the personal demands of traumatized persons to dominate or overwhelm the congregation.

Introduction

The primary purpose of this consultation has been "to surface issues related to bondage and deliverance from a variety of perspectives with a view toward developing some kind of consensus across disciplinary lines." We see our task as a Findings Committee as reflecting the points of convergence and divergence that we noted in the course of the consultation rather than coming up with some kind of position statement.

General Observations

1. Compassion for individuals who are possibly demonized makes us seek knowledge and experience from all possible healing resources for them, yet also makes us cautious about how and what kind of healing measures we employ.

2. Because we represent a range of disciplines, life experiences, and faith communities, we come with particular orientations which affect how we see and how we describe what we see as we look at severely troubled persons in need of healing and discern the appropriate care. We thus come with particular terminology which may not communicate clearly to persons with backgrounds different from our own.

3. We are grateful for the spirit of openness and respect we have observed among the participants in the consultation. We recognize that we need each other in order to come to a fuller understanding of the reality of evil and the ministry of deliverance to those in bondage, incorporating the wisdom of practitioners and theoreticians in a variety of fields.

4. We note high interest and concern in relation to this subject. This is reflected in the unexpected number of participants in this consultation. In the paganized society of North America we increasingly find ourselves in a missionary context, including the spread of the occult, which may call for a "crisis intervention" type of deliverance ministry. With the Charismatic movement's reemphasis on the Holy Spirit has come a greater awareness of the spirit world, including evil spirits. The inadequacy of the modern scientific models and of traditional understandings of the demonic push us to seek new models of understanding which integrate the material, social, and spiritual dimensions of life. We have noted that an existential hunger for that which transcends our mechanistic existence is being expressed both inside and outside of the church.

5. Christian world views stand in tension with the modern scientifically influenced world-views which we discussed in that Christianity acknowledges both the seriousness of evil and the possibility of redemption from different perspectives. This tension includes issues of epistemology.

Areas of Convergence

1. We look to the Bible as a starting point and source of knowledge for understanding spiritual realities. We note that the Bible contains continuities and differences between the Old and New Testaments as well as in relation to the cultural contexts in which they were written.

2. Evil has both individual and corporate manifestations; therefore, healing is needed both in persons and in corporate systems.

3. Evil has far-reaching effects in social and family systems and across generations.

4. Deliverance is one form of healing which is part of Christ's larger work of establishing the Kingdom of God in the world.

5. Guidelines for discernment of spirits and for intervention with demonized persons are not widely known and agreed upon, but are needed.

6. Testing and consultation within an interdisciplinary team is recommended for discernment and healing of demonized persons.

7. Evil is powerful, but the resources of God are infinitely more powerful. Important pastoral resources for dealing with demonized persons include: (a) the use of the authority given us by Christ, (b) the sacraments, (c) the ministry of teaching, (d) stressing an obedient walk and a functioning faith and (f) preparation for, support during, and extensive follow-up after deliverance in the context of a caring community with sustained pastoral care.

8. Deliverance ministry should not occur in isolation but in the context of the church with the authority and counsel of the church and its prayer support of both the one in bondage and the minister of deliverance.

9. Deliverance ministers should display spiritual maturity, emotional stability, relational wholeness and humility and operate within structures of accountability.

10. Care is needed to avoid excesses in deliverance ministry. We affirm the medical injunctions, "Do no harm" and "Be responsible." We need to be sensitive to the possible abuse of power.

11. We affirm the importance of repentance and the need for individuals to take personal responsibility for their sins.

12. We recognize the importance of maintaining for ourselves and in our church communities regular practices of vital worship, prayer, praise, and mutual care for all sisters and brothers as the best prevention and defense against the demonic powers.

Areas of Divergence

1. We observed divergences among us in the following theological issues (a) the nature of evil and good, (b) various emphases in interpreting the nature of Jesus' victory and model for us stressing such features as his incarnation, his suffering servanthood/way of the cross, his resurrection and exaltation as Sovereign, and his embodiment in the church, (c) the nature and use of the sacraments and sacramentality, and (d) understandings of demons, Satan, spirits, angels, human nature, and flesh.

2. We diverge over the way the biblical account is normative for us or needs to be contextualized to fit our present-day situation in describing the spirit world and dealing with spirits.

3. We diverge on how a world view which embraces the biblical understandings of the demonic relates to contemporary psychological and sociological understandings, especially as these are used in the practice of counseling and mental/emotional healing.

4. We diverge on the extent to which Jesus transcended his world and the world-views of his time and the extent to which he enables us to transcend ours.

5. We diverge in our understandings of how patterns within social and family systems are related to evil and/or evil spirits.

6. Differences and questions surfaced regarding individual responsibility for working at changing negative personality traits or habit patterns over time versus taking a possible "shortcut."

Ongoing Agenda

Recognizing that the above divergences among us call for ongoing work, we note also the following ongoing agenda items:

1. Note that this topic is only one slice of the much larger questions of what is meant by Shalom/health/wholeness/ salvation and of what is the deeper nature of illness in its many forms and its multiple causes.

2. Explore the nature and role of angels and their relation to the Holy Spirit.

3. Present a diverse representation of deliverance case studies, including some which were not successful and noting possible reasons for effectiveness or failure.

4. Study carefully sociological factors, such as incidence and demography and social status in regard to why some people become demonized.

5. Take a serious look at Bondage and Deliverance from a transcultural perspective in interpreting the biblical material, the practice of psychiatric counseling, and the implications of this for our own understanding of the phenomena.

6. Gather guidelines for discernment and deliverance ministries which have been developed among Roman Catholics and other segments of the church. We need more help in learning about various "categories of bondage," distinctions between "simple and solemn exorcism," between "bondage, oppression and possession," concerning hierarchies of spiritual beings, between the demonization of a Christian and of an "unregenerated unbeliever," and between "deliverance" and "casting out demons."

7. Take a fuller look at Anabaptist history in dealing with evil and evil spirits and note its positive contributions in this area.

8. Acquaint ourselves with other patterns of pastoral care which do not use exorcism yet are effective in confronting evil.

9. Study what makes some persons susceptible to demonization and recognize that some people may be demonized and delivered in response to the power of suggestion.

10. Study the ways in which Jesus' ministry of exorcism was unique and in what ways it can be replicated by contemporary disciples.

11. Develop patterns of preventive work which make members resistant to the influence of evil, recognizing, however, that the deeper one grows in the spiritual life, the more one may be the target of spiritual attack.

12. Find preventive ways of working with children in confronting evil and helping them especially in the midst of family breakups today.

13. Explore further whether the ministry of deliverance is given to all the saints or to an appointed, trained, and ordained few. Who is to be entrusted with authority to work at what levels? Consider also the hazards to and the recommended care for ministers of deliverance.

14. Explore how exorcism and psychological or psychiatric work can interface with each other.

15. Provide opportunities for further dialogue concerning the creative tension in our attempts to understand and use both the systems of Christian faith and scientific knowledge.

16. Do further academic exegetical work on the NT noting that exorcism is not listed in the gifts of the Spirit, exploring the issue of exorcism practiced with a believer, and pursuing the further implications of the inter-testamental material identified by Josephine Ford.

17. Clarify how we understand human freedom of the will in relation to Bondage and Deliverance.

Conclusion

We have listened and heard but cannot say that we have emerged from this consultation with one mind. We were disarmed and engaged by the story of one who has experienced release from bondage through deliverance ministry and we rejoice over her freedom. We also recognize that some efforts in ministries of deliverance have not yet succeeded and that hurt has resulted. We acknowledge a need to know what it is that we are seeing and become more effective in our care-giving both through rational/empirical channels and through spiritual gifts which all come from God. We need to keep listening to each other and continue to learn from each other. Jesus Christ is Victor. Hallelujah! Amen.

Findings Committee: George R. Brunk III   Sally Schreiner
                       Lois Edmund   Elsie Steelberg
                       David Helmuth   Erland Waltner
                       John Lehman

AFTERWORD

Were this volume to include an account of the actual discussions and "consulting" which took place at the consultation, the number of pages would doubtless have more than doubled. The discussions reflected the rather wide range of expectations, convictions, and perspectives which the participants brought to the consultation. A verbatim account would have expressed that range in greater detail and with more specificity than is possible in a findings report. But it could hardly have captured either the intensity which characterized many interventions or the tentativeness intimated in others.

Each day began and concluded with worship: singing, Scripture reading, litanies or a homily, and prayer. Most sessions began with a summary of a paper and a (usually) concise response. The remainder of the time was devoted to plenary discussion which included questions for clarification, additional commentary on the particular subject at hand, and dialogue and debate between presenters and participants or between presenters or between participants. Conversations continued over refreshment breaks and meals together. Care was given to insure that both participants and presenters were correctly understood, particularly when differing views and genuine disagreements threatened to impede mutual listening.

Plenary discussion during the last half-day focused on the findings report, which does authentically reflect the discussions during the consultation. The committee members had met between sessions and worked long into the last night. One member of the committee continued working until breakfast, in order to collate and type the findings as well as make copies which were then distributed to all participants. Agreement on additions, corrections, and modifications short of final formulation was reached in plenary session. The findings committee edited the revised draft subsequent to the consultation. Both the participants and the findings committee have agreed that the findings report appropriately represents both the divergence and the convergence of views in the consultation. Both have also agreed however that it does not represent a common position statement.

The agencies and institutions which sponsored the consultation are exploring the possibility of convening a small group of "practitioners" to engage in a series of conversations. Such a group would include persons who are engaged in deliverance ministry, pastoral care, or psychiatric therapy. Such a group would seek to examine and assess specific cases from the perspectives of therapeutic, pastoral, and deliverance practices. If such a project is realized, a broader consultation on the subject might again be planned.

Finally, the sponsoring committee has also recommended to the Mennonite World Conference that a consultation be planned in conjunction with the next conference in Winnipeg, Manitoba in late July 1990. One suggestion is that such a consultation be a one-day event before the World Conference program begins. The intent of the consultation would be to include persons ministering in a variety of cultures and settings who might share with and learn from each other.

Marlin E. Miller

Selected Bibliography
(for July-August 1987 Consultation)
by Willard M. Swartley
updated March 1988

I. **Basic.** Several of various types are selected, with leaning toward
those working with the biblical texts.
Bubeck, Mark. *The Adversary* and *Overcoming the Adversary.* Moody
Press, 1975 and 1984. Stresses spiritual warfare as part of
Christian victory and pastoral ministry.
Churchman 94.3 (1980). A British Anglican journal which prints four
studies on demons and exorcism from different disciplines of
analysis:
    Graham Dow, "The Case for the Existence of Demons."
    James D. G. Dunn and Graham H. Twelftree, "Demon-Possession
    and Exorcism in the New Testament."
    Myrtle S. Langley, "Spirit-Possession, Exorcism and Social
    Context: an anthropological perspective with theological
    implications."
    M. J. Barker, "Possession and the Occult—a psychiatrist's
    view."
Cosby, Gordon (Interview by *Sojourners*). "A Prayer of a Chance:
Taking Evil Seriously." *Sojourners*, June 1986, 15-18. Shows the
reality of demonic evil in the structural and personal dimensions
of people's lives; a practical, pastoral perspective.
Dickason, C. Fred. *Demon Possession and the Christian. A New Per-
spective.* Chicago: Moody Press, 1987. Comprehensive on Bible
texts and practice. See also his work on *Angels: Elect and Evil*
(Moody, 1975).
Ferguson, Everett. *Demonology of the Early Christian World.* New
York/Toronto: Edwin Mellen Press, 1984. Important scholarly
study. See his excellent bibliography for biblical research.
Gelder, David W. van. "A Case of Demon Possession." *The Journal of
Pastoral Care* 41, 2 (June 1987), 151-61. Case study analysis of a
possessed sixteen year old boy with theological and psychological interpretations.
Isaacs, T. Craig. "The Possessive States Disorder: The Diagnosis
of Demonic Possession." *Pastoral Psychology* 35, 4 (Summer, 1987),
263-73. Includes a diagnostic description of possession in present categories of DSM.III. Used in Ruth Lesher's paper.
Kallas, James G. *Jesus and the Power of Satan.* Philadelphia:
Westminster, 1968. This together with his four other titles deals
extensively with the biblical literature. See especially *The Significance of the Synoptic Miracles* (1961) and *The Satanward View:
A Study in Pauline Theology* (1966).
Kamp, Timothy James. "The Biblical Forms and Elements of Power
Encounter." M.A. Thesis: The Columbia Graduate School of Bible
and Missions (Columbia, SC), 1985. AMBS Library. Presents the
broader biblical theological background of the divine encounter
with evil, in which exorcism is but one expression.
Kelley, Henry Ansgar. *The Devil at Baptism: Ritual, Theology and
Drama.* Ithaca, NY: Cornell University Press, 1985. Provides
important documentation of the early and medieval church's understanding of the relation between baptism and exorcism.

Kelsey, Morton. *Discernment: A Study in Ecstasy and Evil.* Paulist Press, 1978. Ch. III deals with the reality of a spiritual world, both angelic and demonic.

Koch, Kurt. *Christian Counseling and Occultism.* GR, Mich: Kregel, 1972. This is the more thorough and careful of his writings (*Demonology: Past and Present* [1973] and *Occult Bondage and Deliverance* [1971]).

Kremer, Emile. *Eyes Opened to Satan's Subtlety.* M.O.V.E. Pres, 1969. With some connection to French Mennonite circles, Kremer presents a bold statement that casts the net of Satanic influences quite wide, e.g. acupuncture.

McCasland, S.V. *By the Finger of God.* New York: Macmillan, 1951. Holds that what went for demon possession in first century we would rightly classify and treat as mental illness today.

Linn, Matthew and Dennis, eds. *Deliverance Prayer: Experiential, Psychological and Theological Approaches.* New York/ Ramsey: Paulist Press, 1981. Ten essays from a variety of authors and contexts sympathetically exploring an offering guidance on the deliverance ministry. Important for consultation. Includes two appendices: "Exorcism in Catholic Moral Theology" and "Gender Identity Change in a Transsexual: An Exorcism," the latter a scientifically verified case-study.

Mission-Focus 15,1 (March 1987). Two important case analyses from mission experience: "Spiritism in Brazil" by Valdemar Kroker and "A Pauline Power Encounter Response to Umbande" by Raymond Peter Harms-Wiebe.

Montgomery, John Warwick, ed. *Demon Possession.* Minneapolis: Bethany, 1976. Consists of 24 papers presented to "A Medical, Historical, Anthropological and Theological Symposium" at Notre Dame, Jan., 1975.

Pattison, Mansell. "Psychosocial Interpretations of Exorcism." *Journal of Operational Psychiatry* 8 (1977), pp. 5-19. Appears also in a collection of essays under the title, *Magic, Witchcraft, and Religion: An Anthropological Study of the Supernatural,* ed., by Arthur C. Lehman and James E. Myers. Palo Alto: Mayfield Pub., 1985. A provocative analysis of the relationship between the role of the exorcist and the psychiatrist.

Peck, M. Scott. *People of the Lie: The Hope for Healing Human Evil.* New York: Simon and Schuster, 1983. A perspective out of psychiatric practice and relatively new Christian commitment. Helpful for case studies and method employed--more than theological analysis.

Richards, J. *But Deliver Us From Evil.* Seabury, 1974. Represents efforts to come to terms with bondage and deliverance in Anglican tradition.

Smedes, Lewis, ed. *Ministry and the Miraculous: A Case Study at Fuller Theological Seminary.* Pasadena: Fuller Theological Seminary, 1987. Assesses the role of the miraculous theologically and practically; study arose from course on the "Miraculous and church Growth" at Fuller.

Twelftree, Graham H. "The Place of Exorcism in Contemporary Ministry," *St. Mark's Review* (Sept 1986), 25-39. One of the best short
pieces available.

Twelftree, Graham H. *Christ Triumphant: Exorcism Then and Now.*
London *et al.*: Hodder & Stoughton, 1985. A careful study of the
biblical data with awareness of theological issues and contemporary implications.

Webber, Robert E. *Celebrating Our Faith: Evangelism Through Worship.* San Francisco: Harper & Row, 1986. Gives excellent historical and theological perspectives on relation of worship to
victory over Satan.

Wink, Walter. *Unmasking the Powers: The Invisible Forces that
Determine Human Existence.* Philadelphia: Fortress, 1986. Vol.
II is a series of three on "The Powers," this study develops the
interrelationship between both spiritual and psychic realities
and personal (inner and outer) and corporate systemic "possession." Use Jungian categories for analysis.

Note: While few Mennonite writings have addressed this topic, the following should be noted:

Entz, Loren. "Challenges to Abou's Jesus." *EMQ,* Jan. 1986, 48-50,
and *The Mennonite.* A story testifying to Christ's power over the
demonic power. See also Timothy Warner's following article,
"Teaching Power Encounter," in *EMQ,* 66-70.

Finger, Thomas N. *Christian Theology: An Eschatological Approach,*
Vol. 1; Thomas Nelson, 1985/Herald, 1987. Vol. II; Herald, 1989.
Significant in showing the relation of Jesus' ministry and atoning death-resurrection to the demonic in Vol. 1 (283ff.) and the
relation of sin to the demonic in Vol. 2(ch. 7).

Jacobs, Donald R. *Demons.* Herald, 1972. Informed by African missionary experience, Jacobs shows the need both for missionaries
to take deliverance ministry seriously and what such might mean
in the North American context.

Miller, Paul M. *The Devil Did Not Make Me Do It.* Herald, 1977.
Concerned that exorcism is a cop-out on personal responsibility
and that we can become too consumed by and fearful of demons;
sees need for a holistic pastoral ministry to demonized persons,
rooted in Christ's victory and the caring community.

Yoder, Amzie. "Pastoral Care and Exorcism." An AMBS Independent
Study under Marlin Miller. N.d. Pp. 41 + 20 Appendix. Appendix
is the Clergy Manual for Christian Healing developed by "The
International Order of St. Luke the Physician."

II. Further Study, More Broadly Based

Augsburger, David W. "Possession, Shamanism, and Healing Across
Cultures: A Theology of the Demonic." Ch. 9 in *Pastoral Counseling Across Cultures.* Philadelphia: Westminster, 1986. A
phenomenological analysis of "possession" across cultures.

Aulén, Gustaf. *Christus Victor: An Historical Study of the Three
Main Types of the Idea of the Atonement,* New York: Macmillan,
1961. Holds that the classic view, that of the early church, was
Christ's victory over Satan and evil.

Bibliography

Augustine, "The Divination of Demons," trans. by Ruth Wentworth Brown. In *Saint Augustine: Treatise on Marriage and other Subjects* (the Father of the Church), ed. by Roy J. Deferrari. New York: Fathers of the Church, Inc, 1955. Discusses extent and limits of demon's knowledge.

Bender, Philip. "The New Testament and Holy Warfare. AMBS MAPS M.A. Thesis, 1987. Thoroughly investigates the warfare theology of Pauline literature and, more minimally the Synoptic Gospels. Important theological sub-stratum for this topic.

Berkhof, Hendrik. *Christ and the Powers.* Trans. J. Yoder. Herald Press, 1962, 1977. Basic work in relating the "powers" to corporate structures; roots Christian witness to structures in Lordship of Christ.

Betz, Hans Dieter, ed. *The Greek Magical Papyri in Translation, including the Demotic Spells.* Chicago and London: U. of Chicago Press, 1986. Shows the extent of use of magical formulae used to ward off demons in the Hellenistic world.

Böcher, Otto. *Das Neue Testament und die dämonischen Mächte* (Stuttgarten Bibel-Studien 58). Stuttgart: Katholisches Bibelwerk, 1972. Excellent treatment of the NT data, including both active and passive resistance to demon power. Accents Jesus' victory over the demons and the Christian's consequent resource for victory.

Brown, Peter. "Sorcery, Demons and the Rise of Christianity: From Late Antiquity into the Middle Ages." In *Religion and Society in the Age of Saint Augustine.* New York: Harper and Row, 1972. Pp. 118-146. Careful analysis of sources; holds that power over demons was a significant element in the authority of the early church leaders and in the growth of the Christian community.

Derrett, J. Duncan M. "Legend and Event: The Gerasene Demoniac: An Inquest into History and Liturgical Projection." In *Studies in the New Testament,* Vol. III. Leiden: E. J. Brill, 1982. Pp. 47–58. Critical analysis with bold statements about possession: propensity is cultural and learnt; "a histrionic gift;" two kinds--spontaneous and artificial (self-induced); akin to suggestibility as in hypnosis; those possessed "know what will 'de-trigger' them," exorcist must discover demon at work and "by reason of having the same demon or a more powerful one(!), expel him, often into an animal or object;" primitive psychiatry. See also his lengthy comments on Mark 5 in *The Making of Mark,* Vol. 1, 1985.

Douglas, Mary, ed. *Witchcraft, Confessions and Accusations.* London *et al.:* Tavistock Pub., 1970. Eighteen essays representing worldwide settings; analyzes power factors sociologically; some essays relate rise of sorcery to misfortune. See also her earlier work, *Purity and Danger* (1966) which is a major study of taboo.

Fairbairn, W. R. D.. "The Repression and the Return of Bad Objects (with Special Reference to the 'War Neuroses')." In *Essential Papers on Object Relations,* ed. by Peter Buckley. New York and London: New York University Press, 1986. Pp. 102-107, esp. 113-118. Other essays, 3, 14, 18, are also helpful. Used much in Gerald Kauffman's paper.

Ford, Josephine M.   "The Social and Political Implications of the
Miraculous in Acts."   In Dr. Horton Festschrift, ed. by Paul
Elbert.   Sees Luke's redactional purpose including the use of
signs to vindicate Christian faith against rival claims; each
manifestation of the Holy Spirit is contrasted to "the false use
of supernatural power."

Langton, Edward.   Essentials of Demonology: A Study of Jewish and
Christian Doctrine, Its Origin and Development.   London: The
Epworth Press, 1949.   Most thorough, clear and reliable in description and correlation between time periods.   Most thorough
treatment available on OT.   Author also of Good and Evil Spirits
(1942), another exhaustive study of Jewish and Christian thought.

Lehman, Arthur C. and Myers, James E.   Magic, Witchcraft and Religion: An Anthropological Study of the Supernatural.   Palo
Alto/London: Mayfield Publishing Co., 1985.   Ten topical sections
with 4-5 essays in each.   Section 6 has 5 essays on "Demons,
Exorcisms, Divination, and Magic" including the Pattison essay
(Part I above) and another on "The Psychodynamic of Demon Possession."   A university-type text.

Lind, Millard.   Yahweh Is A Warrior.   Herald, 1980.   Important in
setting forth the basic model of God's role and the human role in
warfare.

Mallow, Vernon R.   The Demonic: A Selected Theological Study; An
Examination into the Theology of Edwin Lewis, Karl Barth, and
Paul Tillich.   New York et.al: U. Press of America, 1983.   Analyzes the works of three theologians to show alternative models
of resolving the problem (origin and nature) of evil.

Martin, Malachi.   Hostage to the Devil: The Possession and Exorcism
of Five Living Americans.   Bantam, 1977.   Five case studies, but
sensationalized and fear-producing, in my judgment.

Meissner, W. W.   Psychoanalysis and the Religious Experience.   New
Haven and London: Yale University Press, 1984.   Some parts very
helpful.   Used in Kauffman's paper.

Nugent, Christopher.   Masks of Satan.   New York: Sheed and Ward,
1983.   Exposes demonic in five major time periods from ancient to
modern world, including Nietzsche and Hitler (includes primary
source documentation).

Oesterreich, T. K.   Possession: Demonical and Other, Among Primitive Races, in Antiquity, the Middle Ages, and Modern Times.
Trans. D. Ibberson.   Seacaucus, New Jersey: University Books,
1966.   Includes many primary source descriptions of "possessions"
across time.   First published in 1921, it takes a dim view toward
exorcism and hopes for more scientific knowledge of parapsychic
states.

Ollenburger, Ben C.   Zion, the City of the Great King: A Theological Symbol of the Jerusalem Cult.   JSOT Supp. Series 41.   Sheffield, England: Sheffield Academic Press, 1987.   Zion is a powerful symbol of Yahweh's defense, calling for human trust and
refusing pride, military alliances and weapons of power.

Parkin, David, ed.   The Anthropology of Evil.   Basil Blackwell, 1985.
Fourteen essays; theological analyses, including theodicy.
Includes Buddhist, Hindu and Muslim views.

Robinson, Lillian H., ed. *Psychiatry and Religion: Overlapping Concerns.* Washington, D.C.: American Psychiatric Press, Inc., 1986. Some helpful essays.

Russell, Jeffrey Burton. *The Devil: Perceptions of Evil from Antiquity to Primitive Christianity.* Ithaca, NY: Cornell University Press, 1977.

_____. *Satan: The Early Christian Tradition.* Ithaca, NY: Cornell University Press, 1981. Two books are basically descriptive with some critical analysis.

Sargant, William. *The Mind Possessed: The Physiology of Possession, Mysticism and Faith Healing.* Penguin Books, 1975. Recommended by John W. Miller to work at question of relation between mental and spiritual. Not available to me.

Schlier, Heinrich. *Principalities and Powers in the New Testament.* New York: Herder and Herder, 1961. A good earlier study of the powers, with sections on Christ's victory and the Christian's relation to the powers.

Smith, Jonathan Z. "Towards Interpreting Demonic Powers in Hellenistic and Roman Antiquity." In *Aufstieg und Niedergang der römischen Welt* II. 16.1. Ed. W. Haase, Berlin/New York: Walter de Gruyter, 1978. Pp. 425-439. Description of Hellenistic their world-views, showing levels of intermediaries (charts), no theological analysis or comparison to NT.

Stevens, B. A. "The Divine Warrior in the Gospel of Mark." *Biblische Zeitschrift* 31,1 (1987), 101-108. Shows how the Ancient Near Eastern and OT views of divine warrior climax through transformation in the Son of Man who gives his life a ransom for many.

Suenens, Leon-Joseph Cardinal. *Renewal and the Powers of Darkness,* Malines Document, 4, trans. Olga Prendergast (Ann Arbor: Servant Books, 1983).

Van Dam, W. C. with J. ter Vrugt-Lentz. *Dämonen und Bessessene: Die Dämonen in Geschichte und Gegenwart und ihre Austriebung.* Aschaffenburg: Paul Pattloch Verlag, 1970. A comprehensive and careful study.

Van der Loos, H. *The Miracles of Jesus.* Leiden: E. J. Brill, 1965. Pp. 339-78. Good treatment of exorcisms in context of Jesus' miracles as a whole.

Vögler, Werner. "Dämonen und Exorzismen in Neuen Testament." In *Theologische Versuche* XV ed. by J. Rogge and G Schille. Berlin: Evangelische Verlagsanstalt, 1985. Basic overview of NT data, mostly synoptics.

Note: Four recent scholarly studies relating Jesus to the contemporary worldview on magic and miracle are reviewed in *Religious Studies Review* 12, 1(Jan. 1986). The books are by Eugene V. Gallagher (*Divine Man or Magician?*), Howard Clark Kee (*Miracle in the Early Christian World*), Harold Remus (*Pagan-Christian Conflict over Miracle in the Second Century*) and Gerd Thiessen *The Miracle Stories of the Early Christian Tradition*). The reviews are by William R. Schoedel and Bruce J. Malina.

CONTRIBUTORS

Harold Bauman served for 13 years as Director of Congregational Leadership and Worship for the Mennonite Board of Congregational Ministries, Elkhart, Indiana.

Thomas N. Finger, a teacher of systematic theology and author of *Christian Theology: An Eschatological Approach*, is now pastor of the North Bronx Mennonite Church.

Josephine Massyngbaerd Ford is Professor of New Testament on the Faculty of Theology at the University of Notre Dame.

John A. Hostetler, sociologist, is Scholar-in-Residence at Elizabethtown College, Elizabethtown, Pennsylvania.

Gerald Kauffman, psychiatrist, is Clinical Director of the ELMS Unit at Oaklawn Hospital in Goshen, Indiana.

Richard A. Kauffman is Administrative Vice President and teacher of theology at Goshen Biblical Seminary, Elkhart, Indiana.

Gayle Gerber Koontz is Assistant Professor of Theology at Associated Mennonite Biblical Seminaries, Elkhart, Indiana.

Ruth Lesher is Chair of the Department of Psychology at Philhaven Hospital, Mt. Gretna, Pennsylvania.

Jacob A. Loewen, a former MB missionary and mission consultant for the United Bible Societies, does research and writing in areas of anthropology, missiology and translating.

Dennis Martin is Assistant Professor of Church History at Associated Mennonite Biblical Seminaries and Assistant Editor of the *Mennonite Encyclopedia V.*

Marlin Miller is President and Professor of Theology at Goshen Biblical Seminary, Elkhart, Indiana.

Robert L. Ramseyer, former Director of Mission Training Center and Professor of Missions and Anthropology at Associated Mennonite Biblical Seminaries, is currently on assignment in Hiroshima, Japan.

Robert T. Sears, S.J., is Adjunct Professor of Theology at the Institute of Pastoral Studies at Loyola University, does spiritual counseling and leads retreats on healing and spiritual growth.

Marcus G. Smucker is Associate Professor of Pastoral Theology and Coordinator of Spiritual Formation at Associated Mennonite Biblical Seminaries, Elkhart, Indiana.

Mervin R. Smucker is Clinical Associate Professor (Psychology) at the University of Pennsylvania, Philadelphia.

Willard M. Swartley, Director of the Institute of Mennonite Studies, is Professor of New Testament at Associated Mennonite Biblical Seminaries, Elkhart, Indiana.

Timothy M. Warner is Associate Professor of Missions and Director of Professional Doctoral Programs at Trinity Evangelical Divinity School, Deerfield, Illinois.

Mark Winslow is pastor of the First Mennonite Church in Allentown, Pennsylvania.